Self-University

Self-University

*The price of tuition is the desire to learn.
Your degree is a better life.*

Charles D. Hayes

Autodidactic Press

Published by Autodidactic Press.
P.O. Box 872749
Wasilla, Alaska 99687

First Printing, 1989

Library of Congress Catalog Number 89-80280

ISBN 0-9621979-0-4

Printed in the United States of America

10 9 8 7 6 5 4 3 2 1

First Edition

Cover design by Connie Hameedi

Typography by Visible Ink, Inc.

This book is dedicated
to James H. Herriage

Contents

Preface

Seeing the truth consisteth in the right ordering of names in our affirmations, a man that seeketh precise truth had need to remember what every name he uses stands for, and to place it accordingly; or else he will find himself entangled in words, as a bird in lime twigs; the more he struggles, the more belimed.
                                        —Thomas Hobbes

In 1960 I dropped out of high school in Irving, Texas to join the U.S. Marines. I was seventeen years old. At the time I considered high school a mind-numbing experience. I thought most of the curriculum was irrelevant. I had been led to believe that school was preparation for life. It was not. High school did not prepare me for the Marines or my work life afterwards. It left me, as it has thousands of others, with a disdain for formal learning.

The hierarchical nature of military rank causes one to examine the way those in charge become qualified. Serving on Okinawa, I became acutely conscious of my lack of a high school diploma. I began a self-study program designed for servicemen, and learned more on my own in six months than I had in the previous three years. In a short time I realized that the simple desire to know was far more powerful than anything I had developed in my formal classroom experience. I passed the GED test with a score high enough to enter almost any college in the country, yet I had always been a C student.

The U.S. Marine Corps is the ultimate experience in conformity. The difference between traditional education and the Marine Corps is that, as a Marine you never doubt that conformity is expected or that you are being indoctrinated. The Marines demand conformity, whereas the traditional educational institution speaks of individuality even as it molds. The Marine knows himself to be the product of conformity. The graduate still sees himself as an individual without realizing the extent to which he has been made like others, or as Ivan

Illich might have expressed it, he would not realize the extent to which he had been "schooled down to size."

I was discharged from the Marines in 1964. My intention was to attend college. I visited the University of Texas at Arlington. I was no sooner in the door than the dreaded feelings of disgust with traditional education returned. I left the campus wondering how I could possibly have thought that I could subject myself to such an environment again.

In 1966 I took the civil service test for police officer for the city of Dallas, Texas. I passed the test and was subsequently hired. Up to this point I had gradually become aware that I could tell little, if any, difference between the performance of individuals with or without college degrees. Yet, I had been taught to expect that there was indeed an enormous difference. I felt inferior to those with a degree, and, when they failed to live up to my expectations, I gave them the benefit of the doubt. I thought that their action or inaction was probably due to some type of superior knowledge.

In the meantime the disparity between the implied rewards due those with a college education and those without deepened my feelings of being somehow inadequate. So in 1968 I enrolled in El Centro College in Dallas to pursue a degree in Police Science and Administration. The negative feelings that I associated with traditional education returned, but this time it was different. I was an adult. I was definitely interested in the subject matter, and I was going to school with fellow police officers. It was not an exhilarating experience, but it was tolerable. Then it changed completely.

The college administration hired a new criminology professor who turned out to be unlike any teacher that I had ever had. He exemplified the era of the Sixties, and instead of the standard curriculum, he threw the book on the floor and challenged us on the level of our basic values about justice and equality. He treated us as equals, but he continually attacked our ideas and our long-cherished beliefs about authority in a democracy. The classroom atmosphere bordered on anarchy. Instead of the usual quiet, calm, conforming classroom environment, we maintained a level of tension near the point of physical altercation. Shouting and storming out of the room were common occurrences. I remember wondering if it were wise for us to be armed as we always were, even though we were off-duty. It was an emotionally wrenching experience, but it was the greatest learning experience in formal education that I had ever had. I suddenly realized that in all my experience with traditional education I had never been required to think. Most of traditional education in the Forties and Fifties consisted of exercises in short-term memory. It wasn't thinking—it was a substitute for thinking, and I had never realized that a difference existed. I had always trusted my teachers, accepting what I had been taught on the basis of their authority and position. Until my experience with this nontraditional teacher, I never realized or had any inkling that I might have been subjected to an education in the form of indoctrination. Yet when my beliefs about justice and authority were attacked, I realized they had no foundation. I believed as I did simply because someone in authority whom I trusted had said that I should. The unconventional professor didn't last long. When he left school, I followed. But the experience in his class changed forever the way I think about the process and role of education.

The late Sixties had a similar effect on the nation. The dissonance created by the Vietnam War attacked the fundamental beliefs of all Americans. I remember thinking that those individuals who publicly burned their draft cards should be imprisoned and possibly even shot. I viewed the protestors as most Americans did at the time, as traitors. During the Tet offensive I was overcome with a sense of guilt about not being in the war. I wrote a letter of resignation and submitted it to the police department so that I could re-enlist. I was talked out of going through with it. And gradually the nightly news from Vietnam, showing the suffering faces of women and children said to be the enemy, began to take its toll. I began to question the legitimacy of our involvement in the war and to doubt the judgment and authority of those who decided we should be involved. Millions of Americans shared a similar experience. It was a painful lesson in democracy. It seemed that thousands had died for no greater reason than that millions would be given the opportunity to think. The Vietnam War experience left me with a visceral distrust in the authority of others to make decisions that affected my future without my involvement. For the first time, I questioned the wisdom of representative democracy in a nuclear age.

I left the police department in the early Seventies to make more money and achieve a higher standard of living. I believed strongly in the American Dream. I believed that through hard work a person could achieve practically anything. I worked as a factory worker, a salesman, an independent contractor, a sports promoter, and a publisher.

In 1979 I was hired by a major oil company at Prudhoe Bay, Alaska at a salary that placed me in the top two percent income bracket in the U.S. Once again I was acutely aware of not having a degree, but the unique work schedule (one week on and one week off) gave me plenty of time to pursue my own self-education. Over a period of twenty years the external orientation of my own motivation gradually changed to internal. In 1983, shortly after my fortieth birthday, I suddenly developed an insatiable appetite for information and knowledge. My desire to know became a rage to know. I began to read and study at an ever-increasing pace, and that continues to the present day. I have read literally hundreds of books about philosophy, psychology, sociology, history, management, and technology. At first I began by reading magazines and books about the possibilities of technology. I distrusted any title over three years old. I subscribed to computer data bases so I could receive up-to-the minute information. But after a while I began to wonder if I was just being swept along with the current of trendy information. Perhaps I was being led again by my learned dependence upon authority. So I went back to the beginning. I started with the philosophy of the ancient Greeks. I studied the life of Socrates as written in the dialogues of Plato. I studied Plato and the works of Aristotle. I was startled by the wisdom of the ancients and surprised at their contempt for participative democracy. I read the works of Thomas Aquinas, Machiavelli, Hobbes, Bacon, Descartes, Spinoza, Locke, Hume, Montesquieu, Rousseau, Smith, Kant, Mill, Hegel, Darwin, Marx, Engels, James, and many others. I read the works of contemporary philosophers such as Mortimer Adler, James Feibleman, John Dewey, Will Durant, Joseph Campbell, Bertrand Russell, Alan Watts, and Sidney Hook. And then I followed psychology from Freud to Adler and Jung, to the behaviorism of Watson and Skinner, to the humanism of Abraham Maslow and Carl Rogers.

I am convinced that there is no greater way to learn than the process of self-directed inquiry. I am also convinced that, in America and in many other countries of the world, traditional education continually short-changes its recipients by its failure to empower them with sufficient knowledge of self to be self-determining. In traditional education we learn about everything but ourselves. Since educators cannot be absolutely sure of the human elements of self-discovery, they ignore them entirely.

The logical approach should be just the opposite: that which we do not know for sure should maintain our attention. We spend hundreds of hours in school studying material of questionable utility, and virtually no time in attempting to understand the human needs, drives, motives, and emotions that we live with every day. We leave these to experts, who have differing opinions, who do not understand themselves because they also were not empowered with the tools for self-discovery early enough to make them an integral part of their personality. Even though the "personal sciences," as I refer to them, are not exact disciplines, it is ludicrous to exclude them as tools for self-discovery and self-determination.

Aside from the dissonant experiences discussed in Chapter Seven, I attribute three reasons to my insatiable interest in self-education. The first has to do with life-stage theory. I found Erikson's life-stage of generativity to be especially applicable to my own life (see Chapter Four). My own mid-life stage arrived with a resolute desire to add value.

The second reason is describable in terms of Abraham Maslow's hierarchy of needs theory. Earning a high salary over a period of years enabled me to focus on my own special interests to such an extent that I have become less intimidated by the lower needs such as security. It was the same phenomenon that causes many people who have few outside interests (other than financial) to become disillusioned when they suddenly achieve wealth — namely that the rewards of material wealth are not self-sustaining without an adequate sense of personal growth and development.

Finally, I attribute the third reason for my interest in self-education to environmental causes, the kind of environmental stimulation that one receives from moving to Alaska. Alaska has a frontier psychological quality that encourages high expectations. It is a spirit that rejects rigidity and conformity. Alaska is home to a rich blend of people, people from many ethnic cultures, and many who came here without jobs. All they had was a sense of adventure and the determination to succeed in an environment of their own choosing. The newness of Alaska lends itself to new ideas, to the kind of attitudes that lead one to find more reasons to do things than excuses why not. I believe, however, that your own Alaska can exist wherever you wish it to be. The secret is in finding an environment you deem suitable and stimulating, and in discovering your niche instead of trying to fit where you wish not to be.

I went through all my first years of formal education without ever being introduced to philosophy. To totally ignore philosophy in the first twelve years of education is to fail to plant the seeds of critical inquiry. The philosophers' continual historical dialog about the great questions confounding humanity is a part of human inheritance, and we have a right to it when we are young. It doesn't matter that young minds cannot offer solutions for profound questions. What matters is that young minds are offered the legitimacy of questions to which no one seems to have the answers. To offer such is to instill in the young the ideas that inquiry is a natural process which is never complete and that one can achieve comfort with ambiguity.

The vast majority of self-help material on the market today assumes that the only road to success is through the accumulation of wealth. No doubt affluence is preferable to poverty, but wealthy individuals without the benefit of the tools of self-discovery and self-knowledge are often the most unhappy. Once they reach their goals for material success they are disillusioned. The fleeting satisfaction of material rewards sends them in desperate circles in search of something that really matters, while the poor look to wealth as the solution to all problems. People who climb Maslow's ladder discover new social needs which they are totally unprepared to handle. Self-education is the crux of understanding human needs and development.

The process of my own self-education has profoundly changed my views on a myriad of subjects. I find this to be most disturbing, because it seems that the more I reach for objectivity, the more radical my ideas sound to others. I grew up with conservative values and with political attitudes shaped by family and friends. I still ascribe to many of those, but my basic definition of the term "value" has changed dramatically. I believe a definitive consensus of value is the premise for achieving a better future.

Discovering the essence of what we value is a life-centering experience. Many of us work at jobs for which we are unsuited, pursue leisure which we do not enjoy and let decades pass without learning any more about what we want to do. Knowledge is the ultimate freedom. I believe that expanding perceptual awareness, a key to growth and development, is a genetic nexus directly wired to the human capacity for experiencing quality of life.

The great paradox of self-education is that when you think you know, you don't; when you know you don't, you do, and the more you learn, the more comfortable you become with how little you know. Meanwhile you gain an extraordinary amount of intrinsic satisfaction with the whole process.

I have much more time invested in this book than is required for a college degree. I hope you will find it useful.

Acknowledgments

Grateful acknowledgment is made to the following for permission to reprint previously published material.

Addison-Wesley, Inc.: Excerpt reprinted from *The Creative Edge*, by William C. Miller. © 1987, by Addison-Wesley, Inc., Reading, Massachusetts, p. 109. Reprinted with permission.

AMACOM: Excerpts reprinted from *The Plateauing Trap*, p. 71, by Judith Bardwick. © 1987 Judith M. Bardick. Published by AMACOM, a division of American Management Association, New York. All rights reserved. Reprinted with permission of the publisher.

Delacorte Press: *Teaching as a Subversive Activity*, by Neil Postman and Charles Weingarten. © 1969 by Neil Postman and Charles Weingarten. Reprinted by permission of Delacorte Press, a division of Bantam, Doubleday, Dell Publishing Group, Inc.

Dial Press: Excerpts from *McLuhan Hot and Cool*, Gerald Stearn, ed. © 1967 by Gerald Stearn and Marshall McLuhan.

Doubleday: Excerpts from *The Brain*, by Richard M. Restak. © 1980 by Richard M. Restak. Excerpts from *The Power of Myth*, by Joseph Campbell with Bill Moyers, Betty Sue Flowers, ed. © 1988 by Apostrophe S Productions, Inc., and Alfred van der Marck Editions. All excerpts reprinted with permission of the publisher.

Bill Draves: Excerpt from *The Free University: A Model for Lifelong Learning*, by Bill Draves, c/o Learning Resources Network (LERN), 1554 Hayes Drive, Manhatten, KS 66502. © 1980 by Bill Draves. Reprinted with permission of the author.

Encyclopaedia Britannica: Excerpt from *The Great Conversation*, by Robert M. Hutchins from *Great Books of the Western World*. Reproduced with permission from Encyclopaedia Britannica, Inc.

Facts on File: Excerpt from *De Bono's Thinking Course*, by Edward de Bono. © 1982, 1985 by Petancor B.V. Reprinted with permission of Facts on File, Inc., New York.

Harper & Row, Inc.: Excerpts from *Deschooling Society*, by Ivan Illich. © 1970, 1971 by Ivan Illich. Excerpts from *The True Believer*, by Eric Hoffer. © 1951 by Eric Hoffer. All excerpts reprinted with permission from the publisher.

Houghton Mifflin: Excerpt from *Personality Types*, by Don Rich-

Personal Acknowledgments

Thanks to the following people who offered criticism or input on numerous drafts of this work, some which continues still: Mike Chmielewski, Ken Donajkowski, Dave Snyder, Luz McDade, Cheryl Hayes Wright, and my wife Nancy.

A special thanks to: Beth Burgos, whose copy editing and research assistance over a long period of time has been invaluable; Martha Head and the staff of the Matanuska Community College Library, for outstanding support in obtaining hard-to-find books; and LuAnne Dowling, whose editing and organizational advice has been indispensable.

And finally, I'd like to extend my gratitude to the many people with whom I worked at Prudhoe Bay. My long association with them has contributed significantly to my attitudes and opinions about education, management, and life in general. They are: Joseph Alecknavage, Guy Aldrich, Keith Axelson, Mark Arkens, Robert Barndt, Bill Batchelor, Joe Beckwith, Bruce Bratain, Chuck Boe, Mike Boone, Bill Brodie, Luci Brown, Bruce Cameron, Larry Carie, Wayne Connelly, Dave Corry, Guy Cummins, Larry Dely, Bill Devine, Rick Domine, Wayne Ellis, Glen Erickson, Eddie Ezelle, Bobbie Farnsworth, Ray Flick, Curtis Foster, Chris Frost, Tony Gann, Velmar Gray, Michele Hartline, Bob Hempstead, Inga Henry, Dan Hildebrand, Bill Hiler, Pat Holdsworth, Paul Jackson, Carl Johnson, Carl Jumper, Cindy Keegan, James Kley, Fred Knack, Bill Lasher, Sue Mimms, Rick Montgomery, Henry Moser, Pat Murry, Ron Meyer, Ronald Nelson, Ray Olson, GraceAnn Owings, Kevin Owen, Mack Padgett, Rod McDonald, Brad Mothershead, Eric F. Olson, Eric T. Olson, Pat Patterson, Elbert Pittman, Paul Peterson, Randy Presley, Jim Proell, Dale Riley, Julian Ragula, Tom Ragula, Tom Rhodes, Michael Rodriguez, Cathy Satterfield, Charlie Schaef, Fred Schomberg, Charles D. Scott, Loucretia Sellers, Mark Smole, Susan Springer, Ray Standridge, Mary Stevens, Bill Stock, Robert Talbot, Wendy Talbot, Greg Taylor, Kim Tengberg, Al Topkok, Wyatt Towner, Bennie Traylor, Ann Van Dorn, Chuck Washington, Chris Watkins, Tom Whitstine, Barbara Withers, Victoria Williams, Nathan Whittom, Clarence Willoya, and Bruce Younker.

Introduction

"I haven't been educated," people will say, as if the process were something that is done to them, rather than something in which they actively participated. Or they say, "I haven't got a good education," as if it were a commodity that must be purchased.

I assert that both these modes of thought are erroneous, even damaging to our society. I am convinced that there exists no method superior to self-education for accomplishing one's goals, whatever they may be. The reason for this is simple: When you control your own education, you also control your own destiny. And the only tuition is desire.

A person need not be apologetic about any lack of "formal" credential, because what's possible through self-education can be so much better. Throughout history some of the greatest contributions to mankind have been made by people who educated themselves. Abraham Lincoln, the sixteenth president of the United States, was self-educated. He had little more than one year of formal schooling. Herbert Spencer, one of the most famous philosophers of the nineteenth century, remained an uneducated man until the age of forty, at which time he educated himself. Thomas A. Edison, technological genius and holder of over a thousand patents, had only three months of formal schooling. R. Buckminster Fuller, philosopher, engineer, architect, inventor, and poet, clearly one of the most original thinkers of the twentieth century, never completed his formal education. In *Critical Path*, the late Buckminster Fuller wrote:

> I am certain that none of the world's problems—which we are all perforce thinking about today—have any hope of solution except through total democratic society's becoming thoroughly and comprehensively self-educated. Only thereby will society be able to identify and intercommunicate the vital problems of total world society. Only thereafter may humanity effectively sort out and put those problems into order of importance for solution in respect to the most fundamental principles governing humanity's survival and enjoyment of life on Earth.

Much has been learned in this century about the learning process, but little of this knowledge has been used. For years, educators have known that students have individual learning styles, that they assimilate information differently according to perception and method. Educators have known for decades that people require varying amounts of time to learn, and that this time has nothing whatsoever to do with hourly classes, semesters, eight years of primary school, four years of high school, or four years of college.

Self-education takes place when the learner perceives a need. In the absence of a felt need we are likely to perceive new information as being irrelevant or as arbitrarily forced upon us, in which case we subliminally categorize it as forgettable. And yet, in spite of this fact, today's system of formal education is designed to discredit the autodidact – a self-educated person.

When I refer to someone in the context of this book as self-educated, I mean a person who has pursued his or her education outside the traditional educational system, but this is not a complete definition. I assert that a person becomes an autodidact when he assumes total responsibility for his own learning and the primary drive to know comes from within and not as a result of others' expectations. I consider all the people quoted in this text, as well as those who work inspired it, to be self-educated, regardless of their educational credentials. Self-education neither depends on, nor is necessarily hindered by, traditional education.

(I have tried to address the problem of gender and awkward language as fairly as I know how without butchering sentences. When I have used he to mean that person or a certain person, or mankind to represent the human race, I have done so only for the sake of sound and clarity and not with a gender bias.)

Self-education is a purposeful endeavor in which we are aware of the perceptual process and its effect on our judgment. We discipline ourselves to favor objectivity regardless of the nature of inquiry, especially when the answers we seek reveal results with which we are uncomfortable. Self-education is a perpetual process in which a left step of self-discovery leads to a right step in self-knowledge, which in turn leads to further self-discovery and more self-knowledge. As we gain momentum we become empowered with the ability to positively affect our environment, and at that point we are capable of self-determination.

Self-University Core Curriculum Questions

Each of us is unique in our acquisition of knowledge and our need to learn. Self-education is person-centered education. Subject matter assumes fluid, non-hierarchical relationships that are forever in a state of flux. Imagine the subheadings in this book as being in constant motion, changing pages and chapters at random, while never appearing in quite the same context more than once. If you keep this in mind as you review the following core curriculum questions, you will gain a sense of the definition of self-education as it is used in this book. These questions are fashioned by my own interests. As you proceed through this book, you may want to replace them with your own.

- How has my experience with traditional education influenced my attitude about learning?
- How do I define reality? Do I see things as they are or as I want them to be?
- Do I understand how I relate to authority?
- Are my values affected by the advertising industry?
- How well do I know myself? Is my self-knowledge adequate for a full life?
- Do my attitudes about intelligence, creativity, genius, expertise and the way I use my memory affect my self-image?
- Do I know how the major theories of human nature square with my own experience?
- Am I aware of my philosophy of life?
- What are the duties and obligations of citizenship in the United States of America?
- Do I understand the management philosophy at my place of work either as a manager or as an employee?
- Do I understand the nature of credentialism in America?
- Should I go back to school? Why?
- Do I really know what I want to do with my life?
- Do I understand the dynamics of competition and cooperation?
- Do I understand other cultures? Do I need to?
- Does busyness always constitute value?
- Am I ready for the future?

A major theme here is that traditional "passive" education, designed to be concluded when we are young adults, is inadequate. Not only is it insufficient for solving today's problems, but it is a dangerous way to embrace the future. Unfortunately, for many people the process of formal education has been a source of learned limitations.

The mission of *Self-University* is simple: To empower *you* with the confidence, conviction and desire to create *your own* Self-University. It is possible to document and prove the learning you have attained through "nontraditional" methods, both what you have already earned and that which you gain as you go. These personal credentials can aid you in getting the promotion you want, changing careers, or simply enhancing your own quality of life as a human being.

It is my belief that self-education through self-directed inquiry is a natural way to gain control over your life. Self-education leads to self-empowerment. Self-empowerment is the ability to provide your own definition of success, thereby allowing you to know when you have reached your goal and have become a "graduate student" of Self-University. My intent is to demonstrate that:

- a formal education tends to ignore that which is most important to us: the development of self-knowledge.
- the study of media is necessary in order to understand ourselves.
- self-knowledge is an anchor necessary for social equilibrium.
- self-directed inquiry is one of the greatest empowering principles there is.
- a liberal education is no longer a luxury, but is in fact a necessity for ourselves as individuals as well as a nation.
- a person can be an expert without academic credentials.
- the satisfaction derived from self-directed inquiry can be one of the most exhilarating experiences of being human.
- the means to an education superior to the college experience is possible in half the time and at a fraction of the cost.
- average people can and should become intellectuals, since the survival of democracy may depend on it.

Though we have each had different experiences, most of us who are adults today endured a passive education in the sense that we were told what to study. Not only were we supplied with answers, but, even more importantly, we were also given the questions. Since we did not formulate the questions, the exercises often had little meaning.

Aside from the process of socialization, the greatest lesson we learned was that of "conformity." We learned how to be instructed, where to stand, where to sit, what to think, and when to talk. We learned that the invitation to ask questions, though sincere by a few teachers, was not in the long term to be taken seriously. We learned to accept authority without question.

The tragedy of the educational experience in America is that new knowledge about learning is simply not being applied as it comes to light. When pioneers in the aviation industry made new discoveries in aerodynamics, for example, they used the knowledge to make better airplanes. The result was that man has been to the moon and back.

By contrast, when educators make new discoveries about learning they seem unable to penetrate the monolithic bureaucracy of the educational system. The result is more of the same. No change.

Futurists and economists assert that technology and shifts in world economic developments are rapidly changing the structure of American society. We are becoming a "knowledge society." The experience is having profound effects on the way we live and work. In a knowledge society education is a "capital" investment. In a knowledge society critical thinking, problem solving, creativity, and innovation are prerequisites for participation regardless of how a person defines success. In *Critical Path*, Buckminster Fuller suggested that we have the technological capability to live as a planet of four billion "billionaires."

I would argue that, if we had achieved only twenty percent as much progress during the past two hundred years in education as we have in technology, today we would be a planet of four billion intellectuals. I think that Mr. Fuller would probably have agreed that intellectual development on a massive scale is a prerequisite to billionaire status for the average citizen. Educated people demand accountability and equitable treatment. Poor, uneducated citizens are unable to articulate their needs and are therefore not taken seriously.

Education is as much a requisite for citizenship as it is a means of earning a living. Instead of using the educational process as a primary means of qualifying for jobs, we must be sure that we are educated to the extent that we know which jobs should be performed.

We are on the cusp of a technological revolution that promises to incrementally eliminate the drudgery of work and exponentially produce products that enhance the quality of human life. A potential for achieving the greatest quality of life in human history is counterbalanced with the opportunity for catastrophe. Paradoxically, the edict of "severe consequences" in which the harshness with which actions are dealt has come full circle. For example, in primitive tribal communities an argument between two individuals that led to a minor physical injury might have meant the ultimate death of the injured party. But the process of civilization has all but eliminated the risk of death from minor injuries.

Today however, a small misunderstanding between countries

could conceivably lead to the destruction of all human life. The price for citizenship and protection of democracy in such a rapidly changing world is that we must develop our minds, or increase the likelihood that humanity will perish.

This book consists of four parts. Part One discusses why we are the way we are: Why the way we are taught affects how we behave, how media affects our lives (often without our ability to detect its influence), and how our attitudes about such attributes as intelligence, creativity, genius and expertise affect our attitudes about ourselves and our abilities.

Part Two discusses the personal sciences and the people sciences, including theories of human behavior, motivation, life stages, the search for meaning, sociology, politics, management and a range of topics associated with being human.

Part Three discuss the difficulties of credentialism: how credentialism restricts opportunity and often protects incompetent practitioners instead of the consumer whom it is supposed to protect; how the credentialing process exacerbates the difficulty of finding employment for which we are suited. Part Three also examines the possibilities of tomorrow, the humanization of technology and how our attitudes about the future will, in fact, shape the future.

Part Four offers practical advice ranging from understanding personality theories and improving your memory to creating your own credentials and deciding whether or not you should go back to school.

Because this book is the result of my own self-education, it is heavily biased and highly opinionated in favor of my own study and experience. I have no formal credentials, but the fact has not stopped me from being successful or from creating my own Self-University. I challenge you to not accept my ideas without argument, but to create your own Self-University so that we may agree, or, if I am wrong, you might have the opportunity to change my mind.

Part I

CHAPTER ONE

Why We Are the Way We Are

*In our days we receive three different or
contrary educations, namely, of our parents,
of our masters, and of the world. What we
learn in the latter effaces all the ideas of the
former.*
　　　　　　　　　　—Charles de Montesquieu

All humans are born into the world with the capacity for unconditional love and compassion.[1] It is through ignorance of nurture that
these qualities are lost. If just one generation across the planet would
use what is known about the nature of humans in the nurture of
their children, and would ensure that each child was taught the
method of such nurture so that each acquired a comfortable level of
self-knowledge, it would be the beginning of the end of war. But
instead, each society, each culture, is slow to pass on any discoveries
in the nurture of children that do not lend themselves to the perpetuation of its accepted lifestyle. It's as if each culture decides that the
way that they themselves were raised is appropriate for their own
children. "If it was good enough for me, it is good enough for them."

In America the most precious knowledge that education can
produce is not even discussed until long past the time that students
realize something critically important in their education is missing.
This precious knowledge is knowledge of self. It is knowledge about
feelings, needs, expectations, interpersonal relationships, social obligation, and the meaning of physical urges ("Am I normal, or am I the
only person alive who feels this way?").

In the process of cultural development, society has perverted
a natural inclination to study what is most important to us. What
we don't know for sure about ourselves should be on the front
burner of human inquiry, but we don't even put it on the stove.
Human behavior is not an exact science, so we dwell on less urgent,
more exact subject matter. We teach only what we think we know for
sure. If our culture did nothing more than make it clear to young
people what is not known for sure about the nature of being human,
we would be much less confused. Instead, we franchise that which is
not known for sure into a profession, so that psychiatrists and

psychologists (who learned little of themselves when they were young) can help the rest of us cope with the same problems. Indeed many people enter the behavioral sciences for the underlying purpose of developing self-knowledge, but the high suicide rate among psychiatrists and psychologists testifies to the need for learning about ourselves when we are young enough to include what we have learned into our repertoire of behavior.

Because we received an education that ignored what concerned us most when we were young, we learned to have little tolerance for ambiguity. As a result we are in constant search of certainty. What we don't find in religion we seek in tarot cards, astrology, crystal balls, channelers and a growing company of self-appointed gurus. Anyone who claims to know what is going on and seems pretty well convinced of it can gain our attention and, unfortunately, our confidence as well.

Pedagogy

Primitive man taught his offspring in the same manner as beasts, by the example of individual instruction. The objective was simple: Learn or perish. As knowledge increased exponentially, it became necessary to tender the young to the care of others for their education. The objective was still preparation for life, but as civilization grew, the consequences for not learning became less severe. Thus, pedagogy was born. Pedagogy is a Greek word meaning the art and science of teaching children. Schools born of pedagogy have existed in similar forms for over four thousand years.

The educational system in the United States is the residue of a pedagogical system established to serve an agrarian society. There were modifications to the system when this agrarian society gave way to industrialization, but the system has changed little from its inception.

Pedagogy is like strong medicine: it has side effects. Millions of Americans are so negatively affected by the process that as soon as they have completed their required years in formal education, they make a decision to stop learning, either consciously or unconsciously. While not directly attributing the cause of this decision to pedagogy, Philip B. Crosby said in *Quality Is Free*:

> There is a theory of human behavior that says people subconsciously retard their own intellectual growth. They come to rely on cliches and habits. Once they reach the age of their own personal comfort with the world, they stop

learning and their mind runs on idle for the rest of their days. They may progress organizationally, they may be ambitious and eager, and they may even work night and day. But they learn no more. The bigoted, the narrow minded, the stubborn, and the perpetually optimistic have all stopped learning.

I assert that for many people this decision to stop learning is based directly on the ill effects of the pedagogical experience.

Another destructive aspect in the nature of pedagogy is that it perpetuates the notion of its own importance in the learning process. In other words, pedagogists ignore the fact that more learning takes place outside the classroom than within, and this learning from experience is ignored.[2] Students are treated as if their heads were empty containers and anything they might offer as having been learned by direct experience is inferior to the curriculum.

In his book, *Deschooling Society*, author Ivan Illich wrote:

School initiates, too the Myth of Unending Consumption. This modern myth is grounded in the belief that process inevitably produces something of value and, therefore, production necessarily produces demand. School teaches us that instruction produces learning. The existence of schools produces the demand for schooling. Once we have learned to need school, all our activities tend to take the shape of client relationships to other specialized institutions. Once the self-taught man or woman has been discredited, all non-professional activity is rendered suspect. In school we are taught that valuable learning is the result of attendance; that the value of learning increases with the amount of input; and, finally that this value can be measured and documented by grades and certificates.

For decades students in American schools have endured the indignation of forced ranking. Identified and labeled by letters, A's learn the pleasure of conformity, F's feel the sting and stigma of failure. Clearly the objective in grading is to evaluate performance. But the result in the classroom experience is that students integrate this often arbitrary grading system into their personal evaluation of self-worth.[3] This system of self-assessment and process of measuring one's malleability follows the student his whole life, from the classroom into the corporation or workplace. Classroom behavior becomes corporate behavior.

The attributes of democracy are championed in the physical

confines of a classroom dictatorship. This problem is compounded by a paradox not readily apparent to us as students: Although the teachers appeared to be totally in charge, they often had little control over their work and were themselves treated as children in pedagogical fashion. The effect was often a thick layer of classroom frustration whose origin we could not sense.

Students learn quickly to distinguish between what the teacher says and what the teacher does. Teachers routinely ask if there are any questions, but the packaged curriculum doesn't allow time for questions. Even if it did, the student might fear appearing dumb by exposing his or her ignorance. Experience teaches the student that few teachers expect the invitation for questions to be taken seriously. There are teachers who sincerely make the offer (and indeed some attempt to establish a Socratic dialog), but they are in the minority. Moreover the reversal of a student's preconditioned behavioral response is not usually spontaneous. In other words, one positive experience will not stand up against ten bad ones.

For years, I thought that the silence that followed "Are there any questions?" meant that I was the only one in the class who had any. When I finally began to ask questions, I could tell that other students had the same ones. They were glad that I had asked, because they wouldn't have. It was a great personal discovery to find that I was not necessarily less intelligent than everyone else.

Gradually the natural sense of curiosity is overridden by a need for acceptance. Socially adept students intuitively perceive that it is easier to learn the teacher than the subject matter.[4] Pleasing the teacher is rewarded behavior. It is as simple as providing the teacher with what he or she is looking for. At this point an important social lesson is learned, and the conditioning tract is set. For many students any natural pleasure that might have been derived from learning is from then on subordinate to a focus on their behavior. In other words, learning is really "behaving," not thinking. Doing what is expected by an authority figure is rewarded. It has a higher priority than thinking, and coincidentally, it is the path of least resistance. Success in classroom learning becomes a simple exercise. It is the ability to demonstrate the recollection of what is said to be fact. In *Teaching as a Subversive Activity*, authors Neil Postman and Charles Weingartner discussed an unacknowledged, but clear message from the aims of classroom teachers:

- Passive acceptance is a more desirable response to ideas than active criticism.

- Discovering knowledge is beyond the power of students and is, in any case, none of their business.
- Recall is the highest form of intellectual achievement, and the collection of unrelated (facts) is the goal of education.
- The voice of authority is to be trusted and valued more than independent judgment.
- One's own ideas and those of one's classmates are inconsequential.
- Feelings are irrelevant in education.
- There is always a single, unambiguous Right Answer to a question.
- English is not History and History is not Science and Science is not Art and Art is not Music, and Art and Music are minor subjects and English, History and Science are major subjects, and a subject is something you take and when you have taken it, you are immune and need not take it again. (The Vaccination Theory of Education?)

Students instilled with a strong sense of self-worth sometimes refuse to learn the teacher and try to maintain a sense of self-determination, only to have their zeal for exploration systematically eroded by the demand for right answers. These are sometimes appropriate, but after years of providing right answers, students begin to believe each question has only one right answer. The world becomes black and white. To demonstrate this phenomenon you have only to mispronounce a word in public. People will be rude to one another in order to be the first to correct your pronunciation, regardless of whether they know the meaning of the word. The point you were trying to make may actually be overridden and nullified by the fact that you made a mistake. You mispronounced the word; therefore you were incorrect. And as a result of your error, those who did not even know the meaning of the word in the first place were vindicated for their lack of knowledge. Such behavior is adopted because it is inherent in human nature to judge ourselves and others by the same criteria with which we are judged. As author Ivan Illich wrote in *Deschooling Society*:

> People who submit to the standard of others for the measure of their own personal growth soon apply the same ruler to themselves. They no longer have to be put in their place, but put themselves into their assigned slots, squeeze themselves into the niche which they have been taught to

seek, and, in the very process, put their fellows into their places, too, until everybody and everything fits.

Regardless of how we perceived the process of our early experience in school, the majority of us found learning in the pedagogical sense to diminish the human experience. We were jaded by conformity and the mind-numbing sameness of the experience. It left an indelible mark on our self-esteem. Maybe that is why we believed those who proved highly adaptable to the dehumanizing experience of school to be a little "odd." We called them book worms, eggheads and other names too numerous to mention. Thinking of them as "nerds" offered some relief and rationalization about our own lack of ability to adapt.

In 1897 educator-philosopher John Dewey said, "The school is primarily a social institution. Education, therefore, is a process of living and not a preparation for future living." But when I went to school in the Fifties we thought of school as a natural means of preparing for the future, not for living in the present. Later we found it to be neither. Little of what my generation learned prepared us for the present or the future, and none of it had anything whatsoever to do with preparing us for the decisions we would face as adults.[5] The greatest thing to come out of education in those days was that almost everyone learned how to read.

The classroom was more likely than not our greatest source of learned, self-limiting behavior. The classroom experience taught us how to be taught, how to compromise our interests, how to flex our short term memory, how to accommodate, how to conform, how to bend the rules and how penalties for creativity might be excised.[6]

We were under the mistaken assumption that ability and effort were the same thing. We thought that if we worked hard enough we would be "smart."[7] The idea that we each had our own individual learning style never occurred to us, so we blamed ourselves, not the teachers or the system that failed to adapt to our needs. When we worked hard and still fell behind, we decided we were somehow inadequate. As we advanced to higher grades, we became acutely conscious of the need for speed in achievement. We felt inadequate if we didn't catch on as fast as others. The feelings from these perceptions of being less than whole set many of us on a perpetual treadmill of underachievement. We have all been affected by the formal learning experience in varying degrees. Some will recover gradually, some spontaneously after many years, but most of us will always exhibit some scars. The behavior viscerally molded and reinforced thousands of times is now part of our personalities.

Obviously, some manage to survive the process of formal education functionally intact or we would not be the most technologically developed nation on earth. Still we have an ongoing argument about the quality of contribution. At issue is whether or not a majority of the scientists and technicians responsible for today's technology have an education sufficiently balanced to keep our technological tools in social perspective.

I don't offer this indictment of pedagogy to undermine the dedication, sincerity and effectiveness of our most deserving educators. We have always had excellent teachers at all levels in the educational system. More often than not they were the source of inspiration that led many of us to experience the enjoyment of self-education. These excellent teachers were merely the previous generation of students damaged least by the experience. Many of them entered the system determined to change it. A few are trying, but most have given up.

It is possible to change this negative orientation to learning, and in fact, it is necessary for finding a successful niche in today's society and for ensuring a place in the future. Adults who naively believe that their education is behind them automatically assume a passive role in society. Even retired people abdicate control of the remainder of their lives with the assumption that their learning years are over. Day-to-day decisions increasingly call for informed choices. Financial decisions, medical decisions, lifestyle decisions, and political decisions that protect the rights of the senior citizen dominate the lives of today's retired persons.

Indoctrination

The first twelve years of school are presented in the form of indoctrination, in pedagogical fashion, from parent to child. It is not until the college experience that we are encouraged to question and examine the origin of beliefs, if then. The implications are obvious. If, as educational statistics suggest, only one-fifth of society attends college, then eighty percent of the population, by the nature of its learning experience, is likely to be comfortable doing what it is told. People are more willing to change their minds based on authority than by their own assessment. Examples of this are often observable on television interviews when citizens are asked questions about politics. They often display assurance that those in government are bound to know what they are doing by the very nature of the positions they hold.

The American Society for Quality Control claims that sixty-one percent of Americans who have not attended college believe American products to be of better quality than foreign made goods, while only 45 percent of people with some college and 39 percent of college graduates believe this to be true.

Epistemology is the study of the nature and origin of knowledge. When we are very young epistemological thought is part of our nature until it is "hammered" out by the educational experience and the nurture of parents who know little of parenting. Thus indoctrination is accomplished by nature of the fact that the student is told what is true, what to think, what is important, and what will be necessary to remember.

In theory, the college experience is supposed to open the student's mind to a perpetual search for objective truths, but in practice the system-induced "pedogenic illnesses" acquired during the first twelve years can hardly be expected to suddenly reverse themselves.[8] After twelve years of indoctrination in a totalitarian environment, one cannot be expected to suddenly demand a democratic process. Indeed a democratic process even in college will not likely be tolerated by a faculty who were themselves educated in a totalitarian classroom environment. Whether the college experience is a questioning environment is dependent to some degree upon the institution. The student should be forewarned not to make the mistake of questioning the teacher or the methods of instruction. For many, college is merely a continuation of the high school experience.

If we have not been abused by an indoctrinational educational process, how else can we explain how citizens of the most technologically advanced nation in the world routinely:

- Make a conscious decision to stop learning?
- Allow the self-educated person to be discredited?
- Accept one religious doctrine without examining others?
- Believe that the search for truth is the folly of philosophers?
- Spend decades in jobs for which they are ill-suited?
- Accept a "storybook" fashion of history texts and movie media as life representations when these don't remotely approximate human experience?
- Almost without exception lose the sense of curiosity that dominated their early childhood?
- Let others dictate the course of their studies without intuitive course correction?
- Accept the assertions of teachers without insisting on active discourse?

- Assume that elected representatives, elected by a minority of the electorate, of whom only a few are acquainted with the issues, will act in their best interest without the benefit of council and active participation?

The list is endless. Create your own by adding to this one, and see if you conclude as I do that much of our behavior, influenced at least in part by the formal educational process, is ludicrous.

Authority

To understand how critical education is to the future of democracy, it is important to examine how our education affects the way we relate to authority. A majority of Americans have assimilated an unacknowledged philosophy based on a shallowly-rooted belief system. This system is shallow not because of the content, but because the beliefs are unexamined by the holder. They are accepted on faith, without question and, for the most part, rest solely on the authority of others. Beliefs accepted on the basis of authority are likely to be regarded as absolute. Philosopher James K. Feibleman in his book *Technology and Reality* wrote, "Men who find themselves in the grip of an absolute belief will slaughter other men without the slightest compunction, as indeed they have done for millennia, and as fascists, communists and other religious fanatics are still doing at the present time."

People are led to such absolute belief by the process of indoctrination. And once indoctrinated, a person who holds on to his or her beliefs via the authority of others will more easily change those beliefs by accepting the authority of yet another rather than by using his own initiative. People who "believe" on the basis of authority are easily manipulated. They are trusting. Indeed, it is easier for them to do what they are told than to examine their beliefs and think for themselves. Hitler's Nazi officers carried out atrocities without question on the sole basis of his authority. Were they manipulated? Were they indoctrinated? Did they trust in the authority of their Fuehrer?

Belief that is based on faith must be acknowledged by the believer as having its origin in faith and not fact. To do otherwise is to deny the legitimacy of those who do not share the same beliefs. Alan Bloom, author of *The Closing of the American Mind*, argues persuasively against this, saying that our attempts to understand other cultures have led to a decay of our own culture because we have adopted an attitude of "openness" in which anything and everything goes. However, I am not advocating that we not hold strong moral convictions. On the contrary: The whole point of examining our beliefs is to plant both feet on firm ground, to maintain our convictions from the basis of awareness and understanding. Yet when the people of any culture deny the rights of others to believe as they choose, their actions inevitably lead to the kind of behavior that causes conflict. The conflict often results in war.

Belief is often a source of comfort, just as doubt is often a source of discomfort. It should be easier to live with the discomfort of doubt than the righteous feeling of having destroyed others in the name of faith. The history of human experience demonstrates that we should exercise the greatest doubt when the desire to believe is the strongest. Throughout human history millions of people have died in wars fought for every conceivable reason while each side assumed God to be on their side. Reality suggests that the majority of humans on this planet prefer indoctrination to the discomfort of uncertainty.[9] Conformity is the path of least resistance. The result is blind adjustment.

Denise Winn, author of *The Manipulated Mind*, wrote:

> Indoctrination is an emotive word. Perhaps for most people it is most commonly associated with the rather blatant process of persuasion that goes on in totalitarian regimes or the systematized thinking encouraged in minority political groups or religious cults (that other people belong to) where slogans or catchwords, such as "state control" or "enlightenment" encapsulate central concepts. It has a bad flavor, a bad feel, implying that the indoctrinated person has taken on board the conclusions of others instead of coming to his or her own. It flies in the face of free thinking, the rational weighing up of arguments and all such ideals that we think we hold dear.
>
> But indoctrination, defined at its simplest, means to imbue with a doctrine. To "imbue" means to permeate or to saturate, implying a process that can be much more subtle than the repetitious reciting of approved slogans. As authors who have been concerned by the concepts of coercion and behavior manipulation show, most of us are indoctrinated throughout our lives, often without even knowing it. Beliefs almost "grow" into us. They are then sustained and protected, usually unconsciously, by the physiological and psychological processes of perception.

Millions of young Americans are indoctrinated each year at home, school and through a variety of institutions. The conclusions of others are accepted as fact. It is a subtle method of programming and maintaining the status quo, because those indoctrinated today are indoctrinated by those who were indoctrinated a generation before, who were themselves indoctrinated by a previous generation and so on into antiquity.[10] The passing on of values and ideals from one generation to another subsequent generation in part explains why we are so slow to change the process of education. What is learned rationally is not always passed on, but what is learned emotionally is. In other words many teachers believe intellectually in the educational agenda of today, but their actions reinforce the educational values of their own student days. We learn by what our teachers do, not by what they say.

What would be the consequence if each generation were nurtured into developing exceptional powers of reason? How would authority be maintained? Who could guarantee that the current system would remain intact? Philosopher Francis Bacon (1561–1626) wrote:

> Again, for that other conceit that learning should undermine the reverence of laws and government, it is assuredly a mere deprivation and calumny, without all shadow of truth. For to say that a blind custom of obedience should be a surer obligation than duty taught and understood, is to affirm, that a blind man may tread surer by a guide than a seeing man can by a light. And it is without all controversy, that learning doth make the minds of men gentle, generous, maniable, and pliant to government; whereas ignorance makes them churlish, thwart, and mutinous: and the evidence of time doth clear this assertion, considering that the most barbarous, rude, and unlearned times have been most subject to tumults, seditions, and changes.

I am not suggesting that the intent of American teachers is to withhold learning about government or any other subject from students. But the process of presenting the curriculum to students during the first twelve years of school without discourse is to plant seeds without preparing the ground, especially when it is known that a large percentage of these students will not go to college.

A society made up of people who are storage repositories of

unrelated facts is easily manipulated. These people have been subjected to enough educational process to think of themselves as being educated and autonomous. Such people have great difficulty distinguishing between fact and opinion and yet, because they consider themselves to be educated, they also believe themselves to be above, and therefore untouched by propaganda.

To a large extent authority is preserved in societies by a knowledge dependency based on faith in the relationship between those who claim to know and those who don't. Spinoza (1632–1677) wrote:

> Hence it happens that the man who endeavours to find out the true causes of miracles, and who desires as a wise man to understand nature, and not to gape at it like a fool, is generally considered and proclaimed to be a heretic and impious by those whom the vulgar worship as the interpreters both of nature and the gods. For these know that if ignorance be removed, amazed stupidity, the sole ground on which they rely in arguing or in defending their authority, is taken away also.

Sometimes the maintenance of authority is protected under the guise of a character trait such as discipline. We are so conditioned to conform that almost any time we have trouble adjusting to a group or an organization the fault is thought to be ours. We are under tremendous pressure to fit. Focus is shifted to emphasize self-discipline. Thus, there is no longer a need to question, only a need to perform.

This advocacy toward performance is so pronounced in Western society that we have come to distinguish between people as "doers" or "thinkers." Our admiration is reserved for those who "do." One doesn't want to be seen "thinking." We are so caught up in this fallacy that almost any action is preferred to inaction. The philosophy, "Do something even if it's wrong," will allow forgiveness. Thoughtful reflection that leads to the conclusion that no action is appropriate will lead to scorn and admonishment. Heroes in Western society are people who "do," not people who "think." A movie I saw several years ago portrayed a situation that called for action. A huge character was introduced, his brawn obviously being offered as a solution to the problem at hand, and the main character introduced him. He said: "This is Chuck. Chuck don't think, he just do." The audience cheered.

A degree of conformity and discipline is necessary for the

existence of civilization. But if the average citizen cannot protect himself against becoming a Nazi in the name of patriotism, then his freedom is near its end. Protection from such influence comes from self-education via the process of self-directed inquiry with an emphasis on reason and critical thinking. For the purpose of living practically, it is necessary to reach an equilibrium between respect for tradition and a healthy disrespect for authority.

Reality

What is reality? It is a philosophical question worthy of investigation and discourse, but the definition used here is simply that reality is what we perceive it to be. Accepting this premise means there are as many realities as there are people. But reality doesn't stop with people; each species has some sense of perception even though we humans have no way of knowing what that might be. And how would we perceive reality if, in addition to our five senses, we could pick up radio signals and space noise, or feel the presence of neutrinos as they penetrate the earth? Our perceptual senses are deceptively limited; we perceive two eighty-degree summer days as being exactly the same, but there are so many subtle differences between them that they make long-range weather forecasting by computer virtually impossible.[11] If you use your imagination you can add thousands of dimensions that would alter human perspective. What about ESP and the cornucopia of metaphysical experience claimed by the New Age proponents?

The point I am trying to make is that there are many ways of perceiving reality and for the most part each of us, with the help of our friends, family and associates, has created his or her own version. We partition our respective realities with a cultural learning process that leads to prejudice. Since the publication of *The Closing of the American Mind*, it has become fashionable to use the word "prejudice" with a positive connotation. For example, one might say that strong prejudices are merely visions of the way things are or should be.[12] The word prejudice is used throughout this book in the negative sense: an adverse opinion without just grounds.

A major thesis of this book is that we should use the process of self-education to see things as they "are" and as they "should" be, but, in light of the way we are formally educated in America, for me to be objective requires that I devote a disproportional amount of space to skepticism. The process of our education encourages that we build walls of arbitrary prejudice without being conscious of the constructive process, or of the existence of such walls once they are in place.

For our purposes here, objectivity means the ability to see through these walls of prejudice without regard to our own wishes or cultural bias. The search for truth is merely a desire to achieve an intuitive instinct in favor of objectivity. Self-education is a journey in the search for truth. It is learning to acknowledge the existence of these walls, to see through them, to view life through the realities of others and to tear down the walls made of arbitrary prejudice. The ability to see from many perspectives is a tremendously liberating quality because it enables one to be free of the frustration of negotiating differences with others. It leads to understanding, which in turn leads to the acceptance of differences, which eventually leads to empathy. It is an empowering exercise and experience.

We think of ourselves as a rational society, as being fair, practical, objective and caring. But are we? How do the following facts fit your perception of reality?

- There are approximately five billion humans on the planet earth.
- There are enough food resources in the world in grains alone to provide everyone on the planet with more than 3000 calories per day.[13]
- In the twentieth century, billions of people have died as a result of starvation. Almost all of these people had "dark" skin. "White" people do not die of starvation.[14]
- Each day 40,000 children die for lack of an adequate diet.
- Human starvation on earth could be eliminated with an amount of food equivalent to one-half of what is eaten each year by rodents.[15]
- Since 1776, 575,068 Americans have died on battle fields around the world in wars fought under the American flag.[16]
- Each year 50,000 or more Americans die in traffic accidents.[17]
- Every decade the number of Americans killed on the highways is roughly equivalent to the number killed in all the wars in the history of the U.S. A significant percent of these annual deaths could be prevented if everyone wore seatbelts. And an additional significant percentage of these deaths could be prevented if manufacturers built safer cars.
- Each year 350,000 Americans die from illnesses related to smoking cigarettes. The medical cost associated with these deaths is astronomical, yet the United States government

spends over 400 million dollars each year to subsidize the growing of tobacco.[18]
- Each year nearly 500,000 Americans die from cancer.[19]
- Each year the federal budget expenditure on defense spending compared to cancer research is almost 300 to 1.[20]
- This year (you fill in the blank) _____ Americans died in battle.

We have enough armaments to destroy our perceived enemies a thousand times over. Yet, each year our expenditures do not reflect the incredible disparity in cancer fatalities versus those occurring from war. This discrepancy would seem hard to explain to the person dying of cancer. Each year we lose almost as many people to cancer as have died in all the wars ever fought by our countrymen. Granted we need a strong defense, but wouldn't it be a more rational response to use some of the emotional enthusiasm that we have for the preparation for war toward preventing millions of deaths by declaring a real war on cancer? I am not ignoring the fact that thousands of people have engaged in cancer research or that we are making some progress, but consider what our response might be if we were suddenly thrust into circumstances where we started to lose nearly 500,000 people a year to a new phenomenon. Substitute the word terrorism for cancer in the sentences above and see how the perspective changes. In such a case, would a 200 to 1 budget be more appropriate, or 100 to 1 or maybe even 5 to 1? Consider what the attitude toward curing cancer would be if we spent 20 percent of our defense budget on the fight against cancer. The intensity of the effort would ensure that there would be a great demand for young people to enter the field of research. The effect would create a great sense of national urgency.

I would argue that our current irrational budget priorities would not have been possible if our sense of awareness had not evolved slowly. The evolution of communications media has gradually elevated our awareness of the number of people dying from cancer. Like the frog in a pot on the stove, if the water is heated slowly the frog will wait until it is too late to jump out. Likewise we have grown used to the escalating deaths from cancer. We now accept it as normal that one person dies about every sixty-four seconds from cancer and that about 30 percent of us will get the disease.

What will we do about AIDS? Will we focus on the numbers in typical bottom line fashion and watch them rise continually because we regard AIDS as a moral dilemma, or will we focus on prevention with a budget that is practical in light of the potential catastrophe?

Nothing that you or I ever learned in school owned up to the economics of human mortality. We were culturized to deny that human deaths are permissible according to an economic formula. Yet such formulas exist. All we would have to do is apply statistical analysis to our current spending and we would discover the arbitrary economic values we place on human life in a variety of circumstances.

Suppose on today's evening news it is announced that a famine and economic chaos have struck suddenly in a foreign country and thousands of people are on the verge of immediate starvation. And the people are white. World reaction is totally predictable. There would be a unanimous cry of "outrage" and "indignation." The very thought that such an atrocity might be allowed to happen is incredible. Citizens from countries around the world would mobilize immediately and dispatch logistical forces to the scene with food and medical supplies. If one child were to starve to death before supplies arrived, the world would mourn together via satellite, while grief-stricken anchormen extolled the child's virtue to news audiences.

Such a disaster would slap the face of reality. White people do not allow white people to starve to death. How, then, did we allow ourselves to be culturized to accept the fact that thousands of "nonwhite" people starve to death each day? It is reality, but we choose not to see it. For eight days in the fall of 1988 world attention focused on efforts to rescue three whales trapped in an ice pack off Point Barrow, Alaska. The American-Soviet effort cost more than one million dollars, during which time 320,000 nonwhite children starved to death in Third World countries. We rationalize starvation with the notion of scarce resources, but there is clearly enough food for everyone in the world. Further, we have only to look at our own history to know that populations stabilize with prosperity. When we really began to prosper in this century, the number of traditional large families dropped dramatically.

Cultural Illusion

We learn to see what we expect to see. It's a natural part of growth and development. If we see something that does not fit with our preconceived expectations, our mind will create a version that does fit. In our personal constructions of reality we set about to experience reality in a manner which suggests that the only things which are "real" are those with which we are preoccupied.

Buy a new car that you think is unusual, and all of a sudden it will seem as if everyone has one just like it. The Alaskan Eskimo learns to recognize over twenty different types of snow. Most of us see snow as simply wet or dry.

Another example is our current battle against cancer. If we were suddenly thrust into having to make decisions about a similar threat to humanity, we would likely consider our current response to be a form of madness, if it were not for the gradual manner that our culture has become accustomed to such losses. We see over, under, beyond, beside, or around that which does not fit with our perception of reality.[21] We look directly at that with which we do not agree, but we do not see. Our personal biases perpetually distort reality. For example, smokers who adamantly believe in their right to smoke wherever they please suddenly comprehend the right not to breath secondhand smoke when they themselves become nonsmokers.

In *The Brain*, author Dr. Richard M. Restak wrote:

> The perception of reality is best understood as a constructive process by which the brain builds useful models of the world. All of us possess useful internal models of what a room looks like, or how tall or small a person may actually be. We can spend a lifetime, and most of us do, without encountering a situation where our perceptual model of rooms and people are thrown into conflict. But such conflict situations can be constructed with rather haunting philosophical implications. If our perception can be wrong, what does this tell us about the conclusions that may result from our logical thought processes? If we examine our beliefs, would they be just as paradoxical?

The way we learn to appreciate music is a good illustration of how we construct our own perceptual models of reality. We learn music appreciation in a long process through the help of others. After we adopt our style of music we cease to be receptive to other kinds. Our response is automatic—if the music doesn't match our style, there is no deliberation. We simply turn it off. What we don't realize is that we respond similarly to a vast array of attitudes about how we see the world. We think of ourselves as being open to suggestion, though our perceptual construction has already made up our minds. But we know that through effort we can learn to appreciate new types of music; likewise we can also change our views of the world. Paradoxically, we often find that our greatest satisfaction rises from a new view which had been hidden from us before. An underlying element in philosophy of self-education is the importance of learning to see through the artificial barriers of culture, to see things as they are from many perspectives, and not just as we would like them to be.

In the book, *McLuhan Hot and Cool*, writer John Culkin wrote:

> All perception is selective. We are all experts at discerning other people's patterns of selectivity. Our own is mercilessly hidden from us. Our own personal experience sets up one grid between us and reality. Our culture adds one. Our language and our media system tighten the mesh. No one man, no one culture has a privileged key to reality.

The greatest practical influence in the development of our individual realities is provided by the accident of birth. If we are born to a culture that wears a bone through the nose, then we will do so. If we are born in a society that believes that cows are reincarnated relatives, then we will also believe it. In America we are nurtured to believe that the process of competition will, through natural selection, see that we reach the station in life that we deserve. But practical experience demonstrates that our station in life is more easily predicted by who our parents are than by any other indicator.

Thus we are born into strata of social reality. Some people move up and some fall from grace into lower strata. Some do so by accident, some by luck, some by privilege and some by hard work, but for the most part our options in life are set by the accident of birth. Each of the strata is protected by a cultural membrane covering which we are culturized to accept as reality. As we grow, the membrane gradually falls away and is replaced with prejudice. Where there was once a barrier to protect us from seeing anything that did not fit with our particular stratum, there is now a strong opinion or vision that will act in place of the membrane. It will help us filter out all else. In time we develop a psychological need "not to know" anything that does not fit with our stratum of reality. Thus, we look at the man with the bone in his nose and pronounce judgments based on that which matches our prejudices. We do not see his reality, nor does he see ours. Instead we see mirrored reflections based on what each of us perceives as being real.

If you are saying to yourself at this point "By God, I am where I am because of hard work," I would say that you may be correct, but I would also add that if everyone else had worked equally hard, most of them would still be in the same job, and have the same social status. It takes more than hard work to change the nature of society. We have to try to understand it first. And it is a paradox of human nature that if we perceive an injustice and subsequently benefit from it, we will no longer perceive it to be an injustice.

To be truly educated is to be able to tear away the prejudice that we have been taught and which has been culturally molded into our being, as well as to replace it with the ability to see at least some of a multitude of realities. It is the ability to see the world from the point of view of the rich, the poor, the oppressed, the homeless, the blind, the paraplegic, the helpless and our friends and adversaries.

At one time or another humans have believed just about anything and everything. Unlike animals, humans can be molded and made to adapt to almost any place and any conditions, which, when assimilated by an individual or group, will be defended not only as normal, but also as being "correct." We know this of ourselves, yet we question little of our own cultural conditioning. We make navigational adjustments because we know that true north is not where the compass says it is, but we do little to alter our attitudes even though we know a lot about the tremendous effects culture has in shaping them. Each society believes itself to be lucky for being born into "correct" behavior. And each society feels some sympathy for others who are unfortunate to have been born into "incorrect" behavior. Some whose behavior is thought to be particularly bizarre may even be perceived to have less value as humans for their ignorance. Each society believes itself to be luckily born into the only religion worthy of worship, and in believing so will likely use religion as a justified substitution for thinking itself.

With such knowledge of ourselves, how can we be so sure of the nature of our correctness? How can we be sure that the attitudes we hold are based on truth instead of a bias to protect a narrow view of reality?

What if all mankind were suddenly transported to a new planet with no memory of any previous experience from having lived on this one? How would we decide what was to be done or who was to do what? It is likely that we would reach conclusions that would be radically different from the way we live today.

What if everyone in the United States suddenly acquired the benefit of a graduate degree education? How would we decide which Ph.D.s would flip hamburgers and which would have the franchise of a profession? What would we point to as the solution to our economic problems? Would there suddenly be enough jobs for everybody because all were educated?

The turmoil caused today by the clash of our realities with those of others has us so confused that we routinely hire experts to tell us that which afterwards we call "common sense." For example, we are totally confused today about the nature of work. A popular management term used to describe efficiency is called "working smart." We are told that if we work smart instead of hard, we will be more productive. But if we do work "smart" then we are likely to have idle time, and if we are idle we will likely be thought of as being lazy or worthless.

The ancient Greeks considered work to be a curse and to be beneath the dignity of free men. The Hebrews considered work to be atonement for sin. Early Christians thought of work as a middle ground between penitence and religious virtue. Thus, most Americans have been nurtured to see work as a sort of salvation. And we seek this salvation by competing to be the first to turn our work over to machines. What happens as we begin to succeed? We have been nurtured to disdain those who do not work. If we are as successful with our technologies as we have been with agriculture we might someday be able to accomplish all the work that needs to be done with only two percent of the people working. If we were to reach such a point and be no better educated or able to appreciate the differences of others than we are today, we would likely destroy ourselves over how to distribute the wealth in a work-free society.

A perceived redeeming value in the sufferance of work has created an attitude of normality in which a large part of the work force is franchised into poverty. They are the working poor. Would it not be possible for us to condition ourselves to believe that anyone who worked at a full-time job in America should be able to earn a decent living? We embrace the illusion that the excellent worker always rises in direct proportion to his or her contribution, while at the same time we encourage the boss to hire our brother-in-law for the next position that opens up instead of the person who has been striving to gain the position.

Buckminster Fuller argued that we have long had the technology and the resource capability to live as a planet of billionaires. The evidence bears him out. We have no shortage of food or material for shelter. Our shortage lies in the virtues we are born with and lose because of the process we call socialization. Much of our success in the future may depend on our ability to unlearn that which we believe to be true, but is in fact cultural illusion.

Summary

All humans are born into the world in malleable form, and are then nurtured with only a fraction of the knowledge about influences on human behavior. We are then schooled to fit and perform. The salient message is: Fit or fail. Schooling that does not recognize that learning is an individual experience based on the learner's particular style and unique time requirements becomes an exercise in self-limiting behavior and conformity. Schooling that does not recognize that the first priority of humans is learning to be human routinely sends the graduated students forth without the slightest idea of what they want to do with their lives. Even more incredible is the fact that it offers little insight as to how to find out.

If traditional education were founded on the principle that people really mattered, anyone who graduated from high school or college would have a basic understanding of human behavior. A college graduate would know what behavioral science practitioners know, regardless of the subject he or she majored in. Moreover, such an educational priority would ensure that both the high school and college graduate would know the limits of knowledge about behavior and where the boundaries of speculation and theory begin.

People with such a sense of themselves would be less susceptible to the indoctrinational aspects of education. They would be less likely to yield to authority without discourse. People with such knowledge of themselves would be able to relate to others with empathy and understanding. They would be less likely to build walls of prejudice and more likely to accept others for their human qualities regardless of nationality, race, or religion. If we were educated in such a manner, we would still be limited to our own individual perceptions of reality simply because we are human, but we would be empowered to see the reality of others without the frustration that inevitably follows when people know little of themselves and even less of others.

The way we are taught is in many cases more important than what we learn. For education to serve its purpose it must empower the recipient to continue the process. Or as behaviorist B.F. Skinner observed in *Upon Further Reflection*, "The task of education is to build a repertoire of behavior that will eventually have reinforcing consequences in the daily and professional life of the graduate."

CHAPTER TWO

Media and Manipulation

All media exist to invest our lives with
artificial perceptions and arbitrary values.
— Marshall McLuhan

In order to remain free, people have to be intellectually free from the influence of manipulation and knowledgeable enough about the nature of indoctrination to recognize it. As the saying goes, "If you are not part of the solution, you are part of the problem." Becoming a part of the solution requires self-education. Self-education depends upon the ability to think objectively. Objective thinking calls for an understanding of the perceptual process, which requires investigation into the ways we actively perceive each other.

In the preface of *The Great Conversation*, Robert M. Hutchins wrote:

> We believe that the reduction of the citizen to an object of propaganda, private and public, is one of the greatest dangers to democracy. A prevalent notion is that the great mass of the people cannot understand and cannot form an independent judgment upon any matter; they cannot be educated, in the sense of developing their intellectual powers, but they can be bamboozled. The reiteration of slogans, the distortion of the news, the great storm of propaganda that beats upon the citizen twenty-four hours a day all his life long mean either that democracy must fall a prey to the loudest and most persistent propagandists or that the people must save themselves by strengthening their minds so that they can appraise the issues for themselves.

Are we being bamboozled? Do we know as much about ourselves as do those with the power to use the media to influence us?

In 1958 Bertrand Russell wrote in *The ABC of Relativity* that our perceptions of reality are primarily based on our sense of touch. In the early Sixties Marshall McLuhan asserted that all media are extensions of human senses and that the low definition of the television image causes us to perceive it as an extension of the sense of touch. Throughout the early Sixties McLuhan argued that "the medium is the message," meaning that how we use our senses in respect to media is more important than the content we receive. It was, and is, a profound assertion. The simplicity, yet profundity, of McLuhan's observations incurred a media blitz of criticism, but even his severest critics acknowledged that his claims were worthy of discourse.

McLuhan argued convincingly that primitive man perceived the world through the dominance of his aural and tactile senses (hearing and feeling) and that these tendencies later gave way to the dominance of visual sense perception because of writing and print technology. Reading and writing enabled people to detach themselves from association with others and allowed them to develop privately and independently. In other words, reading and writing "detribalized" society. According to McLuhan, modern man is impaired in discerning the effects of media upon himself. The difficulty is in understanding the nature of media. In his book *Understanding Media* he wrote:

> The electric light escapes attention as a communication medium just because it has no "content." And this makes it an invaluable instance of how people fail to study media at all. For it is not till the electric light is used to spell out some brand name that it is noticed as a medium. Then it is not the light but the "content" (or what is really another medium) that is noticed. The message of the electric light is like the message of electric power in industry, totally radical, pervasive, and decentralized. For electric light and power are separate for their uses, yet they eliminate time and space factors in human association exactly as do radio, telegraph, and TV, creating involvement in depth.

McLuhan argued that the nature of electronic media, including television and its involvement of the senses, is in effect "retribalizing" society. Retribalizing means that the way we associate with one another is becoming more and more as it was when we were all members of tribes and lived in villages. Thus, the term "global village" was born. It is important to understand that retribalization does not mean a return to a state of harmony among people, but is in fact the opposite. In a dialog with G.E. Stearn in *McLuhan Hot and Cool*, McLuhan said:

> The more you create village conditions, the more discontinuity and division and diversity. The global village

absolutely ensures maximal disagreement on all points. It never occurred to me that uniformity and tranquility were the properties of the global village. It has more spite and envy. The spaces and times are pulled out from between people. A world in which people encounter each other in depth all of the time.

The tribal-global village is far more divisive—full of fighting—than any nationalism ever was. Village is fission, not fusion, in depth. People leave small towns to avoid involvement. The big city lined them with its uniformity and impersonal milieu. They sought property and in the city, money is made by uniformity and repeatability. When you have craftsmanlike diversity, you make art, not money. The village is not the place to find ideal peace and harmony. Exact opposite. Nationalism came out of print and provided an extraordinary relief from global village conditions. I don't approve of the global village. I say we live in it.

If McLuhan's assertions are correct, survivability in the technological future will depend more on our interpersonal and social relations than our technical ability.

In his book McLuhan divided media into categories of "hot" and "cool" to explain how media affects the senses and how we relate to media. He wrote:

There is a basic principle that distinguishes a hot medium like radio from a cool one like the telephone, or a hot medium like the movie from a cool one like TV. A hot medium is one that extends one single sense in "high definition." High definition is the state of being well-filled with data. A photograph is, visually, "high definition." A cartoon is "low definition," simply because very little visual information is provided. Telephone is a cool medium, or one of low definition, because the ear is given a meager amount of information. And speech is a cool medium of low definition, because so little is given and so much has to be filled in by the listener. On the other hand, hot media do not leave so much to be filled in or completed by the audience. Hot media are, therefore, low in participation, and cool media are high in participation or completion by the audience.

McLuhan argued that the processes of media alter the human sense ratios, thus changing the way in which we perceive and conceptualize realities. If he was right, then it is imperative that we understand how such processes affect our perceptions so that we may be protected from manipulation.

The Television and Film Industry

If you accept McLuhan's premise, you must also acknowledge that the different media could possibly have different effects on the user according to the levels of participation required. From a sociological point of view McLuhan was probably right when he said, "The medium is the message," but for you and me, both the medium and the message are relevant because each has an intimate effect on our daily lives. If we are to be self-determining, we have to be able to discern the reality of each, from many different perspectives. We have to be able to discern the effect that media have on us as an extension of our senses and how we react to the content. Are we aware of issues because they really are important, or are we aware because media have directed our attention in such a manner as to make us believe that they are? And what is the effect of television on our imaginations and creative abilities? Do we lose creative ability by spending hour after hour watching what is in essence a product of someone else's imagination? And if so, can we alter the process and ensure that we use media to enhance our abilities?

Television and the film industry have had a profound effect on society. We have become a nation of impulsive "watchers." The phenomenon of television may in part explain why we have become so "passive" where our political interests are concerned. The fast pace of the cool medium of television and the lack of intellectual substance that it offers the viewer leave little time for reflection, nor is it necessary in most cases. Television is powerful because it requires participation of the senses. This elicits a strong emotional response from its viewers, as was the case in the Vietnam War. Television added a spectrum of reality to war that had never before been possible for nonparticipants viewing from a distance. It personalized the horrors of war. In the late Sixties, television brought the race riots of Detroit and Los Angeles into our living rooms. We saw racism for what it is – a moral disgrace.

It is often the case that the casual viewer of television who sets out to watch merely for entertainment becomes a compulsive watcher, hooked on a "stuporous" level of brain wave stimulation somewhere between thinking and genuine amusement.[1] After years of such stimulation, many people discover that television has become a crevice of escape. The viewer watches, and time passes; there is little reflection and little remembrance of the time that has passed. The experience is neither real, nor imaginary. It exists somewhere in between. In time, reruns are preferred over reflection and thought.

On the other hand, carefully crafted films (hot medium) have an incredible power to imprint and influence. Thus, the viewers' trance-like existence is "punctuated" with meaning. The high definition and low participation of the movie prepares the viewer for an intensely emotional experience. This is why we perceive movies to be so much better on the big screen in a theater. When we are involved emotionally with the experience of a movie we mesh it into memory with all emotion intact. It explains why the musical themes from powerful movies can fill our senses with the same feelings we experienced during the movie years afterwards. The imprint is not as deep when we see a movie on television because we use all our senses to participate. One sense is not overwhelmed, so there is no heightened sense of impression. On the other hand, if we see a movie in the theater first and then see it on television the second experience will have more similarity to the first because the memory is already in place.

For many people, television and movies are a primary vehicle for developing social attitudes. Some media observers speculate that the thrust of the self-help movement in America may have been spawned as an unconscious reaction to throw off the passivity induced by television. Television is a high sensory participatory experience, but since the experience is shallow in intellectual stimulation, it creates in young people who have been raised in front of a TV a natural willingness to shift into second gear with electronic games. Electronic process matches how they use their senses; it is a natural evolution from the passive watching of TV to the visual participation of electronic games. Without an adequate reward stimulus of intellectual nourishment, high participation-low reward leads to electronic boredom.

Television is not without a positive side. It can comfort, inform, instruct, teach, and genuinely entertain. Public television (PBS) produces top quality programing, but the power of television as a major tool in education has yet to be discovered in the formal sense. Still, by the time a child of today is an adult, he will incur the sense experiences of ten sets of great-great-grandparents.

He will have literally been assaulted with information.

Freedom of the print media is guaranteed under the authority of the U.S. Constitution and similar implications exist for the emerging electronic media, although these safeguards are less clear. Media supported by advertising revenue are to some degree a safeguard for freedom. It is certainly preferable to media supported by government, but the difference between support and control calls for continual scrutiny.

Advertising

Advertising is somewhat analogous to fishing. The advertiser is the fisherman. The media specialists are the tackle makers. And you guessed it: We are the fish. Only most of the time we don't bite for keeps, we just nibble. In the marketplace we nibble with our pocketbooks; in political matters we nibble with our approval. It is a symbiotic relationship, and for the most part we enjoy the sport; we think of ourselves as picky, discriminating fish while the advertiser thinks of himself as a crafty fisherman.

Like real fish we have to be convinced that the bait is real and worth the effort or we withhold our actions. All is well until the sport becomes one-sided. When it does, the odds are always in favor of the fisherman, because most of the brain power in media is devoted to catching fish. McLuhan said, "Far more thought and care go into the composition of any prominent ad in a newspaper or magazine than go into the writing of their features and editorials." Today the fishermen know more about us than we know about ourselves. They tell us when, where, and how to swim; the irony is that they make us think that it is our idea. You see, the fishermen fired the old-fashioned tackle makers and replaced them with "psychographic" specialists.[2] Now, when the fishermen cast bait into the waters, we can no longer see the line. They even know that the higher our level of traditional education, the less likely we are to perceive ourselves as susceptible to being hooked. The well-educated are special sport: they only require the light line.

Psychographics is the study of people profiled into like categories by demographic data and is conducted by psychiatrists, psychologists, sociologists, and a myriad of social engineers who study human behavior. These specialists analyze demographic data, looking for known behavioral habits and searching for clues that might influence future actions. They study the desires, likes, hopes, fears, ambitions, and aspirations of groups of people and match these traits with past purchasing or voting history. The techniques gleaned from this process are available to almost any commercial enterprise or political group with the means to purchase them.

No natural balancing forces exist to offset the influence of advertising. To protect ourselves, we must keep up with technique and study the nature of advertising and its effects on human behavior. Advertisers with more knowledge of us than we have of ourselves set our standards as to what constitutes a good life.

VALS Typology

In the late Seventies the Stanford Research Institute (SRI) developed the values and lifestyles (VALS) profiles: nine identified lifestyles in the U.S. discernible by demographic data that includes information identifying our aspirations as well as our greatest hopes and fears. Seven of these groups are the targets of advertisers and political groups. Starting at the bottom and moving up the VALS double hierarchy typology chart (see Figure 1) we first find the need-driven group. They are the "survivors" and "sustainers." Survivors and sustainers make up approximately 11 percent of the population. They have some political significance, but as far as Madison Avenue is concerned, they do not exist because they have so little money.

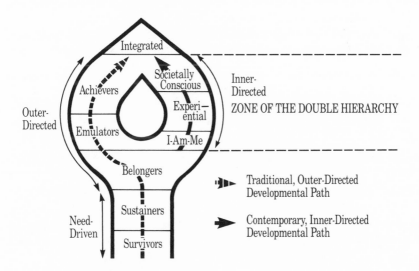

FIGURE 1.
The VALS™ Double Hierarchy.

Reprinted with permission from *Nine American Lifestyles*, by Arnold Mitchell.

Next is the largest block – the outer-directeds, (externally motivated), consisting of "belongers," "emulators," and "achievers." Belongers make up roughly 35 percent of the population, emulators 10 percent and achievers 22 percent. They are traditionalists, generally classified as being middle-class. Belongers need to fit in. Generally speaking they are the happiest of the groups.

Emulators are psychologically more mature than belongers, but as a rule they are not as happy. Emulators are intensely ambitious and highly impressionable. They are easy to influence. They want desperately to become "achievers," even though they really do not understand the attributes of those they emulate. They are at the highest level for the outer-directeds. Achievers are likely to be in charge. They tend to be conservatives, who are self-made individuals. Achievers are the architects of the American Dream.

On the other side of the ladder from the outer-directeds are the inner-directeds (internally motivated). The people who make up this division are categorized as having an internal sense of self. They tend to march to the beat of their own drums, caring less what others think. The inner-directeds begin with the youngest group, the "I am me's." The "I am me's" are characterized as being rebellious of the outer-directed lifestyle. They may be the children of outer-directeds. The "I am me's" are young and impulsive. In his book, *The Nine American Lifestyles*, author Arnold Mitchell said that the "I am me's have developed whims of iron."

Next up the double hierarchy are the "societally conscious." The societally conscious are similar to achievers except that they are more emotionally mature. They are likely to be concerned with world problems. This group makes up only eight percent of the VALS typology, but its ranks are growing rapidly.

And finally at the top are the "integrateds" – a combination of the inner- and outer-directeds. The integrateds are people who have their act together. They are psychologically mature and likely to be financially comfortable.

The VALS typology is worth studying in greater detail. You should know how you are identified as a target group so you will be less vulnerable to manipulation. And you should know how to use the VALS typology and similar future studies to understand and relate to others. (See bibliography for additional information.)

Media Reality

I am not trying to paint a portrait of advertising as a great evil that is out to destroy society; however, advertising and the general programming that is sponsored by it is responsible for creating a perpetual distortion of reality. Advertising and television media create a collective "unreality" which we all tune into, and in doing so, we lose ourselves. We aspire to a collective illusion through hours of viewing what we know to be unreal to start with but in time cannot separate from practical experience. This is important to understand because even if you don't watch television, it's likely that most of your friends and associates do. Advertising and regular television programming is so heavily biased toward human "wants" that millions of viewers with little self-knowledge cannot distinguish them from "needs." And satisfied wants are the primary substance that we use to insulate ourselves from the realities of others. We do this by justifying what we do as long as we get what we want. The products we purchase serve as status symbols which distance us from those without them. The point is that people who have little self-knowledge and even less knowledge of others are not likely to distinguish between needs and wants. Thus they do not understand their own primary motivations, and they misunderstand the positions of others. Actions prompted from such confusion are likely to cause conflict among people who mis-read the intentions of others. The actions of individuals who fail to understand their own motivation resemble the dog that chases its own tail. For example, a compulsive desire to keep up with the Joneses without understanding why is similar to being a prisoner of the advertising industry without knowing how to escape.

The intent of advertisers to influence is never in doubt. We take it for granted at a conscious level. But if the intent to influence can slip by undetected by the observer, it is doubly effective. The intended target views the message, fails to detect he's being influenced, and therefore assumes that the newly acquired belief or action comes from his own volition. If he is subsequently accused of being influenced, he will defend the new position as if it were a long-cherished belief. In doing so he drives the convictions deeper.

I am not suggesting that we are being unduly influenced by a subliminal form of advertising. I am saying that we are dealing with people whose knowledge of human behavior is far superior to ours. We are dealing with people who know how to use our fears and emotions, our hopes and dreams, to achieve results that prioritize their goals over our own. They sing. We dance. They create an illusionary world that does not exist except in our expectations of what we need to live a happy, productive life. We begin to associate self-esteem with the products or services that we purchase. Without them we are less than adequate. Do you think you're not affected? Think again. We have lived with the glitter of Madison Avenue for so long that our vision is impaired. We think of ourselves as discriminating consumers who dictate our desires to the marketplace, when in fact the reverse is true. We have teenagers who are ashamed to go to school without a designer label on their bluejeans. In the Seventies insecure young Americans by the hundreds of thousands rode into Marlboro country with the Marlboro man and in doing so suffered and continue to suffer the consequences of respiratory illness. These Marlboro riders were "emulators"—targeted because of their insecurity. Today the Marlboro man is riding tall and proud in Third World countries. Most Third World countries do not require a warning label on cigarette packages, so the tobacco companies happily leave them off.

If educated Westerners can be bamboozled, what about the citizens in Third World countries? What are the political consequences of media advertising? In *Global Reach*, Richard J. Barnet and Ronald E. Muller wrote:

> It is disingenuous to talk about the "dictates of the consumer" when the consumer is so thoroughly subject to the dictation of the modern technology of manipulation.
>
> What are the long-range social effects of advertising on people who earn less than $200 a year? The peasant scratching out an existence on a tiny plot, the urban slum dweller subsisting on odd jobs and garbage scavenging, and the army of low-wage domestics, harvesters, and factory hands receive most of what they learn of the outside world through the images and slogans of advertising. One message that comes through clearly is that happiness, achievement, and being white have something to do with one another. In mestizo countries such as Mexico and Venezuela where most of the population still bear strong traces of their Indian origin, billboards depicting the good life for sale invariably feature blond, blue-eyed, American-looking men and women. One effect of such "white is beautiful" advertising is to reinforce feelings of inferiority which are the essence of a politically immobilizing colonial mentality.

We cannot be in control of our lives if advertising specialists know enough about us to control our behavior, without our knowledge, but with our complete cooperation. We become like the mechanical bear in a shooting gallery. Each time we are zapped with an electronic signal we take off in a new direction. And in a short time we become dependent upon the stimuli. We begin to operate on automatic pilot. If the reasoning ability of the average citizen is subordinate to media technology then citizens become chess pieces whose moves are negotiable according to market price.

Much has been learned by advertising media specialists about influencing human behavior from studying the experiences of American prisoners of war. In World War Two and the Korean War the methods used were similar. The technique to coerce confessions and admissions of guilt later became known as "brainwashing." This term is misleading and inaccurate. It incorrectly implies a process where the victim can do little if anything to prevent it. Brainwashing is in fact a process in which knowledge of human needs and cultural conditioning is exploited to make the victim "feel" and act rather than "think" and reflect. Prisoners were subjected to extremely high levels of stress because such practice was discovered to produce a state of "suggestibility." This state is thought by some researchers to be the same phenomenon that produces religious conversions when evangelical preachers rouse their audience to high levels of emotional stress.

Another fact discovered by the American captors, and also thought to contribute to the phenomenon of sudden conversions, is that we are culturally conditioned to be incapable of dealing with great amounts of ambiguity and uncertainty. When the stress of doubt becomes unbearable a new belief that provides certainty and structure is welcomed wholeheartedly.

Sensory deprivation is also known to be a means of converting people from one belief to another. It seems that we have an innate need for novelty.[3] When deprived we become desperate for stimulus. Thus we reach a state of suggestibility based on deprivation rather than induced stress. Knowledge of this technique could be an invaluable tool for television media specialists. Indeed, television is often guilty of subjecting its viewers to a form of sensory deprivation by virtue of its "sameness."

Today's media behavioral specialists know that if a person can be persuaded to commit himself to an idea or product, the commitment can be driven deeper simply by attacking that commitment. Politicians have used such methods to influence unsuspecting audiences for decades. Likewise it is also known that you can obtain a large favor from someone by asking for and receiving a small one first. Thus, the solicitation of a favor and the attacking of one's position can be used in tandem for political or commercial ends.

Advertisers know from studying the "psychology of commitment" that if they can enlist a participant's efforts in filling out a coupon or writing the name of a product on a plain piece of paper, then the participant will increase his commitment to the product, if for no other reason than to keep from appearing foolish for having done so.[4] Indeed, the American distaste for appearing or feeling foolish is the principle upon which the "money back guarantee" works. In other words, we would rather keep a product that did not live up to our expectations rather than admit we might have acted foolishly by purchasing it.

Subliminal Suggestion

Today's advertisers know that the majority of us will respond to sheer repetition, meaning that almost any ad they produce will show sales results if people see it numerous times. Likewise, they know that a great many of us ask to be deceived. They know that we will respond consistently to advertisements that offer great results without any personal effort on our part. The success of miracle weight-loss products and subliminal self-help tapes are examples of this great desire to be deceived. Subliminal tapes are said to have a message that is undetectable to the conscious mind, but is fully recognizable and understood by the subconscious.

An articulate salesman stands before an audience where he slowly and carefully builds them a vivid picture of how the human mind works. He uses metaphors such as a storage room for the subconscious and a guard at the door to represent the conscious. The pitch is based on half-truths in psychology, derived from scientific knowledge and assumptions; it contains enough logic to sound as if the claims amount to common sense. The narrator sums up the pitch by saying that all you have to do is listen to the tapes over and over again and your subconscious will turn you into a thin person, improve your self-esteem, give you the confidence to be an effective public speaker, or anything else that you wish to achieve as long as you use the tape with the appropriate message. All you have to do is purchase the tapes, listen to them regularly and you will achieve your desired results without any effort on your part. Who would not want to believe it? Problem solved. No effort. Simply by allowing the subconscious to listen to a message repetitiously will override years of learned behavior.

We have all heard about the power of subliminal suggestion. Most of us have heard or read about the experiments in the Seventies where movie theaters were supposed to have used subliminal messages hidden in film to sell popcorn and soft drinks. And after all, you are in fact at this moment reading about the dangers of media manipulation. So why can't you expect an effortless cure for what ails you with a simple appeal to the subconscious? You have nothing to lose, the offer is even made with a money back guarantee. I would argue that you cannot expect a cure, because the behavior you are trying to change has been learned over many years and is embellished into memory by a vast range of emotions. It will not likely be reversed by a simple appeal to the conscious or subconscious mind. I am not suggesting that there is something virtuous or particularly effective about the amount of effort required to change our behavior. I am simply suggesting that emotionally learned behavior conditioned over time is not likely to respond to a simple non-emotional appeal played over and over at a frequency that is in itself questionable. I do not deny that subliminal perception is a valid field of study or that we cannot use similar techniques to assist in changing behavior, but I do assert that the sellers of these tapes are more successful in marketing than they are in altering behavior.

When we apply reason and logic to this question we realize that if such changes of behavior were this simple, the sellers of these tapes would not have to advertise. Word of mouth advertising would be sufficient. For example, successful diets spread like wildfire. These tapes, on the other hand, are sold through a carefully orchestrated sales presentation. A breakthrough of such significance in the modification of human behavior would be headline news for months, a great cause for celebration. This hasn't happened yet.

I would argue that the testimonials used by the sellers are the result of the natural force of the "law of expectations" and that anyone achieving success does so by the nature of his faith and the expectation that he will succeed. In other words, he succeeded by nature of the "placebo effect." Anything can serve as a means for achieving the end result as long as the participant can "believe."

The law of expectations is an incredibly powerful force, and unlike the tapes, it is free. The nature and methodology of the power of expectations will be discussed thoroughly in Chapter Five.

Propaganda and Destructive Persuasion

Propagandists know that the repetition of true or false information can produce a conditioned response in which reasoning is circumvented in favor of recollection. This method is used to distract those whom it is intended to influence by focusing attention on information that is false.[5] In other words, slogans and cliches are offered in hope that they will be used as substitutes for thinking. Most political campaigns in America are conducted primarily by the use of cliches and simple slogans.

In *Mein Kampf,* Adolf Hitler wrote, "All propaganda must be so popular and on such an intellectual level that even the most stupid of those towards whom it is directed will understand it. Therefore, the intellectual level of the propaganda must be lower, the larger the number of people who are to be influenced by it."

By using demographics to discern the perceived needs of "like" groups, advertisers and politicians can tailor products and ideas in the form of precise solutions. They know that a need that has been long unfulfilled will lead to conditions in which the subject is receptive to radical ideas and methods for resolution.[6]

It is embarrassing to admit the extent to which we are the victims of persuasion without being aware of it. We form realities based on illusions intentionally presented to us by those who would have us act favorably in their interest. Another dangerous aspect of mass media is access. If there is no means for airing dissident views, then there is no means for making rational judgments.

In *The Anatomy of Illusion,* authors Thomas and Jacqueline Keiser wrote:

> Strange as it may seem, destructive persuasion embodies processes identical to those found in education. It is the *motive* or *purpose* of the persuader that differs from that of genuine educators. Fascist propaganda and the Constitution of the United States are both learned in the same way. The persuader, however, does not seek to inform but to control. An educator's motive is to destroy illusion and she does so by presenting as much accurate and relevant information as possible. A destructive persuader seeks to distort his victim's reality for his own gain. If a relevant source of knowledge exists, an educator, if aware of it, informs her student and suggests that he explore it. Her goal is simply what it appears to be—to survey a problem from as many angles as possible in order to achieve

knowledge which will serve an adaptive purpose. The function of information in the educational process is to *inform*, its use in destructive persuasion is to *control.*

In destructive persuasion, what appears as merely factual is always promotional. Highly charged emotional images are used to appeal to needs and provoke fears in order to move individuals along a predetermined course of action.

We have grown dependent upon the advertising industry. Advertising is not necessarily a bad thing. When we are informed of a new product and it meets our needs, we are grateful. But we have to know more about advertisers than they know about us or they begin to manipulate our values by setting the standards for our behavior. When we begin to think less of ourselves and others for lack of a product, advertising becomes a threat rather than a service. In such case the line between advertising, destructive persuasion and propaganda becomes blurred.

Media and Citizenship

If America is to continue to be a democracy, Americans as "patriots" must develop a healthy, respectful distrust for media, not as a paranoia of people who see themselves as victims, but as a citizenry that will not accept coercion and destructive persuasion. Distrust for media and authority must grow until Americans no longer accept simple cliches and slogans in response to questions from elected officials. We must adjust our sense of values so that we do not view the need to question and to demand answers as an unpatriotic act. When reporters ask the administration in power embarrassing questions many of us cry "foul play," suggesting either that deference is due by nature of the office held, or that such matters are none of the public's business.

In his essay "On Liberty" philosopher John Stuart Mill (1806–1873) wrote:

> Strange it is, that men should admit the validity of the arguments for free discussion, but object to their being "pushed to an extreme;" not seeing that unless the reasons are good for an extreme case, they are not good for any case. Strange that they should imagine that they are not assuming infallibility, when they acknowledge that there should be free discussion on all subjects which can possibly be doubtful, but think that some particular principle or

doctrine should be forbidden to be questioned because it is
so certain, that is, because they are certain that it is
certain. To call any proposition certain, while there is any
one who would deny its certainty if permitted, but who is
not permitted, is to assume that we ourselves, and those
who agree with us, are the judges of certainty, and judges
without hearing the other side.

During this century people who question authority in America
often incur the wrath of those who are obedient–those for whom
remaining silent would be an admission of guilt for not having
spoken up earlier themselves. The existence of a quiet, obedient
citizenry and nonresponsive government officials is a threat to
democracy through the guilt of both parties. Montesquieu indicated
this in an essay titled "The Spirit of Laws." He wrote, "Excessive
obedience supposes ignorance in the person that obeys: the same it
supposes in him that commands, for he has no occasion to deliberate,
to doubt, to reason; he has only to will."

Critical scrutiny of political power is democracy's greatest
strength. If you doubt it, watch the news on Soviet television. The
Soviets have always had what some Americans seem to be clamoring
for: a society in which the views of those in authority are not
disputed. Soviet news is beginning to change with the policy of
glasnost (openness) and *perestroika* (restructuring), but since its
inception it has consisted largely of hour after hour of monotony.
Party leaders discuss progress and production in industry and agriculture while the camera pans continuous footage of factories and
collective farms. It leaves the viewer with no avenue of recourse and a
sense of hopelessness and helplessness.

The portrait of the American Dream is painted with the colors
of individuality, initiative and the freedom to be self-determining, yet
almost one-third of the adult population is classified as semi-literate.
Barely 75 percent of U.S. students graduate from high school and
only one in five Americans has a college degree.[7] This disparity of
education poses an immediate danger of decidedly sharpening the
divisions of social class in America. As the gap grows larger between
"haves" and "have nots" the foundation of democracy weakens. A
liberal education is necessary not only for social mobility, but to hold
media in perspective.

John Stuart Mill said:

One of the greatest dangers, therefore, of democracy, as of
all other forms of government, lies in the sinister interest

of the holders of power: it is the danger of class legislation; of government intended for (whether really affecting it or not) the immediate benefit of the dominant
class, to the lasting detriment of the whole. And one of
the most important questions demanding consideration,
in determining the best constitution of a representative
government, is how to provide efficacious securities
against this evil.

The media enable the holders of power the means to enact such class
legislation. A self-educated citizenry able to discern the political
effects of media is the greatest insurance we can have for the
preservation of freedom. The estimated one-third of society classified
as being semi-literate are not stupid people, they simply are unable
to read well. And reading is a key to education. Many are in fact so
intelligent that they can hide their inability to read from the literate.
Many of the young people who cannot read well fit the criteria of
McLuhan's retribalized society: They are individuals who have spent
most of their childhood within ten feet of a TV. They have a different
sense ratio of experiences in perception than people who rely heavily
on print media for information. They are not dumb, they just perceive
differently. But perhaps the most tragic aspect of all is that young
people who grow up with a painful void of knowledge of self use the
media to fill in the blanks. They adopt "Madison Avenue" values that
include the assumption that all problems can be solved in one hour
with plenty of time left over for commercial breaks. The conclusion
then follows that a good life is possible through instantaneous
solutions to complicated problems. In other words, there is little
reason or need to sacrifice the present for future rewards.

In 1964 Marshall McLuhan wrote:

The drop-out situation in our schools at present has only
begun to develop. The young student today grows up in an
electrically configured world. It is a world not of wheels
but of circuits, not of fragments but of integral patterns.
The student today lives mythically and in depth. At school,
however, he encounters a situation organized by means of
classified information. The subjects are unrelated. They
are visually conceived in terms of a blueprint. The student
can find no possible means of involvement for himself, nor
can he discover how the educational scene relates to the
"mythic" world of electronically processed data and experience that he takes for granted.

Today's drop-out rate tends to bear out McLuhan's assertion. It is a political and economic tragedy that millions of Americans are so turned off by the process of formal education that they have yet to discover the power and superiority of self-education. It is tragic in the political sense because the greatest danger to democracy is a large body of citizens left out of the American Dream; in an economic sense we will pay for the inequity one way or another. For the uneducated, the electronic media of today is a mysterious mass of stimulation and sense experience. It is both captivating and alienating. But the salient force is that it is manipulative.

For the self-educated individual, wise in the method and madness of media, the excitement of today is exceeded only by the expectation of tomorrow. All methods of media are merging into what will finally evolve as one described by McLuhan as an electronic "consciousness." The world is being "wired" at a breakneck rate.

If the world were totally dark except for the new "link ups" in communication technologies, from a short distance in space our planet would appear to be engulfed in the grip of a massive electric storm. Bright flashes of lightning would dominate the West in the connective arcs between new telephone lines, computer connections, modems, cable hook-ups, fiber optics and a myriad of electronic associations. In the East and West alike the surface of the earth would appear to be struck repeatedly by space lightning as satellite transmissions streak to and from contact points. From such a point of view the earth would appear to be host to a perpetual storm. And if the present rate of electronic associations continues, in a few years the appearance of a violent storm will give way to a dimly lit pulsating sphere that continually grows brighter.

The study of media, and our political, social, and personal relationship to them, is a necessity if we are to be self-determining individuals in control of our lives. It is an ideal curriculum for the self-educated person because traditional education has all but ignored the sociological aspects of media. During the Sixties the popularity of Marshall McLuhan's assertions kept the effects of media a popular subject. Today some of his arguments may seem a little naive, but his questions do not. McLuhan's assertions about the global village effect remain obscure, but we are clearly engaged in day-to-day relationships with media that are not only changing our sense ratios, but promise to dramatically change the way we live and the way we relate to each other.

Summary

We are clearly the objects of propaganda. It is in the interest of politicians that we approve their actions. It is in the interest of advertisers that we buy their products. If we do not understand how we respond to what our senses take in, we run the risk of being manipulated by those who do. Advertisers load multiple messages into a single commercial because they can depend on our desire to see what we want to see.

The overwhelming characteristic of the "wiring" and "linking up" of the planet is that we will yet be inundated with a myriad of new choices to make in our everyday lives. Such choices will require self-knowledge. Media are for all practical purposes extensions of our senses in the same way that clothing is an extension of our skin. How we use our senses determines who we are and how we get along with one another. Self-educated people must be able to hold media at a distance for critical viewing. We should always be able to distinguish between the content and the essence of the medium itself.

The continuation of democracy depends upon its ability to provide just government. What is just depends on a continual dialog among people who can see themselves clearly in relation to others. For democracy to survive, ordinary citizens must possess powers of reason sufficiently developed to checkmate those willing to abuse the communications media. The push buttons that operate our home electronic media offer the naive an illusion of control.

Democracy demands that we be capable of meeting change through the objectivity of a people committed to the preservation of democracy. And if we are to be a self-determining people we must know a lot more about ourselves than do politicians and advertisers. We must know ourselves well enough to understand our own motives as well as those of our neighbors and our adversaries. And we cannot understand ourselves without continually studying the media that are so much a part of our lives.

CHAPTER THREE

Self-Knowledge — the Foundation
of Self-Education

*For wisdom of behavior, it is by learned men
for the most part despised, as an inferior to
virtue and an enemy to meditation.*
— Sir Francis Bacon

Most of us live our lives in a fashion similar to that of an amateur
sailor who knows little of the sea, nothing of the wind, and even less
about sailing. We weather years of storms and gales before we begin
to develop an intuitive sense for the approach of bad weather.

We drift, with little sense of direction. We continually arrive in
strange ports, quite by accident. We have little sense of where we are
going or where we have been. Thus we are molded by the waves of
experience. We take the tests of the sea, without benefit of the
questions. Without self-knowledge or knowledge of the sea we
become victims and casualties of circumstance and environment.

Six thousand years of recorded human history offers little
evidence of human purpose, yet it suggests a great deal about the
nature of humans. It is incredible that we do not use this evidence.
The knowledge of human experience that is necessary to understand
oneself is, as I have already said, largely ignored by the educational
system. The time to broach the subjects that hold the keys to self-
knowledge such as human feelings, human needs, psychology, motivation, personalities, social interaction, ethnicity, and the art and
science of getting along with others is when we are young enough to
assimilate the knowledge into our behavior. But these subjects are
taboo until such time as we have already become rigid in personality
and behavior. These subjects are inexact sciences and are by their
very nature highly subjective. They do not fit the classroom demand
for right answers. The result is that we ignore dealing with the very
questions which are most important to us. We should intuitively do
the opposite.

What is important to us — even though we are unsure about it —
should maintain our attention. When we are young we may have
difficulty understanding complex subjects open to sharp differences

of opinion, but we have a right to know what the questions are and how the opinions differ. Otherwise we grow into adulthood without any sense of knowledge about ourselves, without the slightest idea of why we feel or act as we do, and without knowing if we are normal or uniquely odd. Simply put, we are starved for emotional literacy. We have no criteria by which we can make intelligent choices. We haven't any idea which occupations might suit us. We don't even know how to find out. We are adrift with a sense of uneasiness. We have been educated to have little tolerance or capacity for ambiguity, so we attempt to conform to the expectations of others, with the hope that someone knows what's going on. We become adults knowing little of ourselves or others. We become Texans, Alaskans, Californians, Floridians, Northerners, Southerners, Easterners, Westerners, and Americans before we are humans. We are socialized in such a manner that we become comfortable only with those who are like us. Sadly, this is not likely to change.

We didn't study behavioral psychology when I was in primary school for the same reason that our children and grandchildren won't—namely that subjects of this nature transcend the boundaries of philosophy and religion, and we cannot agree about what will and will not be taught. Also it is easy for "experts" to argue that such subjects are much too complex for young minds. So young people, void of the nature of nurture, have children of their own without the slightest idea about the importance of their own roles as parents, and the cycle of permitted ignorance continues.

Self-Knowledge and Social Equilibrium

Self-knowledge is an anchor in social equilibrium. If we are comfortable with ourselves, we are less uncomfortable with others. Knowledge of others leads to understanding. Understanding leads to empathy. Empathy enables us to accept the differences of others without resorting to conflict to reduce those differences.

If we have the benefit of self-knowledge we can reach a level of comfort with that which is unknowable. We can distinguish the "truths" that we accept on faith from those that we accept on reason. And finally, self-knowledge enables us to continually examine the methodology of reason itself.

A majority of us go all through the formal educational process without ever understanding how we learn best, or why. We know what we like, at least part of the time, though sometimes we have to check with others to make sure. We know what we dislike, but then again sometimes we still have to check to make sure it's OK. We often have only a vague idea how we assimilate subject matter into knowledge. Self-knowledge is the launching pad for self-education. Marilyn Ferguson, author of *The Aquarian Conspiracy*, wrote:

> *The power of paying attention,* of discovering what works, of facing and transforming conflict, gives one the advantage of being wide awake even in the company of those hooked on our social painkillers: distraction, denial, cynicism. The deliberate transformation of stress is a new factor in history.
>
> So is *the power of self-knowledge.* Until technology freed us from the struggle to survive, few had the time or opportunity to look within to explore the psyche. Self-knowledge leads to a profound change in the individual's definition of power. As the ego diminishes, so does the need to dominate, to win. *Not* engaging in power games becomes a kind of natural power. There is a liberation of the energy formerly channeled into anxious competition: *the power of letting go.*

This feeling of "letting go" is similar to releasing negative baggage we have carried from the pedagogical experience. For example, learning in an authoritative environment taught us to be dependent upon that authority, but when we begin to search for knowledge for its own sake, we find ourselves immune to the intimidation of those in authority. Learning for its own sake has a very natural reward—the thrill of understanding.[1] Scientists believe that this is caused by a release of endorphins in the brain, and it is likely that it has evolved into a natural biological reward to enhance the survival of the human species. It is ironic that in our effort to formally educate, we often override the natural pleasure of learning with the negative effects of pedagogy.

Tools for Self-Discovery

To make maximum use of our natural abilities, we have to examine our human facilities, our predispositions to learning styles, our personality traits and the methods with which we learn. Each new point of awareness is an opportunity for growth and development. We have in many cases accepted the judgments of others too quickly; we have given up too much in deference to authority, and therefore we impose arbitrary limits on ourselves. In other words, we fail to synthesize our own personal experience with the theories of the experts. The following subjects are avenues for introspection and self-understanding. Studying them invites comparison between personal experience and the theories of experts. Making such comparisons ensures that you will remember the analysis.

Psychobiology

Psychobiology is the study of the human brain. We know that the brain is where learning takes place, but we don't know how. We know that we have far more learning capacity than anyone ever uses, and again we don't know why. Many of today's scientists are replacing their views of the brain as an electrically driven computer-like device with the view that it is a gland. This is a radical change in thinking, but it is hardly a new idea: it was suggested in ancient Greece by Plato and Aristotle. If the brain is a gland it is chemically driven and may be subject to regulation by administering hormones. This is a theory that offers a revolutionary new way of thinking about treating mental disorders such as schizophrenia, dementia and depression.

The theory of dissipative structures, for which Belgian chemist Ilya Prigogine won the 1977 Nobel prize, is especially revolutionary when applied to human potential. It offers evidence that the nature of the universe exists in a state of becoming rather than a state of decaying. Prigogine argues that open and living systems continually reach higher states of order. Simply stated, it means that order arises out of chaos. Apply Prigogine's theory to the human brain as some scientists have, and human potential is radically altered in favor of growth.[2]

In *Megabrain*, author Michael Hutchison wrote:

> Relating this to the brain as a dissipative structure, we can say that the brain is able to accept certain amounts of energy input (such as ideas or events) and assimilate them without any serious challenge to the internal organization of the brain. "Yes, yes," we say in response to certain ideas or stimuli, "this all makes sense." However, at a certain level of intensity, the external events or stimuli become too intense, the brain's fluctuations become too great to be damped, and the brain will escape from its old pattern into a new organization of higher order and coherence. First, things no longer make "sense," then, with a shock of recognition, they make a new type of sense, sense of a sort we had never before imagined.

We have experienced a "brainstorm." When the sky clears the landscape is changed.

Just think of it: If the brain is a dissipative structure then we can continue to grow as individuals and reach higher states of being until the moment of death.

Brain Hemisphere Function

We know that the brain performs different functions in the left and right hemispheres. The left hemisphere governs logic and analytical functions and is the primary home of language and verbal skills. The right hemisphere is intuitive and performs synthesis. Because we think with the software of language and use language to express our thoughts, the left brain dominates our school activities. Indeed our whole educational process centers on left brain activities.[3]

The separate functions of the different hemispheres are at the heart of individual learning styles. Each of us is unique in the way that our two hemispheres interact. Some of us can be said to be left brain dominant and some right. We all differ in degrees of dominance and in our propensity to depend on one hemisphere over the other. If we are left brain dominant we might exhibit characteristics of verbal articulation and pragmatism. Right brain dominant individuals are often described as thoughtful and reflective. The right brain handles pattern recognition, while the left brain is the home of reasoning ability.

Some individuals appear to share an equal amount of hemisphere function without either being dominant. And some people, especially those who are left-handed, have the brain functions reversed. The human brain is often compared to a computer, and indeed, we tend to appreciate the functions in the brain that best emulate a computer. However, as a matter of practice, the human brain is inferior to the computer in its capacity to perform linear left brain functions. For example, the computer can perform hundreds of thousands of mathematical calculations in seconds. On the other hand, it has nowhere near the capability of the right brain when it comes to pattern recognition.[4] This capability allows us to recognize someone we haven't seen in twenty years, who has gained weight, lost his hair, developed wrinkles and even had minor plastic surgery.

The biological predisposition with which we are best able to process and assimilate information into knowledge is likely to have been viewed as a character trait, possibly a negative one, during our school years. The left brain dominant people were considered good students, and were thought to be well-behaved, while the right brain dominant students were considered dreamers or idlers with an attitude problem. Thus occurred the first separation of the "doer" from the "thinker."

A case could be made that the high school drop-outs that Marshall McLuhan referred to are the way they are because of their altered sense ratios. They are especially adept at pattern matching, which is a right brain function. So, in effect, right brain dominants (not just drop-outs) are a challenge to computers in that they are good at doing what computers are not. People who are left brain dominant are at risk of being replaced by computers because what we do best (left brain type functions) cannot compare to the power of computers to perform the same tasks.

The term, "whole brain thinking," suggests the desirability of using both sides simultaneously. Scientists suggest whole brain thinking is a sort of oneness with experience, in which an individual functions intuitively with heightened awareness and less self-consciousness. In a sense, the person becomes the experience. Research indicates that the mental states reached during meditation are in fact the synchronization of both hemispheres into matching brainwave patterns. Synchronization adds such force and power throughout the cortex that the process suggests the potential for reorganization of the brain at a higher level.[5] Brain hemisphere theory is not without its critics. Some argue that interaction between hemispheres is so quick that the functions cannot be separated. I would argue that studying the theory is useful, if only in a metaphorical sense, because it isolates our learning dispositions into areas that we can deal with practically.

Intelligence

A first step in taking an inventory of our personal tools for self-education is to re-think the meaning of intelligence. One of the most damaging, long-lasting effects of traditional education has been the perpetuation of the myth that people can be properly identified and tagged by their level of intelligence. This has had the tragic consequence of allowing millions to abandon their effort at higher learning by shifting the responsibility to a biological predisposition.[6] It has led people to think they were simply not born very smart and therefore there was little they could do about it. This was reinforced in the classroom when they perceived themselves to be learning more slowly than others. It didn't occur to them that they weren't comprehending the material because of the method in which it was presented. This view of oneself as not being very bright starts a pattern of self-limiting expectations and behavior. People often allow their IQ score to represent the potential of their probable contribution, regardless of whether it is high or low.

Before we can identify intelligence we first have to define it. Lawrence J. Greene, author of *Kids Who Underachieve*, suggests a good definition: "Intelligence is the capacity to perceive similarities and differences, to analyze information, to solve problems, to associate past experiences with current experiences, to learn from mistakes, and to distill complex variables into a comprehensible schema."

Greene describes aptitude as "a specialized manifestation of intelligence that is reflected in a specific skill or ability." An aptitude that gives one a seemingly natural edge in a particular discipline is not a reflection of general intelligence.[7]

We tend to regard intelligence as a specific descriptive indicator of how smart we are or how successful we will become. But intelligence has many forms, and it often has little to do with the ultimate success of the individual. Sometimes we associate intelligence with the brain itself, but intelligence is merely a manifestation of brain functioning. We have a lot yet to learn about the true nature of intelligence.

Harvard University psychologist Howard Gardner argues that there are seven different types of intelligence. They are: mathematical, linguistic, musical, spatial, kinesthetic, interpersonal and intrapersonal. They are completely different ways of knowing, and as individuals we have them in varying degrees.[8] We may make an unimpressive score on an intelligence test and still be capable of the type of work attributed to a genius, a musical prodigy, or an Olympic athlete. Yale professor of psychology Robert J. Sternberg suggests a triarchical theory of intelligence that incorporates three elements: componential (analytical thinking), experiential (creativity) and contextual (street smarts).[9]

For years scientists have acknowledged the existence of two distinct types of intelligence, "crystallized" and "fluid." Crystallized intelligence is the result of education and experience, while fluid intelligence operates independently of education and experience.[10] It is dependent on genetic or biological structure. Fluid intelligence is sort of a hardwired ability for inductive reasoning, perceptual speed, pattern matching and short-term memory.[11] If you are familiar with computers, an easy way to remember the difference between crystallized and fluid intelligence is to think of fluid intelligence as ROM, or read-only memory; it is a physical component of the computer and does not change. Crystallized intelligence can be thought of as RAM random access memory; like our knowledge, it can be upgraded.

Theories of crystallized and fluid intelligence can be used to explain how a person with little experience can readily assume a task and appear as if he has experience. He may simply have enough fluid intelligence to make up the difference. Likewise, a person with little apparent fluid intelligence may also be able to exhibit superior performance because of the crystallized intelligence he has gained through experience. This flexibility suggests that crystallized intelligence and fluid intelligence are at least to some degree usefully interchangeable.

Crystallized intelligence increases throughout a lifetime in direct proportion to an individual's education and learning experience, while fluid intelligence is thought to begin a gradual decline in the early thirties. The ability to continually increase the amount of crystallized intelligence is thought to be a means of offsetting the decrease in the amount of fluid intelligence that occurs in the aging process.[12] However, if we do not continue to learn, we will also lose our capability for using our crystallized intelligence. In other words, the athletic principle of "use it or lose it" applies to our minds as well as our muscles.[13] There are numerous theories about intelligence, and while we are still puzzled by its elusive nature, we have enough knowledge to be confident that individuals should not limit their view of themselves solely on the basis of an intelligence test score. We know from our attempts at self-diagnostics in personality traits and learning styles that we have many strengths. The self-educated person learns to intuitively build on strengths with the knowledge that in time this strength will bridge his or her weaknesses.

Edward DeBono cautions in his book, *DeBono's Thinking Course*, that we should not be confused by the usual mistaken assumption that intelligent people are necessarily good thinkers. He argues that it leads to the assertion that if you are intelligent, your thinking is naturally OK, and if you are not apparently very intelligent, nothing can be done about your thinking skill. Both are erroneous assumptions.[14] Intelligence is closely associated with capacity, while thinking is closely associated with process. The process of thinking can be taught, but its ability to affect intelligence is arguable. We all know people regarded as intelligent whose actions continually try to prove us wrong, just as we know people who, with the benefit of method or procedure, can figure out just about anything.

Recent research offers evidence that there is a link between intelligence and environmental stimulation. According to Berkeley psychologist David Krech, there is a strong connection between intelligence and sensory stimulation. Studies by a number of scientists have demonstrated that environmental stimulation has led to the enlargement of the cortex (the seat of intelligence) in rats.[15]

If intelligence can be influenced by environmental stimulation and if the brain is a dissipative structure, we have two key insights into our own development. They are dynamic when combined: Change means growth. We can arrest the aging of our brains with stimulating experience.

Change and Growth

Many of us spend our lives resisting change under the erroneous assumption that security is attainable and change is abnormal. What we learn is that a fleeting semblance of security is possible only when the law of "reverse effort" is applied. In his book *The Wisdom of Insecurity*, philosopher-theologian Alan W. Watts said:

> I have always been fascinated by the law of reversed effort. Sometimes I call it the "backwards law." When you try to stay on the surface of the water, you sink; but when you try to sink you float. When you hold your breath you lose it — which immediately calls to mind an ancient and much neglected saying, "Whosoever would save his soul shall lose it."

Concerning security Watts said:

> It must be obvious, from the start, that there is a contradiction in wanting to be perfectly secure in a universe whose very nature is momentariness and fluidity. But the contradiction lies a little deeper than the mere conflict between the desire for security and the fact of change. If I want to be secure, that is, protected from the flux of life, I am wanting to be separate from life. Yet it is this very sense of separateness which makes me feel insecure. To be secure means to isolate and fortify the "I," but it is just the feeling of being an isolated "I" which makes me feel lonely and afraid. In other words, the more security I can get, the more I shall want.
>
> To put it more plainly: the desire for security and the feeling of insecurity are the same thing. To hold your

> breath is to lose your breath. A society based on the
> quest for security is nothing but a breath-retention
> contest in which everyone is as taut as a drum and as
> purple as a beet.

If you apply the law of reversed effort to the search for security, the moment you realize there is no such thing you will be immediately engulfed with a feeling of security based on the realization that it is unattainable.

Another way to think about this in the context of human intelligence is to look at man as a change-driven organism. We are hard-wired with an operating system dependent upon the natural order of change for our growth and development. It is detrimental to our health to view change only as a phenomenon to be avoided or tolerated. We are physically dependent upon change. Without it we wither. Thinking about oneself as a change-driven organism puts Tom Peters' book, *Thriving on Chaos*, in a new perspective. It means that the accelerated rate of change we experience today can be positive. The uncertainty of the future becomes the fuel for growth.

If we find change to be psychologically stimulating and at the same time find comfort and security in ambiguity, we are well on our way to reaching a new sense of self-knowledge that will ultimately lead to the opportunity for self-actualization. When we better understand our needs for security we are less inhibited by them.

Self-knowledge tends to allow us to become more comfortable with intrinsic needs and less dependent on extrinsic demands. Simply put, as self-knowledge develops, we begin to care more about what we think and less about what others ask of us. We begin to trust our own intuition and judgment. We are less dependent upon external demands and more in touch with our natural sense of curiosity and desire for exploration. We feel a natural urge to acquire knowledge. We become confident that higher levels of understanding will result in more pleasure than discomfort. We become comfortable with the knowledge that as we learn more we gain a sense of just how little we really do know. Having become comfortable with ambiguity and uncertainty we can now appreciate that knowledge is a means of personal "empowerment." Armed with knowledge of ourselves we are empowered to replace our subdued spirit of inquiry with a passionate "rage to know." A positive relationship exists between curiosity and intelligence simply because one process complements the other. Likewise, a negative relationship exists between curiosity and rigidity, because one process limits the other—without curiosity people become rigid. Self-knowledge liberates us from the frustration of ignorance, while simultaneously nurturing and supporting our capacity for intelligence.

Objectivity is the essence of intelligence, and also something we seem to lose in the process of being educated. We learn to approach life under the primary inertia of adaptability. We stand prepared to be able to answer questions when we are asked, but we are not compelled to ask them ourselves. The whole of our growing up experience is to become a "part" which will fit into the whole of society, regardless of the nature of the whole. We don't concern ourselves with whether or not certain jobs should be performed for their effect on the environment or mankind; instead we dwell on whether or not we can become qualified to perform them. Once in a while someone comes along who can see clearly through all the pretentiousness. When that person appeals to our intelligence by calling our attention to a greater quality of reality through the use of an innate sense of objectivity, we are momentarily startled. We see clearly for an instant. But then we step back into a shroud of illusion, because our primary function as we have become conditioned to see it, is to fit. For example, while they were alive Abraham Lincoln, Mahatma Gandhi, and Martin Luther King awakened us to self-evident definitions of equality and justice, but after they were gone, many of us chose to forget.

Memory

We base a large degree of our assessment of others on their demonstrated strength of memory. A person who demonstrates an exceptional ability to recall facts is thought to be intelligent. To understand the function of memory, it is useful to break it into three components: registration, retention, and recall. Registration is awareness through sensory perception. Retention is the persistence, prominence or priority of the material that has been recorded. Recall is the process of search and retrieval.[16]

Memory is at the heart of our ability to learn. Without it we would be incapable of adapting to the environment. For all practical purposes our memories are limitless. We record the totality of our experience in our brain and describe the residue as memory. We are born experts at retention, but we have to learn to adjust our methods to develop spontaneous recall.[17]

It's as if in our mind there exists a video and audio camera connected to a computer that never shuts off. Film runs through the camera at a steady speed. The intensity of the image on the film is determined by our senses which serve as detectors. We use emotion and concentration as emulsifiers to embody the image on film. The camera has no on or off button; it runs continuously, even when we are asleep. The control panel on the camera has five dials, one each for vision, feel, sound, smell and taste. On the computer there are two main dials. One is the emotion intensity regulator and the other is the attention control dial that measures the level of concentration. The emotional registry dial is by far the most powerful.

The rules for operating the camera are simple, if your goal is to establish memory. The more dials you use and the higher you turn them, the better off you will be and the more vividly you will recall the experience. Turn one dial high enough, and you will remember the experience; use two, and not only will the image be meshed deeper into the film, but it will be recorded under two or more categories. Use all the dials with high intensity, and the memory will become an unforgettable experience.[18]

We have file storage systems made up of memories so large they are almost incomprehensible. We know there are four additional components of memory: short-term, long-term, declarative, and procedural memory. Declarative memory is demonstrated by the ability to remember facts, numbers, names and dates. Procedural memory is demonstrated by conditioned abilities such as reading, riding a bicycle, driving a car, or solving puzzles. We know that everything that ends up in long-term memory has to go first into short-term memory. Short-term memory acts similar to computer random access memory in that if the machine is turned off before the memory is designated for long-term storage, it will be lost. Forgetting a telephone number before you realize you will need it again is one example of this.[19]

Recent research suggests that forgetting is not so much evidence of the decay of memory, as it is the inability to find the right cue for retrieval.[20] In other words, the memory is still in the film file if we can find the means to look it up. Stress appears to both help and hinder the recall process by inducing the secretion of adrenaline. Depending on the nature of the memory and the severity of the stress, this biological action will either stimulate or suppress recall. The cue to recall for the particular experience may indeed rest in the fact that the experience was registered and recorded under stress. In such cases, a return to a similar state is known to aid in recall.

The cues to recall appear to be so complex as to include the totality of the environment at the time of the experience. For example, if you have an experience during a thunderstorm while seated in your living room with a particular group of friends, the experience may be recalled at a later date by associating it with either the storm, the chair, the living room, or the people. It may be triggered by one association or all of them together. In other words, it might be easier to remember the experience on a stormy day, and easier yet by sitting in your living room in the same chair with the same people.[21]

A strange phenomenon that offers insight into the complexity and how little we know about the retrieval systems of our memories can occur when you lie down on the ground and relax, think about nothing and just watch the clouds in the sky. Soon, the clouds will begin to look like recognizable objects, such as animals, people, places or things. The images of the clouds are subtle cues to images stored as records in memory. They are not exact recollections of specific memories, but are memories of similarities. The older you are, the more experience you have had, the more you are likely to see in the clouds. Another interesting point about this phenomenon is that if you are watching the clouds while tense or under stress, you will see nothing but clouds. (For tips on techniques to improve your memory see Chapter Ten.)

Creativity

Creativity is another characteristic which is often misunderstood. Creativity is not a mystical trait for a select few who are born with the gift for special thinking. The paradox is that we associate intelligence with creative ability and yet many intelligent people do not think of themselves as creative. Thus, they are not.

According to Edward DeBono:

Intelligent people often tend to be conformists. They learn the rules of the game and make use of them to have a comfortable life. At school they learn the rules of the game: how to please the teacher; how to pass exams with minimal work; how to get on with people. Creativity tends to be left to the rebels who cannot or will not play the rules for a variety of reasons. The paradox is that if we treat creativity (in the form of lateral thinking) as a perfectly sober part of information processing then we may get the strange effect of the conformists being more creative than the rebels—because the conformists are also better at playing the rules of creativity. If creativity is no longer a risk then nonrisk-takers may decide to be creative.

William C. Miller, author of *The Creative Edge*, sees five categories of fundamental attitudes that affect creativity. How do these categories compare with your own attitudes about creativity? They are:

1. Leader/Victim. Do you generally feel that you are directing your life or that you are the victim of outside forces? Do you have a sense of personal power?

2. Confidence and Trust. Do you tend to see the world as friendly or antagonistic? Do you have confidence in yourself (and/or a higher power) for having your life "turn out" okay?

3. Talent/Contribution. Do you feel you are exercising your talents and having a positive impact on the world around you?

4. Strength of Expectations. Do you feel "addicted" to having life turn out according to your expectations? Do you problem solve or do you blame others when your goals aren't accomplished?

5. Personal Value. Do you feel you have to prove yourself continually to "earn" self-esteem and the esteem of others, or do you believe in an inherent personal worth of each person?

Miller adds, "Our culture has principles that can also block creativity, including: 'Fantasy and reflection are a waste of time.' 'Playfulness is for children only.' 'Reason and logic are good; feeling and intuition are bad.' 'Tradition is preferable to change.'" Understanding how we have shaped our beliefs about creativity is a fundamental key for advancing self-knowledge.[22]

Genius

What is a genius? Our definition likely affects the standards we set for our own achievement. We tend to think of a genius as someone with a high IQ, or as someone with exceptional creative ability. But history is full of extraordinary feats of genius by otherwise ordinary people. When you consider the self-limiting tendencies of culture, it is highly probable that many of the greatest writers in history were never published, the greatest inventors never submitted their work for patent and the best ideas ever conceived were never discussed. If we start with the assertion that we are all creative, and accept the premise that all humans are capable of genius, we radically alter how we view ourselves, and our expectations follow accordingly. Moreover, we find the path to genius is in complete congruence with the process of self-education because it is directly concerned with objectivity and the search for truth. As Schopenhauer said in his essay, "The Wisdom of Life":

> Genius is simply the completest objectivity,—i.e., the objective tendency of the mind .... Genius is the power of leaving one's own interest, wishes and aims entirely out of sight, of entirely renouncing one's own personality for a time, so as to remain pure knowing subject, clear vision of the world .... Therefore the expression of genius in a face consists in this, that in it a decided predominance of knowledge over will is visible. In ordinary countenances there is a predominant expression of will, and is directed merely by motives of personal interest and advantage.

It is important to bear in mind that the constructive process with which we build our versions of reality is heavily influenced by what we have learned in school. This is another example of how many of these attitudes restrict our daily lives—we haven't yet challenged them through the dissonance of our own experience.

In *Critical Path*, Buckminster Fuller said: "We may soon discover that all babies are born geniuses and only become degeniused by the erosive effects of unthinkingly maintained false assumptions of the grown-ups, with their conventional ways of 'bringing up' and educating their young. We know that schools are the least favorable environment for learning."

Expertise

Self-knowledge enables us to assume and maintain the posture necessary to develop professional expertise which enables us to earn a living. What is expertise? How do we become an expert? A large body of research into the nature of expertise suggests that we become an expert in a particular field when our level of knowledge reaches a point of sophistication where we no longer have to resort to the recollection of rules. An expert responds to problems intuitively. Imagine that the acquisition of knowledge is like sewing. We start by adding a stitch at a time. Each new piece of knowledge is represented by a different color of thread. At first the contrast of bright colors is obvious, but as the addition of knowledge reaches critical mass, colors become indistinguishable. At that point one becomes an expert. Solving problems no longer requires recalling the color of a particular thread for a piece of knowledge. The expert offers a solution that is both accurate and spontaneous. It is a "gut-level" response.

Robert J. Trotter, managing editor of *Psychology Today*, has said, "Experts don't apply rules, make decisions or solve problems. They do what comes naturally, and it almost always works. When they fail it often is because they are pitted against another expert."[23] I would argue that it is precisely this phenomenon that leads people in management positions to want to be seen as decisive and capable of making gut-level, intuitively correct decisions on the spot. It is to our collective misfortune that many of them emulate this behavior without the benefit of expertise.

The more you work at becoming self-educated, the more often you will encounter credentialed experts in fields that interest you, only to find their alleged superior knowledge questionable. When you meet the umpteenth person with a degree who knows less about his field than you do, you will begin to truly appreciate the ineffectiveness of the formal educational system. Remember that a large number of people become certified or degreed by furnishing other people's answers to other people's questions. On the other hand, most experts without credentials settle for just being an "extraordinary" person. Developing expertise without the right orientation has some risk. In *The Plateauing Trap*, Judith M. Bardwick said:

> Mastering something you don't know is engrossing. People usually find the process of learning and achieving more fulfilling than the knowledge that they achieve. In that time when we are fully absorbed and engrossed, mastering the task is a high. Motivated to become an expert in what we do, the paradox is that we are psychologically most at risk when we are expert because that is when we are most likely to be bored and discontent. We are expert, but the challenge is gone. And, if work is the most important sector in our lives, the danger is that no sector feels exciting.

When one adopts the self-image of a self-directed learner whose growth and well-being is dependent upon the stimulation of lifelong learning freedom from boredom is assured. And if we don't take measures against boredom we run the risk of getting off track in the course of reaching our goals.

Individual Learning Style

If you will accept the premise that education is human software, you might possibly agree with my assertion that finding your learning style is discovering how you are programed. Learning then becomes a process of finding software that is suitable for your personal style. Discovering how you learn best is the single greatest self-empowering principle that you can accomplish. It is a lot like learning to read maps: once you have achieved that, you can go anywhere. Another important aspect of determining your learning style is that once you know your learning strengths you will also be aware of your weaknesses. This means you will know what to work on in order to improve.

In a training environment I have often heard it said that we retain 10 percent of what we read, 20 percent of what we hear, 30 percent of what we see, and 50 percent of what we see and hear. In contrast, it is said that we remember approximately 70 percent of what we say and 90 percent of what we say and do. These are just estimates, but they offer some insight into the general methods of learning which can help explain how to best use our own specific learning style to the fullest advantage.

We learn through different perceptual senses in varying degrees. Some of us need to get physically involved in the learning experience through touching and feeling, some of us require high visual content, others may need to hear and then discuss the material being studied. Some of us are "big picture" learners—we have to get a sense of the overall and then use the process of synthesis to assimilate the information into knowledge. Still others take the opposite approach, needing to understanding by learning specifics first and then stringing them together until the big picture emerges. There is an old Chinese proverb that says: "I hear and I forget. I see and I remember. I do and I understand."

Discovering your learning style is a subject worthy of a book in itself. There are many good books and self-administering tests available that you can use to determine your learning style. (See Part Four for additional information.)

Summary

If we acknowledge the importance of self-knowledge, we take the first step in seeing our human traits and capabilities objectively. We are better able to rise above our regional identity and observe the differences of others without feeling threatened. Likewise, when we learn about the nature of human personality to such a degree that we are no longer surprised by the results of self-diagnostic tests, we have a strong sense of personal identity. We are thus empowered to discover intuitively our "right livelihood" – what we are best suited to do for a living.

When we have a firm foundation of self-knowledge we are able to maintain a natural sense of objectivity about brain function, intelligence, the attributes of stimulating change, the characteristics of memory, the nature of curiosity and exploration, and the essence of creativity and genius. Without a strong sense of self, many of us allow our perceptions of these human capacities to become stereotyped categories having more to do with our limitations than with our capabilities. We think we that we are not very intelligent or creative, so we stifle our own curiosity so as to conform to our limited self-image. But when we understand the nature of expertise, we know how to use our human faculties and our own individual learning styles to develop it.

Part II

CHAPTER FOUR

The Personal Sciences

*Knowledge of human nature is the begin-
ning and end of political education.*
                                    —Henry Brook Adams

Personal sciences is a general term intended to encompass the many
different schools of thought about human psychology and human
development. This chapter will look briefly at the major schools of
psychology and the confusion that results from them. It will explore a
major theory of human needs, avenues of personal growth, and the
search for meaning. In addition, since psychology is rooted in philosophy, the subject of philosophy will also be broached.

Major Schools of Psychology

There are thousands of theories about human nature and human
behavior, and they are all concerned with why we behave as we do.
Many of the theories vary dramatically, but they generally fall into
three major fields or schools of thought: psychoanalysis, behaviorism,
and humanism.

Psychoanalysis

Sigmund Freud (1856–1939) was the father of psychoanalysis. Significantly influenced by the work of Charles Darwin, Freud asserted
that man's presence on earth is an accidental fluke of nature, and
believed man to be an animal, a product of the evolutionary process.
He also thought religion to be a mild form of mental illness. The
theories of Sigmund Freud had a profound effect on American society
during the first half of the nineteenth century.

Freud began his work with the study of dreams. He shocked the
scientific community by suggesting that dreams were film clips of
the unconscious, a sort of sneak preview into what is really going on
in the depths of our minds. He argued that man is in perpetual
conflict with himself and others and is in large part driven by his
sexual urges. Freud broke the human psyche into three major components: the id, the ego, and the superego. In this model, the id is the
power source of the psyche, a mechanism of energy propelled by
genetics and biological disposition. As the origin of instinct, it is the

unconscious part of the human mind. The ego is the totality of the conscious mind and acts as a referee between instinctive urges and the consciousness. The third component of the psyche, the superego, is a conscious accumulation of learned behavior based on customs and parental authority.

According to Freud, behavior is a continual balancing act between the id, the ego and the superego. Simply put, the conscious (ego) is always at odds with the unconscious (id). The little voice that we call our personal "conscience" (superego) censures our behavior and keeps us from doing what we feel like when it's not morally or socially acceptable. In other words, we have the gas pedal pushed to the floor with one foot while holding the other foot on the brake. At any moment we have the potential for being out of control without knowing exactly why.

Alfred Adler (1870–1937), a colleague of Freud's and a student of psychoanalysis, split with Freud in 1911 and founded the individual psychology branch of psychoanalysis. Adler originated the idea of the inferiority complex. He differed with Freud's assertion that the sexual urge is the major driving force in human nature, arguing that the desire for power and self-assertion is the primary driving force in man.

Carl Gustav Jung (1875–1961) was a Swiss psychologist who also broke away from psychoanalysis because he disagreed with Freud's belief about the role of the sex drive. Jung contended that a general "life urge" dominated the sexual drive. He also believed in a "collective unconscious" that is hardwired into humans by heredity. Jung originated the terms introvert and extrovert.

Behaviorism

John B. Watson (1878–1958) is the individual primarily credited with responsibility for the second major school of thought in human behavior, which came to be known as behaviorism. While Freud had argued that man was driven by unconscious drives, Watson claimed that man was externally or environmentally driven. The behaviorist point of view was deduced by scientific observation. Watson believed personality to be the residue of habit. Behaviorists offered evidence of stimulus-response theory and conditioned reflexes. Ivan Pavlov's salivating dog and B.F. Skinner's conditioned response experiments are the classic examples.

B.F. Skinner (1904) furthered the behaviorists' point of view when he startled the scientific world with the thesis: "Behavior is determined by its consequences." Period.[1] This assertion led the behaviorists to the conclusion that "will and motivation" are irrelevant. Skinner and his associates argued that all you need to know about someone in order to predict his behavior is a history of his past reinforcements and the circumstances of his present environment. In other words, we are environmentally reliant creatures entirely dependent upon circumstances for our actions[2]. What we think and how we feel are of little consequence. We are, in effect, prisoners of circumstance and environment. Skinner experimented with rats to observe the effects of conditioning. He constructed a box for his experiments in which a rat would learn the connection between pushing a pedal and receiving food. As his work became famous, the term "Skinner Box" became a common frame of reference for operant conditioning.[3]

Humanistic Psychology

Abraham Maslow (1908–1970) is one of the best known individuals responsible for the third major school of thought known as humanistic psychology. This is often referred to as humanistic (Gestalt) therapy or as "third force psychology," the first being Freudian or psychoanalytic psychology and the second being behaviorism. In the Forties, Abraham Maslow and a few others began to have serious difficulty with some of the assertions accepted as truths by Freudians and behaviorists. Maslow began as a behaviorist, but with the birth of his first child he came to view behaviorism as impossible. He simply could not accept the assumption that a child is no more than a conflict of urges and drives or a bundle of conditioned reflexes. Humanistic psychology argues that man has the use of free will and is therefore subject to differing degrees of self-determining choices and behaviors. Simply put, humanistic psychology is a human-centered psychology, asserting that there is a sharp distinction between man and animal. According to humanistic psychology, man is a creature of choice, and animals are creatures of conditions.

Maslow is best known for his hierarchy of needs theory which postulates that we progress in an upward movement from the lower drives such as the physiological needs for food, clothing and shelter, to those for safety and security, to love and belongingness, to self-esteem, to the growth needs of self-actualization. Maslow argued that once a particular need is satisfied it is no longer a source of motivation.[4] He stated that people are motivated toward growth and that upon finding the right level of need with the right nourishment or environment, they will blossom spontaneously into actualizing organisms.

Humanistic psychology has received extensive criticism because of its proponents' failure to produce scientific data to support its premises. Indeed, its theories are difficult to prove because humanistic psychology, by nature, is based on the credibility of human experience.

Confusion from Dramatically Different Theories

In effect, the personal sciences have evolved in neat little hypothe-sized packages made up of small chunks of variables good for the professional life of the producer. Each theorist or practitioner is limited to the number of variables that he or she can explain and take credit for.

What does all of this mean? How can so many people certified and looked up to as "experts" (such as today's psychiatrists and psychologists), be at such odds over the fundamentals of behavior? And, if they can't agree on the basic underlying principles of human behavior, why should we be concerned? Just as self-knowledge is the foundation for self-education, human understanding is the basis for self-knowledge. Without it we have little hope of living a full life. If the basic premises of the personal sciences are disputed by practition-ers who cannot agree on cause and effect between biological drives, environmental stimuli and human aspirations, then we have no choice but to continually address these questions through our own experience.

It is truly a baffling paradox that as a society we allow the credentialing of experts who are in total disagreement with one another about the basic nature of their knowledge. Yet we treat each of them as an expert and defer to them in both simple and complex matters, knowing intuitively that some of them must be totally wrong, and thus not expert at all but merely misinformed. It would be much more practical to certify "theorists" whose credentials would assert their theory and offer supporting evidence for their position. We would be less vulnerable as consumers if, instead of approaching practitioners as experts, we regarded them as fallible.

Our society treats the field of psychology and human behavior as a deeply mysterious endeavor much too complicated for the average person to comprehend, yet our feelings and emotional needs are the only areas in which we have direct experience – even at an early age. If we begin with the premises upon which the experts disagree, then we can apply their assertions to our own personal experiences. If we were treated as if we had a greater capacity for understanding ourselves from early childhood, we would grow into adulthood seeing ourselves very differently from the way we do today. We would seek knowledge instead of hiding from it. We would see ourselves as "thinkers" capable of self-determination. We would be comfortable with ambiguity. Change would be an ally.

Today, people seek professional help from mental health practitioners they believe to be experts, but if they were fully acquainted with the basic principals upon which the discipline is founded, they would be philosophically opposed to it. In such cases, they would probably be better off conferring with a pet.

According to the National Institute of Mental Health, there are 417 different types of therapies. These run the gamut from psychoanalysis, primal screaming, EST, to the answering of open-ended questions for the process of self-discovery. And the most we can say scientifically is that some of them "seem" to work.

Social Psychological Assumptions

These differing concepts and psychological theories have subtle ways of becoming a part of the structural fabric of society. We find residue of unacknowledged assumptions in the workplace, in government, in societal values and in family values. For example, a slip of the tongue during a conversation is commonly called a "Freudian slip," and is accepted by many as the revelation of a hidden agenda of thought. In other words, you are concealing something and with a slip of the tongue you have given an idea of what you really meant to say, consciously or even subconsciously. In the early Seventies folk singer Harry Chapin hit the popular music charts with the song "Cat's In The Cradle." The lyrics dealt with a father and son relationship in which the son was emulating the behavior of his father who was too busy to spend time with him. When the son grew up the circumstances were reversed: Now it was the son who was too busy to spend time with his father. Both father and son were locked into an automatic response cycle determined by their environments. The song echoed the assertions of behaviorism.

If we are incapable of recognizing these common assumptions or understanding the origin of the beliefs, we are likely to experience pressure of being pulled in many directions at once. The result is a feeling of frustration, confusion and a general sense of helplessness or lack of control over that part of our lives which means the most. What of the teacher who does not understand his own position in how he relates to students? Does he see the student as a conflicting bundle of conscious and unconscious drives, an environmentally-controlled organism, or a person having a significant role in his own development and destiny? If he doesn't know, how can he possibly be an effective teacher? How can the students make the most of the experience, if they don't understand the teacher's position in how they are viewed in the learning experience?

This lack of insight into one's actions is analogous to sailing a ship over rough seas using random sail riggings without determining the effects each time a change is made. Choosing the correct rigging for changing weather conditions becomes nothing more than a guessing game. Understanding the fundamental assumptions held by society and how they are able to be in conflict and yet continue to exist simultaneously is like being able to read the elements, the weather and the currents at sea. Without that ability, sailing is uncertain and, at best, hazardous.

Human Needs and Personal Growth

In *Aristotle for Everybody* Mortimer Adler put human needs in perspective when he said:

> Aristotle sums all this up when he says that our success in living a good life depends on two things. One is having the moral virtue that enables us to make right choices from day to day. The other is being blessed by good luck or good fortune. As moral virtue prevents us from aiming in the wrong direction and choosing things that are not really good for us, so good fortune supplies us with real goods that are not entirely within our power to obtain by choice.
>
> A good life it has been said, is one in which a person has everything that he or she desires, provided that he or she desires nothing amiss. In order to desire nothing amiss, one must have moral virtue, but one must also have goods that lie beyond the reach of choice—the goods bestowed on us by luck in addition to the goods acquired by good habits of choice.

To achieve true happiness we must understand ourselves well enough to be able to distinguish between a "want" and a "need." It is incredible that what we have learned of the nature of humans since philosopher-psychologist William James (1842–1910) wrote *Principles of Psychology* in 1890, has not been integrated into our educational system. How can we know others if we don't know ourselves? How can we make personal choices if we don't understand personal cause and effect?

Humans are need-driven beings. We convert needs into drives

by organ deprivation and environmental stimulus. Our inability to know ourselves inhibits our ability to adjust to society. Our reaction is to respond excessively in terms of need reduction. For example, our quest for wealth continues long after we have acquired more money than we can ever spend. We eat more food than our bodies require. We pursue sexual conquests at the risk of our marital relationships.[5] In short, the actions that we take in response to our perceived needs and wants create for each of us our own Skinner Box. We step on the pedal of our Skinner Box as we react to our perceived needs. The result is that our wants are rewarded and our needs are ignored. Not being able to distinguish wants from needs, we are doomed to a lifetime of making the wrong choices. Rat-like, we continue pushing the same pedal over and over.

With little knowledge of ourselves, we have little hope of knowing others. If we can't relate to others, we have little hope of achieving global peace. Consider the difficulty of a political system dependent upon leaders who are unable to understand why they act as they do. How can they know what is good for others if they don't know what is good for themselves? Yet the political system of America and the world is made up of people who know little of their own motivation. When we discover that someone in public office has a tragic personal life, we are shocked to think that this could be the same person with whose image we are acquainted.

Adler continues:

> Thomas Jefferson thought that all human beings, having the same human nature, had the same natural rights. That amounts to saying that they all have the same natural needs—that what is really good for any one human being is really good for all human beings. To this extent, Thomas Jefferson appears to have adopted Aristotle's view that the pursuit of happiness involves all human beings in seeking and trying to obtain the same set of real goods for themselves.

Consider what the results might be if mankind could generally agree about what constitutes natural human rights.

Maslow's Theory of Human Needs

There are many theories regarding the nature of human needs. The one that I find most useful as a means of self-discovery is the five-level hierarchy of needs theory proposed by the late Abraham Maslow. I am not offering this theory as all-inclusive, but only as a means for gaining insight into the nature of needs. It is an excellent formula by which to compare your own experience against the theories of others.

Maslow asserted that human needs exist in an imprecise hierarchy that begins in an upward progression starting with:

1. Physiological needs (food, clothing, shelter, sleep).
2. Safety and security (the need for stability).
3. Social needs (love and belonging).
4. Self-esteem (the need for self-respect, recognition, status, etc.).
5. Self-actualization (the need to reach one's potential).[6]

The non-hierarchical "being values" or Metaneeds, as Maslow referred to them, come into being at this level.

Maslow believed that these needs are satisfied in a hierarchical fashion: once the physiological needs are satisfied the search begins for safety and security, then on to the social needs, and so forth up the ladder. Once a need is satisfied, according to Maslow's theory, it is no longer a source of motivation.[7]

Our needs express themselves as feelings. We feel hungry, thirsty, cold, fearful, safe, curious, unloved, loved, lonely and important. There is no doubt that the lower needs are the most powerful. When we are sufficiently hungry or thirsty we can think of little else. There is a controversial expression with supporting evidence that each man is only about twenty-one meals away from cannibalism.[8]

The lower needs seem to be minimum requirements for growth to a higher level. After we have been fed, we can begin to feel safe and secure because we are assured that food and water will be available the next time we are hungry and thirsty. To feel safe and secure we need a certain amount of consistency and predictability.

Once the physiological and safety needs are satisfied, the needs for love and belonging become salient. Maslow theorized that love involves a healthy relationship between two people, and felt that Freud had made a mistake by suggesting that love was derived from sex. Maslow felt that the absence of love inhibited the growth of the individual.

With the needs for love and belonging satisfied, the needs for self-esteem emerge. These include esteem from others, such as status, recognition, prestige, appreciation and acceptance, as well as feelings of adequacy, self-respect, competence, independence, freedom and mastery. For these feelings to be adequate they must be genuinely felt and must override any sense of inferiority.

Next comes the self-actualization stage—the pinnacle of

Maslow's needs hierarchy. Unlike the previous steady progression upward on the needs ladder, self-actualization may not occur. Maslow argued that in addition to the need to self-actualize, man also has an innate tendency toward inertia, which exists primarily because of the physiological need to rest. To override this tendency to settle for the status quo, humans must be sufficiently challenged or stimulated, and permitted to burst forth with the actions of an organism bent on the process of becoming.

An unfortunate aspect of Maslow's hierarchical theory of needs is that some people tend to use it as a means for rationalizing their superiority over others. Since their own lower needs are satisfied, they see themselves at a higher plane of existence. They believe they are superior because they enjoy a better quality of life. This is a mistaken assumption; it was certainly not Maslow's intention to suggest that some people are better than others based on their level of personal development.

I once pointed out to a mid-level corporate manager the fact that if managers use Maslow's theory literally as a means of control, they may find it effective to ensure that some employees' needs are never met at certain levels. He was silent for a moment. Then a smile broke from ear to ear as he realized he had discovered a new tool. He walked away repeating to himself over and over, "I like it, I like it."

Consider Maslow's theory in a political context. An examination of a country according to the way the majority of the population lives within the hierarchy will bear his theories out. Third World countries struggle on the first and second level, while the middle class of the U.S. is concerned with the social level. The VALS typology developed by the Stanford Research Institute and discussed in Chapter Two was based in part on Maslow's work.

Look at this from another political perspective. Is there a political advantage to preventing a struggling country from advancing up the hierarchy, so that it never becomes politically concerned with more than the basic needs? Does Maslow's theory offer some mechanism for political or organizational management control by anyone who would use it to his advantage? In other words, keep them hungry, keep them quiet.

During the last years of his life Maslow was excited by his insight into the nature of self-actualization which he saw as a sense of mission, a calling or vocation. He argued that this sense of mission is value-driven, with the B-values being the dominant force.

There are fourteen B-values. I studied them for several weeks, alternating between reading and listening to audio tapes of Maslow's lectures. After a time, in a shock of recognition, it all made sense. I understood in a visceral and graphic sense what he was trying to say and why his descriptions of the B-values seem similar to attempting to shoot at a moving target. Most of us spend so much of our lives out of tune that we don't comprehend what it's like to be hitting on all eight cylinders (self-actualizing). I have included a complete description of the B-values because it is the key to understanding their essence. They are:

1. Truth: honesty; reality; (nakedness; simplicity; richness; essentiality; oughtness; beauty; pure; clean and unadulterated completeness).

2. Goodness: (rightness; desirability; oughtness; justice; benevolence; honesty); (we love it, are attracted to it, approve of it).

3. Beauty: (rightness; form; aliveness; simplicity; richness; wholeness; perfection; completion; uniqueness; honesty).

4. Wholeness: (unity; integration; tendency to oneness; interconnectedness; simplicity; organization; structure; order; not dissociated; synergy; homonomous and integrative tendencies).

4a. Dichotomy-transcendence: (acceptance, resolution, integration, or transcendence of dichotomies, polarities, opposites, contradictions); synergy (i.e., transformation of oppositions into unities, of antagonists into collaborating or mutually enhancing partners).

5. Aliveness: (process; not-deadness; dynamic; eternal; flowing; self-perpetuating; spontaneity; self-moving energy; self-forming; self-regulation; full-functioning; changing and yet remaining the same; expressing itself; never-ending).

6. Uniqueness: (idiosyncrasy; individuality; singularity; non-comparability; its defining-characteristics; novelty; quale; suchness; nothing else like it).

7. Perfection: (nothing superfluous; nothing lacking; everything in its right place; unimprovable; just-rightness; just-so-ness; suitability; justice; completeness; nothing beyond; oughtness).

7a. Necessity: (inevitability; it must be just that way; and it is good that it is that way).

8. Completion: (ending; finality; justice; it's finished; no more changing of the Gestalt; fulfillment; finis and telos; nothing missing or lacking; totality; fulfillment of destiny; cessation; climax; consummation; closure; death before rebirth; cessation and completion of growth and development; total gratification with no more gratification possible; no striving; no movement toward any goal because already there; not pointing to anything beyond itself).

9. Justice: (fairness; oughtness; suitability; architectonic qual-

ity; necessity; inevitability; disinterestedness; non-partiality).

9a. Order: (lawfulness; rightness; rhythm; regularity; symmetry; structure; nothing superfluous; perfectly arranged).

10. Simplicity: (honesty; nakedness; purity; essentiality; succinctness; elegance; abstract; unmistakability; essential skeletal structure; the heart of the matter; bluntness; only that which is necessary; without ornament, nothing extra or superfluous).

11. Richness: (totality; differentiation; complexity; intricacy; nothing missing or hidden; all there; "non-importance," i.e., everything is equally important; nothing is unimportant; everything left the way it is, without improving, simplifying, abstracting, rearranging; comprehensiveness).

12. Effortlessness: (ease; lack of strain, striving, or difficulty; grace; perfect and beautiful functioning).

13. Playfulness: (fun; joy; amusement; gaiety; humor; exuberance; effortlessness).

14. Self-sufficiency: (autonomy; independence; not needing anything other than itself in order to be itself; self-determining; environmental-transcendence; separateness; living by its own laws; identity).

Maslow realized he might be on thin ice, but he asserted that the B-values might be a superstructure for joining the spiritual life. In other words, they are the core of our being. The B-values are connected because they are not separate; they are bound as facets of one thing. Each B-value is alike in that it can be defined in terms of all the others, i.e., truth can be good and beautiful, just as good can be beautiful and true.

Maslow concluded that if a person is self-actualizing because of being driven by a force of synergistic values, then he would be most altruistic when he reached the point of being the most selfish. In other words, when you are doing what you have the most talent to do and you also feel that it is important, you will also enjoy it more and thus you will likely be capable of making your most valuable contribution.

American workers are indebted to Abraham Maslow. His hierarchical theory of needs has had a significant influence on American management style. Its broad acceptance by management psychologists forced most managers (though there are still exceptions) to look at workers as human beings willing and capable of superior achievement given the proper environment and treatment.

Beyond Maslow

Let me append five additional points to this theory to help you keep the perspective necessary for the chapters that follow. The first is that of artificial needs. The use and abuse of alcohol and a myriad of legal and illegal drugs has contributed significantly to the complication of human behavior. Alcohol and drugs are profound examples of wants exercising power over needs by physically manifesting themselves and becoming genuine felt needs.

The second point concerns the work of Edward W. Deci in the area of self-determination. Deci has offered evidence which differs slightly with Maslow. He argues that man has an innate need to be self-determining.[9] Self-determination will be discussed further in the next chapter.

The third point is that understanding the conflict among needs is a complex proposition. To gain self-knowledge, to know oneself in terms of individual needs, requires considerable effort. Reading a few articles, taking a couple college courses and attending a few seminars will not be sufficient. To achieve insight and effective self-determination we must develop expertise. Self-knowledge requires overlearning the fundamental approaches to the behavioral sciences. (Overlearning is discussed in Chapter Ten.) It is absurd for humans to abdicate the search for self-knowledge in favor of leaving such matters to experts. To do so is to contribute to our own helplessness.

The fourth important point I want to add is the tremendous significance of the need for novelty in our lives. Relying on my own experience I feel that Maslow's hierarchical need theory falls short in accounting for the importance of novelty.

The fifth and final point is one by Marsha Sinetar, author of *Do What You Love the Money Will Follow*. She said:

> Any talent that we are born with eventually surfaces as a need. Current research on child prodigies—youngsters who, from an early age, are mathematical wizards, virtuoso musicians, brilliant performers—tells us that they possess a burning desire to express themselves, to use their unique gifts. In a similar fashion, each of us, no matter how ordinary we consider our talents, wants and needs to use them. Right livelihood is the natural expression of this need. Yet many of us cannot imagine that what we enjoy doing, what we have talent for, could be a source of income for us or even a catalyst for transforming our relationship to work. But, indeed, it can be. Leaders in

every walk of life (e. g. housewives, crafts persons, entrepreneurs, inventors, community volunteers, etc.) who have
the drive, skill and compelling vision to advance their
ideas, despite obstacles, need to exert their influence as
much as their solutions, energy and enthusiasm are
needed by others.

There are other items to be reconciled, and had Maslow lived
longer he might have been able to address them. One apparent
discrepancy is that, although his theory suggests that infants should
be motivated primarily by physiological needs, medical evidence
shows that they can die without love.

The greatest problem remaining lies in the misinterpretation of
Maslow's work. Unfortunately, Maslow's work has been distorted by
others since his death. Maslow was a dedicated psychologist who had
great aspirations and expectations for mankind. He did not, I am
sure, intend his work to be the focus of a "pop psychology" that
centered on the premise that the world revolves around the "Self" to
the exclusion of all else.[10]

For this reason I was a little reluctant to choose the title of *Self-
University* for this book for fear of being associated with such thinking. I believe that understanding oneself is of extreme importance
and that it is necessary for a full life. But I also believe that the
process of self-education cannot help but place the self in a more
balanced perspective, leading to the discovery that acknowledges
one's interdependence on others and a sense of duty and commitment
to society. E.F. Schumacher said that the essence of education is in
the transmission of values. I would add that an object of self-
education is to discover them.

Maslow has his share of critics. His work, like that of thousands
of others, is incomplete, but even his most severe critics acknowledge
the value of his contribution in helping us to better understand
ourselves. I suggest it as the starting point for your own investigation. Study the hierarchical structure of needs relative to your own
experience. Review the B-values often as you compare Maslow's work
with the work of others. It is a worthwhile effort for self-discovery. A
fundamental thesis of this book is that self-education is the "Up"
button on Maslow's elevator of needs.

Getting Your Ducks in a Row

A simple exercise in gaining insight into your own needs is what I
call "getting your ducks in a row." It works like this. You break up the
"needs" categories as follows: Survival Duck represents your need for

food, clothing and shelter. These are the physiological needs. Safety Duck represents your need for physical health and security. Social Duck represents your need for love and belonging. Prestige Duck represents your need for self-esteem. And finally Dynamic Duck represents your need for self-actualization. Now each one of these "ducks" represents a stage of developmental progress, but each stage may have several components. For example, Social Duck may consist of family and friends (see Figure 2). These subcategories are called "needlings." You can have as many needlings as you feel necessary. The object is simple: all you have to do is line ducks and needlings up in the "V" formation used by wild ducks. This is done by priority:

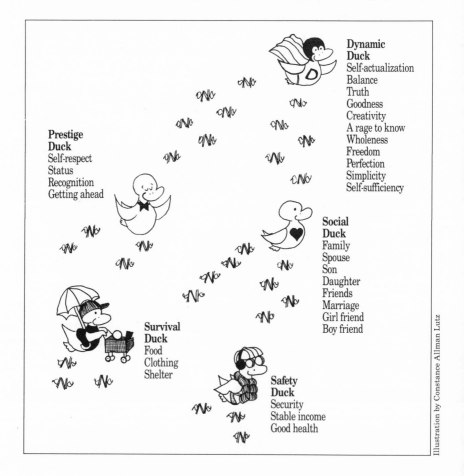

Illustration by Constance Allman Lutz

FIGURE 2.
Getting Your Ducks In A Row.

Your most pressing need is the lead duck, the rest follow in order of their importance. Once you have them in place, ask yourself what it would take for the priorities to change. How far are you away from being in a position to self-actualize? Study the B-values carefully. Do they make sense? Which ones are most important to you?

If lining up your ducks seems difficult, study them for a few minutes and the exercise will begin to make sense. The stage of priority on which you are currently focused will probably be obvious. The main difficulty is often the placement of Social Duck. For example, it is impractical for most of us to even consider that anything has more priority or importance in our lives than our families, even though our actions often suggest otherwise. If you have dissonant feelings regarding this, the exercise is probably worthy of careful consideration. To remedy the problem, line up the needlings under each appropriate duck before you attempt to place them in final formation. Remember there are no limits to the number or type of needlings. At this point, if you still have trouble, simply compare one with another until you are satisfied with the arrangement. The "V" formation allows you to stagger the ducks and needlings in such a manner as to suggest an equal or a slight preference. Do this exercise whenever you are bored or feel the need to doodle. You will be amazed at how revealing it is. After you complete this exercise compare your results with your personality profile from the Enneagram discussed in Chapter Ten. Using Riso's book you should be able at this point to determine the direction you need to take in order to achieve self-actualization. By a careful examination of your felt needs hierarchy you should be able to see what is keeping you from it, if indeed anything is.

The Search for Meaning

William James, a pioneer of modern psychology, considered one of his greatest contributions to the body of knowledge in that field to be his discovery that humans use only a small part of their potential. James was thrilled simply because he had concluded that humans are merely partially developed organisms.[11] Quality of the "perception" of life exists in direct proportion to the level of our individual development. Flowers are designed to bloom. Humans are designed to develop to or near the biological limits of human capacity. Nature made certain qualities of life contingent upon reaching higher states of learning and being in order to ensure survival, but nature also allows us to fool ourselves by not necessarily making a conscious connection with the cause and effect of our own development. We reach higher stages of development, but we have no felt assurance that striving will help us go higher, and indeed it may even jeopardize our present sense of comfort with the progress we have made thus far. New knowledge brings additional responsibility. To seek growth is to put ourselves at risk. It is far easier for most of us to avoid it.

Perhaps our biological need to become a fully developed organism subtly manifests itself as the perceived need for meaning. This may be what teacher-philosopher, Joseph Campbell (1904-1987) was implying when he said: "People say that what we're all seeking is a meaning for life. I don't think that's what we're really seeking. I think that what we're seeking is an experience of being alive, so that our life experiences on the purely physical plane will have resonances within our own innermost being and reality, so that we actually feel the rapture of being alive." In time each of us will come face to face with our own mortality. When we examine our mortality we are faced with the fundamental questions of existence. Who are we? Why are we here? What are we to do? Does life really matter?

Nowhere is our predisposition to self-directed inquiry and our relationship to authority more important than when we begin to search for meaning in our lives. People who hold unexamined beliefs based on authority replace those beliefs by yielding to yet another authority. They tend to look for absolute answers and absolute truth. When their personal beliefs no longer seem able to withstand the perceived reality of circumstance, they replace those beliefs with new absolutes. They trade an old religion for a new one. Traditional religion leaves contemporary questions unanswered so these people look for answers in tarot cards, crystals, horoscopes and trendy mysticism. Each time they abdicate thinking by submitting to a new authority. Such a willingness to mindlessly accept new explanations based on authority is evidenced by the continual stream of new products that are supposed to solve a myriad of life's problems. Ranging from vitamins to crystals to diet patches, these products appear on a regular basis, and with each come hundreds of testimonials about miraculous solutions that would be laughable if they were not so pitifully misinformed.

We know little more about why we are here than we did when the first human asked this question. This is not, however, justification for intellectual suicide. Indeed, we may come closer to spiritual connectedness by searching for meaning rather than by attaining the answers. We accept a part of life based on faith. We have faith in the sunrise of tomorrow, but we don't have to abandon reason in order to do so. Alan Watts said that accepting tomorrow on the basis of faith is in fact an act of openness. Why then do we allow authorities the license to prescribe precise absolute truths as answers to questions that they themselves have no way of knowing except on the basis of faith? If our search for truth is genuine, we must be critical when the need to believe is greatest.

An understanding of the personal sciences, their limitations and their truths, significantly reduces our vulnerability to the various forms of mysticism. A major thesis of this book is that belief must be based on good reasons. It does not mean we can never trust authority, but simply that we should not do so blindly. It is neither practical nor desirable to think we must go through life having to prove everything to ourselves, or that we can never place our trust in others. But it is equally impractical to assume that we will not often require proof or that we should not question the authority in which we have placed our trust. The object is not to weaken belief, but to discover and strengthen it through the maturation of conviction.

Education in Western culture emphasizes external knowledge, while eastern culture centers its educational emphasis on the internal, the search for meaning.[12] From either perspective, everything else is considered irrelevant. Both approaches lack balance. It is easily demonstrable that life is a perpetual balancing act between internal and external forces. Achieving this balance is the goal of self-education.

Of philosophy and the individual, James Feibleman said:

> Only the educated man is aware of philosophy yet it is not only in him that it exists. Civilization functions as a kind of operant conditioning, and the individual absorbs a point of view even in the midst of a humdrum life, for living consists in interacting with the persons and artifacts around him. That such a point of view is fundamental and consistent makes of it what for want of a better term and in more explicit formulations we have come to call a philosophy.
>
> A philosophy in this sense is not something that an individual understands but something by means of which he understands everything else. It lies as far down in his unconscious mind as do the presuppositions of which he remains unaware. When a man holds a philosophy consciously it usually means that he does not hold it very deeply. But when he does not know that he holds it and assumes that when he acts he does so from instinct and not from philosophy, then it is possible to say, with

Parmenides, that he holds a philosophy in the inalienable sense that makes it more accurate to say that it holds him. This, then, is the way I mean the philosophies to be understood, namely, as descriptions of the unconscious fundamental beliefs of the individual at various periods in his career.

Feibleman continues:

Like cows interminably grazing, ordinarily individuals are so concerned with the requisite for immediate survival that they do not have the time to look up from their jobs in order to see just where it is they are going. They do not ask why, and if they belong to institutions with answers, such as churches, they ask only once and never question the replies. They resent the one who does question because he challenges them to think—always a momentous effort for those who are unaccustomed to it—and because he is disturbing to the tidy order in which they had supposed he had a settled part. To raise doubts is to threaten general security, and for this they will fight as they have been trained to do by their very membership in whatever leading institution it is which supports them in their beliefs.

We are driven by what we believe. If we don't understand the nature and origin of our own beliefs, we cannot help being driven by those of others. When we practice self-directed inquiry we learn to get along without having absolute answers. We reverse the fear of ambiguity inspired by the pedagogical process and replace it with a positive anticipation of the future. Jack W. Meiland, author of *College Thinking*, said:

The whole project of college teaching and research—indeed, the whole project of the modern mind—is to base belief only on good reasons. Moderns feel that only this is rational and legitimate. We have banished authority, superstition, magic, and prophecy as bases for belief. We pride ourselves on rejecting these "primitive" and "emotional" reactions to the world. We exalt reason. And what this means is that we attempt to base belief only on good reasons. We are told that in the Middle Ages, people believed things because the ancient Greek philosopher Aristotle said that they were true. They believed these things on Aristotle's authority. This is now seen as illegiti mate; instead we should see for ourselves whether things are true by gathering evidence and finding good reasons for ourselves. Various tribes base some beliefs on the results of magical rites. We regard this as mere superstition. The modern mind rejects all this. And college simply reflects this view about the legitimation of belief by inquiring into the rationality of every belief to find out whether each belief is supported by good reasons.

This view has extremely important consequences. Because every belief ought to be based on good reasons, every belief must be examined. This includes even the most obvious beliefs. In fact, it is especially important to examine those claims and beliefs that are most obvious – it is precisely because something is "obvious" that people will not have examined the reasons behind it. But it may turn out that any particular belief, even an "obvious" belief, is unjustified. It may turn out that although we thought that there were good reasons for that belief, when we take a hard look at the case, there are no good reasons for it.

For practical and obvious reasons it is best to examine commonly held beliefs in a non-threatening manner, suspending judgment until you have enough information to form a new hypothesis. Philosophical questions are the bedrock foundation for the personal sciences. By studying the personal sciences first you have the benefit of your own experience, so that when you trace psychological theory to its origin in philosophy, it's like finding the source of a mysterious river which you were never sure existed. When you are personally involved in the search, discovery can be one of the most exhilarating experiences life has to offer. Reconciling your personal experience with philosophy is a liberating experience, but more importantly it allows some truce between reason and emotion. When we are capable of making decisions and judgments balanced with both reason and emotion, we can trust our decisions.

The wisdom of the ancient Greeks can be seen in the admission of their acknowledged ignorance. Socrates was a man who knew that he did not know.[13] We, on the other hand, who are no match for the wisdom of Socrates, have the audacity to think that some person or computer can provide an answer for almost any question. We believe that we have the power of answers. But power lies in the quality and nature of questions. Learn how to question and you take charge of your education. Period.

Questions for Philosophical Inquiry

I don't pretend to be wise enough to know the answers to these questions, but I have reflected on them long enough to feel confident that they are worthy of deliberation. They can be argued and debated for a lifetime without resolve, simply for the satisfaction of the search. They are questions for your own Self-University.

The first question is: Does man have free will? It seems simple enough, except that it cannot be proved one way or the other. The question of free will is a bedrock issue for psychology and behavioral science.

The second question asks for your personal definition of the concepts Mortimer Adler describes in his book *Six Great Ideas*. What are truth, beauty, goodness, liberty, equality, and justice? When you are finished compare your definitions with his.

The third point to ponder is the question of God and moral virtue – the question of right and wrong. In his book, *The Elements of Moral Philosophy*, James Rachels, Professor of Philosophy at the University of Alabama, Birmingham, wrote:

> 1. Suppose God commands us to do what is right. Then *either* (a) the right actions are right because he commands them *or* (b) he commands them because they are right.
>
> 2. If we take option (a), then God's commands are from a moral point of view, arbitrary; moreover, the doctrine of the goodness of God is rendered meaningless.
>
> 3. If we take option (b), then we have admitted there is a standard of right and wrong that is independent of God's will.
>
> 4. Therefore, we must *either* regard God's commands as arbitrary, and give up the doctrine of the goodness of God, *or* admit that there is a standard of right and wrong that is independent of his will, and give up the theological definitions of right and wrong.
>
> 5. From a religious point of view, it is undesirable to regard God's commands as arbitrary or give up the doctrine of the goodness of God.
>
> 6. Therefore, even from a religious point of view, a standard of right and wrong that is independent of God's will must be accepted.
>
> Many religious people believe that they should accept a theological conception of right and wrong because it

would be impious not to do so. They feel, somehow, that if they believe in God, they *should* think that right and wrong are to be defined ultimately in terms of his will. But this argument suggests otherwise: it suggests that, on the contrary, the Divine Command Theory of right and wrong itself leads to impious results, so that a pious person should *not* accept it. And in fact, some of the greatest theologians, such as St. Thomas Aquinas (ca. 1225–1274), rejected the theory for just this reason.

The fourth point to ponder is a question posed by philosopher Will Durant. Simply stated, is it better to be good or strong?

The fifth and final point is to address the question: Do natural needs create natural rights? This is a fundamental political question for all cultures.

Major schools of philosophical thought for additional inquiry include: Aristotelianism, cynicism, dialectic, empiricism, Epicureanism, ethical egoism, existentialism, humanism, idealism, logical positivism, Marxism, Platonism, pragmatism, psychological egoism, rationalism, scholasticism, skepticism, Stoicism, transcendentalism, and utilitarianism.

Summary

The three major schools of psychology have each contributed strongly to the body of knowledge we call the personal sciences. Psychoanalysis made us aware of the significance of the unconscious. Behaviorism demonstrated the extent to which our habits become a conditioned or automatic response. Humanistic psychology offered the hope and aspirations with which to break the spells of conditioning. Indeed, if we are to move significantly toward self-development we must assume the responsibility for understanding human behavior within the framework of our own lives and personal experience. Practitioners disagree about fundamental issues concerning mental health. Therefore, as a responsibility to ourselves and our families, we should never abdicate the study of psychology to such a degree that we are forced to seek help with psychological problems without being able to discuss them practically and philosophically with the practitioner.

Understanding the nature of human needs and specifically the hierarchical nature of our own needs is a prerequisite for genuine personal growth. Likewise, it is fundamental to relating to the rest of humanity. When we set aside our political bias, we see that we all have the same basic needs. As we study human needs we find that the nature of our needs changes at different times in our lives. This pattern leads to the realization of human life stages, which if used objectively can dramatically ease the transition from one stage to the next.

When we examine our cultural conditioning, the theories we hold about human nature, and our personal experience, and then consider their effects, we are able to see more clearly and objectively in our search for meaning. When we try to understand psychology, the process inevitably leads to philosophical questions which in turn lead to the development of a constructive philosophy of life.

CHAPTER FIVE

Motivation

If we imagine the cause of an affect to be actually present with us, that affect will be stronger than if we imagined the cause not to be present.

—Benedict de Spinoza

The study of motivation is a growing multi-million dollar business. Each year thousands of us attend seminars and read books to learn the keys to our own personal development. Many of these sources promise a lot but deliver very little. Still, we have such an innate desire to know that we persist in buying the books and attending the classes. We are always looking for the one little bit of insight that will put everything in perspective. Most of what we find is similar to candles: they burn for a short while and then they go out. We then continue to search for longer-burning candles.

The information advertising such material promises to help us motivate ourselves and others, but much of it totally misses the mark by one fundamental error—the assumption that any of us is ever "unmotivated." We are all in a perpetual state of motivation. Our individual level of motivation at any given time depends upon the state of flux between our needs, our beliefs, our education and our experience. If you understand someone's hopes, dreams and goals, then you know something of his motivation.

The reason much of our learning about motivation is so short-lived is not that the information is bad, but that each of us has a great void in the area of self-knowledge. We have no personal expertise in human psychological mechanics, so we treat new information as a child treats a new toy. As long as it seems to be working OK, we will use it. But as soon as circumstances change and it doesn't seem do be doing what it is supposed to, we put it on the shelf in the closet to stay. We then look for a new toy.

To use self-education as a process for self-discovery, it is necessary to light many candles, knowing all the while that some places will remain forever dark. For self-education to be effective, self-discovery must be a lifelong process. You start by following up on fundamental questions you have about the nature of your own feelings, needs and aspirations. You will likely find many of the answers in places where you never thought to look, such as college text books. The difference is that it is you and not the teacher who formulates the questions. When you begin to look in earnest for answers to questions that are meaningful to you, you will be able to rekindle the fires of curiosity that were extinguished by the pedagogical process when you were a child. As your natural curiosity is rewarded, the intensity of your desire to know will grow. The process becomes naturally reinforcing, naturally leading to more questions.

There are two key rules to keep in mind when you are trying to develop understanding and to gain more insight to your own motivation. These rules apply to the nature of inquiry regardless of the reason. The first rule is to never fall so in love with a particular theory that it becomes the sole explanation with which you can suddenly interpret everything else, for this becomes a natural mind-closing mechanism. Always leave room for new possibilities and perspectives.

The second rule is to never accept as absolute fact that which you cannot prove to your own satisfaction without irrefutable evidence. Even when you are sure of your facts, reserve some skepticism into the methodology. Again, this is not to undermine your beliefs so that you will never be sure of what you know. On the contrary, it is a maneuver by which you feel assured that you are searching for truth objectively, so that you do not need to fear those with whom you disagree. If we cannot listen objectively to an opposing view, it is often because we haven't examined our own opinion and thus are fearful of discussion.

You are an adult. You have experience. Compare your experience with that of those said to be experts. Matching your experience with their theories ensures that you will remember what you have studied, and it will enable you to develop a sense of authority and trust in your own ability. The educational experience we had during our early years, combined with the nurture of our parents, set us up with a fundamental orientation as to how we relate to authority. It is necessary to understand the nature of this relationship in examining our behavior.

Suppose you are suddenly approached and taken into custody by a police officer. The officer takes you before a judge and jury, where the judge tells you that the world is in a state of crisis. There is only enough food for one-third of the present population; two-thirds of the population must be eliminated or humanity is doomed. The judge instructs you to convince the jury why you should be spared. You turn to face the jury and the foreman asks, "What are your goals?" Seeing that you are a little shaken, he offers you a chair and hands you a pen and a blank sheet of paper. He says, "Here, write them down. You have ten minutes." Put this book down and try this yourself.

The ease or difficulty you have with this exercise can offer a great deal of insight into how much control you feel you have over your environment. Remember the major schools of psychology? Freud believed that we endure a constant state of conflict between biological and intellectual forces, the id, the ego, and the superego. B.F. Skinner asserted that behavior is a result of its consequences. In other words, your present actions are a result of your past reinforcements. And Abraham Maslow postulated a theory of needs in a progressive hierarchy that starts with the need for food, clothing, and shelter and culminates with self-actualization.

If you found yourself speechless before the jury, could it be because you accept the premise that you are being driven by forces over which you have little control? Are these forces internal or external? If you feel that you behave as you do primarily to please others, does that mean that you agree with the Skinnerian view that you are a product of environmental stimulation? If you feel that you are living your life and behaving as you do because of internal forces, does it mean that you agree with the ideas of Freud or Maslow? How does your personal experience relate to the general theories of each?

I make no assertions here. One response is not necessarily better than another, nor does anyone know with absolute certainty that any one of these schools of thought is more correct than the others. This exercise is not scientific, and I am certainly not advocating that some people deserve to live more than others. Rather, the exercise is a startling means of inquiry intended to help you discover your internal or external motivational orientation. If you had a strong case to present to the jury, then it is likely that you perceive yourself as having considerable influence over the events in your life.

Elements of Self-Concept

Each of us has a unique self-concept that is a result of our individual interpretation of the environment and the feedback we receive from it. The process of developing a self-concept which forms into self-esteem is both complex and hierarchical, but it is not hard to gain insight into how it works. When we are very young its hierarchical aspects are apparent because we care more about what some people think about us than others. Behavioral practitioners refer to these people as "significant others." For example, parents are our first significant others, followed by other grown family members, followed by teachers. As we grow and develop we begin to care about how our peers perceive us, and when we reach adolescence, acceptance by our peers becomes critical. Throughout our lives we see ourselves through the eyes of others, almost as if each person we come in contact with wears a mirror in which we are able to see ourselves as the other person sees us. But this is deceiving, because our perception of the feedback from others is the basis of our acquired self-image. We may be totally incorrect in our interpretation. This is why it is crucial to develop self-knowledge, which leads to the ability to read others with some reliability. If we do not, we are likely to develop a self-image that is inconsistent with the reality with which others perceive us. A self-image that is out of touch with reality makes any effort at improvement futile, because there is no way to determine personal cause and effect.

When we started school, teachers were definitely significant others, but we also picked up from our classmates a lot of data about how we were doing as students. A lot of data is necessary for us to develop a multidimensional view of ourselves. This is an important point. Understanding the significance of a multidimensional outlook is a key to understanding how you might have been affected by your own experience in school. For example, in many competitive learning environments students are placed into groups of "like" ability.

Remember those reading groups made up of excellent, good, average and poor readers? Students placed in such groups lose the multidimensional range of natural feedback that they would ordinarily get in a group that reflected the normal range of talents. In other words, an excellent reader with a multidimensional range of experience gets feedback from all the other categories—good readers, poor readers and average readers—and thus is able to appreciate his or her reading talent in depth. Excellent readers grouped with excellent readers are reduced to a status among peers of being only average, just as is everyone else in each of the other groups. Each student loses the ability to see himself clearly in relation to others, he loses the feedback about his efforts—feedback that would have been naturally reinforcing. As a result he may always be plagued with self-doubt, never really sure how he is doing in relation to others.

We didn't spend all our early years in such categories, but when we did, it may have affected our capacity to gain a true sense of our abilities. This may be especially true if we were also often subjected to learning stress, such as repetitive exercises, without being able to detect discernible feedback, either positive or negative. These experiences may have set us up to strive continually without the ability to appreciate a genuine sense of accomplishment; we constantly seek assurance, but it's never convincing enough.

On the flip side is that when we were labeled with a grade, the only distinction we could make between ourselves and others was in varying degrees of perceived effectiveness and ineffectiveness. Many of us internalized this to mean that some of us were better, and in fact more deserving, than others.

The way that each of us learns is different in the ratio of senses that we use to apprehend. The difficulty or ease with which we adapted to the teaching style of our teachers depended on their own learning styles, because teachers usually teach the way that they themselves like to be taught. If our learning style matched our teachers', we were likely to have thought of ourselves as a good student, probably receiving confirming feedback from our peers. If it did not match, however, it probably affected our self-image in a negative way.

Doers and Thinkers

I have no supporting evidence, but on the basis of experience and observation I believe that this phenomenon is at least in part responsible for the dualistic separation between the perceived doer and thinker. I see it as working something like this: When the child who has a big-picture learning orientation (one who learns best by considering whole concepts) is taught by a teacher who has a sequential teaching style (step-by-step process), the big-picture student will likely fall behind. Sometimes this child will discover that if he can enlist the assistance of peers who learn sequentially, he can get the help needed to pass the course. And in ten or fifteen years this talent for subtly enlisting the cooperation of others will be called "people skills."[1] On the other hand, the sequential learner could be engaged in a leadership role, by openly showing the big-picture learner how to proceed. But since there is competition in the learning environment, the cooperation that would occur naturally becomes manipulative—this student does not want to be seen engaging in an activity that might be considered cheating. If the sequential learner gives help "on the sly," his opportunity to receive natural reinforcement as a leader is lost; instead he becomes a doer of favors for others. Thus, the students become separated into doers and thinkers. This could explain why some managers are considered thinkers who don't know how to do anything of a technical nature and why those who are technically oriented are considered doers and choose not to manage.

To summarize, the process of our early childhood development, including our experience at formal learning, had a fundamental effect on our perception of how effective we are as people. A great deal of our personal confidence comes from how we perceive others as perceiving us. We watch them both consciously and subconsciously for clues about how we are doing at any given time with any activity. Our ability to gauge our success depends upon how well we are able to accurately read the reactions of others when they react to us. For these reasons it is easy to see how important it is for teachers to help young people build a positive self-image rather than label them with grades. The obsession with grades that has persisted for so many years has, in my opinion, maimed almost as many children as it has intellectually empowered.

Internal and External Motivation

Early learning at home and school had a pronounced effect on our self-concept and self-esteem, which has become a basic personality orientation. This tendency can be called a "perceived locus of causality," which is simply how much effect we perceive ourselves to have over our life circumstances and environment and whether our reasons are internal or external. In other words, how much confidence do we have and why? You can have a high level of confidence and still be externally motivated. In such case you would simply be responding to an external reward, a social expectation, or perhaps to please someone such as a parent. An internal motivational orientation is simply acting or performing to please yourself. In contrast an impersonal causality orientation, means that you have little or no confidence in your ability to affect your environment, regardless of the reason.[2]

If you have high confidence and internal motivation, you are likely to interpret the environment informationally and as being responsive to your actions. If you have high confidence and an external motivation, you will likely perceive your environment as controlling and demanding. If you have no confidence, you are likely to have little motivation either internal or external. You will probably have the attitude that you have no control over your environment and nothing that you do will have a positive effect on your circumstances. You might be said to have reached a state of learned helplessness.[3]

Each activity that we participate in can be described in terms of how much confidence we have and whether our fundamental motivation is internal, external or a combination of both. Each of us has unique personal levels of internal and external motivational capacity. Simply put, this means we do some things because they please us in an internal sense and others because they please us in an external sense (because of an anticipated reward or to please someone whose approval we seek). Some things we do for both reasons. For example, if you fish because you enjoy it, your motivation is probably internal. If on the other hand, you stop fishing for fun and begin doing it to earn a living, the motivational force becomes external. You may still enjoy fishing, but since you now receive a reward in the form of money, the act of fishing suddenly has a controlling aspect.[4] Your enjoyment is likely to be diminished.

How we relate to authority is a fundamental clue to our motivational orientation. How much deference do we naturally give to others in areas that matter to us? In other words, do we normally assume that others know best? Is the boss or the teacher always right? Do we in fact have free will? Is our life being guided by astrological or divine forces? People who express a determinist view such as, "When it's your time to go," or "when your number is up," have unconsciously abdicated some degree of control over their lives.

Self-Determination

Psychologist Edward L. Deci asserts that of each us has, at least to some degree, an innate need to be self-determining. Self-determination is a natural reward of intrinsic motivation because the process of being internally motivated is in itself an act of self-determination. According to Deci, when we engage in an activity, we receive feedback either in the form of an informational aspect or a controlling aspect. Positive feedback is likely to increase one's internal sense of motivation, thus improving the perceived locus of causality or confidence level. Likewise, negative feedback is likely to decrease one's confidence, just as a controlling aspect tends to diminish our satisfaction.

I assert that the process of self-education is a direct means of increasing a person's general orientation of perceived locus of causality from external to internal. Self-education = understanding = confidence = empowerment. Empowerment enables self-determination. Since empowerment is based on confidence and understanding, it is natural to have faith in your own judgment. To examine your own behavior in any given context, ask yourself questions such as:

- Why and for whom am I really doing this?
- How much confidence do I have?

- Do I have enough confidence to know that I can be successful? And if I do not, what would it take for me to turn the activity into one in which I can gain the confidence necessary to be self-determining?

You can apply the question of intrinsic versus extrinsic motivation and perceived locus of causality to almost any circumstance. It may not make your decisions about what to do any easier, but, in time, it can offer you considerable insight into the reasons for your own behavior. It can help you turn negative experiences into positive ones.

Sometimes appearances can be deceiving. For example, a person with an external motivational orientation might appear to be a hard driving, self-determining individual, but may in fact be someone who is only demonstrating a total commitment to the external doctrines of a higher authority. The higher authority may be an individual, an institution or a myriad of "shoulds" subsumed unconsciously from parents and society in general. These people may be responding frantically to external cues. Many hard-driving, high achievers fit this description. In other words, they are pedaling a Skinner Box constructed by others. Paradoxically, their behavior, which seems to be assertive and selective, is really highly conforming. This propensity for conformity is often an expression of external motivation. People with such an orientation may not realize they are acting solely on the expectations of others until faced with a traumatic event such as a job loss or the death of a spouse. On the other hand, people who seem out of step, a little bohemian, are apt to have an internal motivational orientation. Externals obey archaic laws without question. Internals challenge them. Externals resist self-knowledge. Internals seek it.

When I apply these personality orientations to what I have studied in the field of human health I am struck by the similarities of experience in studies of people who are thought to be terminally ill. For example, the evidence suggests that people with an impersonal orientation die readily. People with an external orientation seem to die on cue or even earlier so as to meet some "schedule." But internals seem to be good at beating the odds and sometimes live long enough to make their doctors look foolish.

Turn back to the VALS topology diagram in Chapter Two, and you will see that terms similar to impersonal, external and internal are used to describe the nine American life-styles. The survivors and sustainers referred, to as "need driven," obviously have an impersonal orientation. The emulators, belongers and achievers, referred to as outer-directed, have an external orientation. And the "I Am Me's," the experientials and the societally conscious, referred to as inner-directed, have an internal orientation. The integrateds represent a balance between internal and external orientation.

Unexamined lives lead to a tendency to seek routine; we become comfortable only with what is familiar. As a result we begin to behave and act automatically. Automatic response to our environment means that we lose the ability to be self-determining.

Time Orientation

Different cultures express a vast range of relationships regarding the concept of time. Members of certain primitive tribal cultures die when imprisoned because of a lack of ability to conceptualize the future. They are so bound to an orientation of living in the present that they have no concept that someday they may be freed. On the other end of the cultural time sense is the monk who spends a lifetime practicing a denial of the present in order to achieve a greater life in a hereafter. Nations themselves manifest a certain affinity in regard to time. Newly founded nations look to their futures with great hope and expectations for future generations. Our founding fathers were visibly preoccupied with the notion of posterity. During their time personal sacrifice for posterity was as noble an effort as any. Third World countries, on the other hand, grappling for a hold on survival, have little concept of the future and thus have no long-range vision. A long-range vision leads to greater expectations. This vision inevitably produces actions that attempt to fulfill the prophecy of the expectations.[5]

Each of us, although physically confined and limited to the present, has a particular time orientation which determines how much of the present can be sacrificed in anticipation of a future reward. For instance, do we have a tendency to require instant gratification? Can we spend four years going to school if we perceive the reward to be worthwhile? Faith in the future is a means of affecting the future – it is the blank slate we use to write our goals. Our very acknowledgement of the existence of the slate enables us to achieve our goals. A fundamental characteristic of time and motivation is that when we are highly motivated toward a task, we reduce our perception of the time required to complete the task. It is true for individuals as well as nations, and both can use this knowledge as a lever for progress. Time orientation changes in relation to one's life stage or sense of accomplishment. And at some point in almost everyone's life near or during middle age there is a shift to the realization that the future is now.[6] A near-death experience will drive this point home like a cold slap in the face.

The Law Of Expectations

The "law of expectations," referred to in Chapter Two, is much like the perceived locus of causality except that one needs to accept it independently. The law of expectations is simply the phenomenon that allows you to get what you "expect" to get, regardless of the orientation of your natural perceived locus of causality (what you've come to expect). If you affirm the law of expectations you can change your perceived locus of causality. This is the principle on which almost all motivational books are written, and it's true. The evidence is overwhelming. Convince someone that he has the power to do what seems impossible, and he will likely succeed. Convince him that he cannot, and he won't even try. Combine the law of expectations with genuine self-knowledge, and we are empowered with a realistic assessment of our abilities; add maturity, and we are able to forgive ourselves when we fail without a heavy burden of guilt. We are culturized to believe that failure is abhorrent and that whenever we fail it is simply because we did not try hard enough. However, failure and success are both the residue of effort, and the fear of one should not discourage the other. When we are afraid to fail, we fail to grow.

The Need for Novelty

Humans have an innate need for novelty.[7] We are nourished by diversity of experience; without it we wither and withdraw. Competition forces many of us to ignore our need for novelty, and the result is stunted growth. Plants do not grow well when they have to compete for nutrients. They thrive in rich soil just as humans thrive in a rich intellectual environment. Consider the difference in perspective between the caterpillar and the butterfly. The caterpillar is condemned to crawl, but the butterfly has the potential to soar under the summer sun with an all-inclusive view of the world. As humans we complete our caterpillar stage when we reach mature physical growth; if we are to soar as the butterfly we must do so through the development of our minds.

How do you ensure your intellectual stimulation? An objective lifelong learning plan will allow you to grow for the rest of your life. Appreciation, acknowledgement and an understanding of your need for novelty and intellectual stimulation will help you devise your own lifelong learning plan. Remember the assertion made earlier that change means growth? If you simply cannot foster your need for novelty on the job, at least you can set about to look for it as a part of your leisure. An objective approach to self-education will ensure that your need for novelty does not allow you to settle into a rut where you respond automatically and lose your ability to be self-determining.

Human Motivation and Behavior

The nature of human motivation has not changed in the past two thousand years. Management gurus find new ways each year to repackage the same old information. It's the same message over and over, year after year: believe in yourself, establish goals, and you can be and do what you want. So why is it necessary to keep repeating it? I would argue that it goes back to the toy principle. As soon as we try something new, circumstances change and we don't have enough knowledge or confidence to continue on our own. We have such limited knowledge about our emotional selves that we live at the edge of a vast, dark void; we have been taught that it's too complex for us to understand. The result is that if we cannot establish confidence in our own ability to affect the environment, we will look for an external source of authority to either obey or emulate. We grope with candles. The premise of self-education is to light enough candles so that we can always see to explore.

Human behavior is everybody's business. It is as much a part of our lives as math, English, history, and science. Freud argued unsuccessfully for a profession of "lay" analysts so that many people could benefit from psychoanalysis without becoming dependent upon doctors.[8] The result of not understanding ourselves is that we are unable to balance our lives. When we find a niche in which we perceive ourselves to be successful, we put all our energy into it to the exclusion of everything else. Many individuals allow their work to become their whole lives. When they retire, they die.

I am not suggesting that we each become practicing self-psychologists, but I am advocating that we assume a much greater amount of responsibility for self-knowledge. Such responsibility requires that we study and understand theories of human nature and behavior. Such inquiry has an empowering effect. It moves our perceived locus of causality toward believing ourselves to have a more significant effect over the events in our lives. It is an automatic buy-in to the natural law of expectations. Self-knowledge allows us to make choices which are self-determining. If everyone undertook such a quest for knowledge, it would not suddenly do away with the need for behavioral specialists. Indeed it would probably increase their practices, but it would enable each of us to be intelligent consumers of professional help and would substantially improve our chances of being responsive to treatment. The most significant effect it would have would be in the empowerment principle. It would give each of us the confidence to light our own candles and lose our fear of the dark.

Perceived locus of causality, internal and external motivation, time orientation, relating to authority, the natural law of expectations, the need to be self-determining, and the need for novelty are all closely related in much the same way, I think, that Maslow's B-values are. Each is describable in terms of the others.

If education were a person-centered experience, if what we already knew had been taken seriously in the educational process, we would take our ability for effectiveness more seriously and have higher expectations for ourselves. But since our education was compressed to keep us at the same grade levels with others, we learned gradually and in varying degrees to abdicate to the expectations of others. If we received significant pleasure from the approval of others during our efforts at learning, the process may have affected the nature of our motivational orientation. We may now feel a greater need to meet the expectations of others than to meet our own. We may have, in effect, become hooked on the need for the approval.

Time orientation is integrally related to internal or external motivation, perceived locus of causality, relating to authority, the natural law of expectations, and the need to be self-determining. We are apt to demonstrate how we feel about these orientations by what we do with our time. For example, if we feel we have little effect or control over our environment, we are likely to waste our time for the fleeting enjoyment of the moment. In other words, nothing that we do is going to improve things anyway, so we might as well live for today. To give up our time to activities which are for the moment unpleasant, but from which we expect a later reward, is a demonstrated act of faith in our ability to exercise control over our environment, regardless of whether the activity is to please ourselves or others.

Life Stages Theory

Like the schools of philosophy and psychology there are many theories about the development stages of our lives. In *The Stages of Human Development*, philosopher James Feibleman said:

> There is no adequate preparation at one stage of life for what is coming in the next. Each has its own autonomy, and the transitions are definite and abrupt. Just when the human individual becomes adjusted to one variety of existence, and finds himself able to meet its demands and derive from it some of its benefits, he is suddenly

catapulted into another variety and confronted with an altogether new set of conditions he is ill-prepared to deal with in any way. He is faced with what life will be for him now by a completely new set of conditions, and he will have to make rapid and adequate accommodations to them if he is to survive and flourish anew. He was a child? But he is an adolescent! He was a youth? But suddenly he will become a mature adult. He had established himself in middle age? It is removed and he is an old man, and thoroughly incapacitated for dealing with most eventualities. The development of the individual consists in a series of seemingly permanent stages and of sudden drops into new conditions bringing him new experiences but with no warning and no time for preparation.

Throughout the whole experience of living, many of us complete all these transitions without using our intellectual ability to fully understand them. The opportunity to know oneself or the possession of a mechanism to gain self-knowledge did not exist in the education afforded those of us who are now adults.

During the Fifties, Erik Erikson offered a life stage theory that is often used as a standard in human development analysis. Erikson subscribed to the psychoanalytic school, but, unlike Freud, he based his stage development theory on the socialization process rather than on the sexual and biological drives. Like Maslow's need theory, Erikson's stage theory suggests that people move in an upward progression, dealing with the conflicts of each stage before moving on to the next.

Erikson's stage theory begins in infancy with the Trust versus Mistrust stage; the child develops an orientation based on his treatment during infancy. The second stage, Autonomy versus Shame and Doubt, begins between the ages of one and three. As the child begins to become independent, doubt and guilt surround his own abilities and his view of the parents' expectations. The third stage, Initiative versus Guilt, occurs during the preschool age. It is a time of tremendous development. Orientation polarizes self-confidence and humiliation. The fourth stage, Industry versus Inferiority, occurs during the early school years. The child's ability to perform in comparison with his peers determines the degree of competence and control the child feels if performance is inadequate. Feelings of inferiority develop accordingly. The fifth stage, Identity versus Role Confusion, begins during the adolescent years. It is an awkward time. The adolescent is too old to be treated as a child and too young to be awarded the privileges of an adult. The reasons for an identity crisis are obvious. The sixth, Intimacy versus Isolation stage, begins in young adulthood. Its orientation depends upon the young adult's success in building social relationships and generally "fitting in." The seventh, Generativity versus Stagnation stage, occurs during the middle years. It is simply a matter of adjustment between one's sense of contribution and one's perception of that contribution or lack of, that pulls toward generativity or pushes towards stagnation. The eighth and final stage, Integrity versus Despair, begins in old age. Orientation during the final years of life depends in large part on the success or failure during the first seven.[9]

In 1974, Gail Sheehy authored *Passages*, based on the work of Erikson and others. *Passages* deals only with adult development and suggests six passages or stages of development. They are:

1. Pulling up roots
2. The trying twenties
3. Catch-30
4. Rooting and extending
5. The deadline decade
6. Renewal or resignation.

As the rate of change accelerates and the complexities of living increase, life stage theories will likely become an obsolete methodology; at least significant changes or variations are likely. *Psychology Today* editors Anne Rosenfield and Elizabeth Stark say:

> What seems to mark our adult years most is our shifting perspective on ourselves and our world—who we think we are, what we expect to get done, our timetable for doing it and our satisfactions with what we have accomplished. The scenarios and schedules of our lives are so varied that some researchers believe it is virtually impossible to talk about a single timetable for adult development.

They go on to quote sociologist Orville Brim Jr., who said, "Stage theories are a little like horoscopes. Vague enough so that everyone can see something of themselves in them."[10]

It is easy to see how life stages will begin to blur in the near future, but is also unlikely that young people will survive early adulthood without experiencing a bout with the "shoulds." This begins in childhood, but during early adulthood it becomes intense. (The study of transactional analysis offers some insight into the development of the "shoulds." This is discussed in Chapter Ten.)

Marsha Sinetar, author of *Do What You Love the Money Will Follow*, argues that before an adult can become a fully functioning conscious person he has to root out and examine the "shoulds" that dominate his life. Sinetar asserts that each of us has a unique, highly personal script made up of "shoulds." She goes on to say:

> There are "Being injunctions" that program a whole life of actions, attitudes and decisions. Some examples of what parents tell their children are: Be Perfect, Be Careful, Be a Winner, Be Polite, Be Docile, Be a Risk-Taker, Be a Loser, Be Smart, Be Dumb, Be Pleasing, Be Irritating. And there are negative commands as well: Don't Trust, Don't Expect Much, Don't Argue, Don't Live, Don't Think, Don't Take Chances, Don't Give Up, Don't Worry, Don't Be Sexual/Humorous/Charming/etc. The list goes on and on.

Sinetar adds:

> We are all lessened as persons when living according to unexamined, unconscious "shoulds." While it may be impossible to be totally free of parental or societal conditioning, it certainly is possible to increase our capacity to consciously choose a life that we value and that is supportive of the best in us. And it is possible for men and women to define themselves.
>
> All of us owe it to ourselves to examine our own lives, the rules by which we live and the values inherent in our choices. We must decide for ourselves who we are, what our conduct should be, and how we wish to use our lives. This is a difficult assignment for everyone because it forces us to confront the "shoulds" and the "shouldn'ts" that run our lives. And yet this confrontation is entirely right and essential, because it aids the growth in awareness that unites us with our own potential. The easiest thing to do is nothing; yet the harder task of self-scrutiny and truthful living is the only way to raise our self-esteem and self-respect.

The progression into our thirties seems to offer some evidence that we have a natural tendency to examine the "shoulds"; perhaps it is inherent in the maturation process. At this stage, life pressures often intensify once again. There is an urgency to feel that we have made the right choices. It is often a time of soul searching and a reevaluation of life's priorities and values. It's as if one suddenly discovers for the first time that life is traveling at full throttle while being stuck on automatic pilot. There is a sense of urgency about the correctness of current course and a sense of fear about taking over the controls.

In the mid-thirties many of us reach what Gail Sheehy called the "Deadline Decade," a time from about thirty-five to forty-five in which exists an opportunity to redefine ourselves. Sheehy argues that those "who make the most of the opportunity will have a full-out authenticity crisis."

My own assessment is that at about age forty we have had enough life experience to put our life cycle in perspective. We compare that perspective with the lives of others and with whatever sense of the "scheme of things" that we have developed. The walls of "shoulds" constructed in the earlier years begin to crumble under the weight of our own individual experiences. This destruction of barriers puts previous life goals and aspirations in a new perspective. We realize that some goals will never be met, that some were merely illusions and others were adopted to meet a definition of success prescribed as desirable by others.[11]

This phenomenon sometimes causes enough disruption in one's life to attract the attention of others. When it does, it is often referred to as "mid-life crisis." My own experience is that it enables us to see from an entirely new perspective. Thoughts such as, what if, why, and what difference will it make in a hundred years, accompany the new identity. The automatic pilot is temporally shut off. We have no choice but to take the controls, at least for a short period of time. It can, and should be, an exhilarating experience.

Marilyn Ferguson, author of *The Aquarian Conspiracy*, said:

> That famous transition, the mid-life crisis, may be due in part to the cumulative effect of decades of denial, the sudden thrust into consciousness of pain that can no longer be sedated. One sensitive observer of the phenomenon said that it manifests as "either a cry or a call"—a cry of disappointment or the stirring call to new purpose—to vocation—experienced by one who has been engaged in introspective, transformative processes for some time.
>
> However intently the person with a vocation may pursue his purpose, he should not be confused with a "workaholic." The workaholic, like an alcoholic, is indiscriminate in his compulsion. He attempts to find meaning by working. The individual with a vocation, on the other hand, finds meaningful work. A vocation is not a job. It is an ongoing transformative relationship.

Later Middle Age

Of this stage James Feibleman, wrote:

> What is here called later middle age is the last twenty of
> the mature years, the period, say, from age 46 to 65. The
> individual experiences at this period the rueful satisfac-
> tion of completing a cycle. It is not difficult to see the end
> from here, and the end is not a satisfaction in any sense.

Indeed, the sense of satisfaction during this age period will likely be
redefined by the baby boomers. With the graying of America, there is
a growing consensus that more should be expected from these later
years. If you think of the brain as a dissipative structure as discussed
in Chapter Three there are no reasons why we should not expect to
grow until the moment of death. Among the people over 50 in
Maslow's study of self-actualizing adults, a common denominator
was found to be their openness to experience.

As we close in upon old age there is a tendency to once again
experience a change in time orientation. In middle age we moved
from a preoccupation with the future into an acute realization that
the future is now, but the diminished capacity of old age shifts many
out of the present and into the past. My own personal observations
suggest people are transformed into this orientation through diminished intellectual activity. They gradually become non-persons. They
no longer see to their own intellectual stimulation and begin to lose
touch with those younger persons around them who begin to treat
them as if they were non-persons. For example, when the old person
says something indicating he is out of touch with the times, insensi-
tive young people will often laugh aloud or try to suppress laughter
by snickering. The still partially perceptive old person realizes he is
just being tolerated and so withdraws even further.

There is much to be learned from studying life-stage theory. It is
obvious there are no absolute answers. But the maps left by those
who have already traveled through life and are now gone are a legacy
of practical experience. It is foolish not to consider their advice.

Summary

If you want to use the self-education process as a means of gaining
more control over your life, the best way to proceed is through the
study of human nature and human behavior. The method that I
have used with the above principles was developed through the
process of my own self-education. You begin with attempting to
understand what the nature of your motivation is for any given set of

circumstances. Develop your own method for understanding your behavior and motivation. Commit enough information to memory to begin a knowledge base. If you subsequently decide that you need professional assistance with your personal or professional development, you can then benefit from the position of an educated consumer. You can read the latest books about motivation and attend the latest seminars with the benefit of a long-term objective, and in doing so you are searching for candle power, not just a single candle. Your intent is to acquire enough self-knowledge to give you the confidence and personal empowerment to take charge of your life and to plan so that you can take full advantage of the natural law of expectations.

Fredrick Engles said, "The definition of lower class is the inability to plan." The American experience tends to bear him out (survivors-sustainers). Many of the people who live in American ghettos have little faith in their ability to affect the future, and that is why many of them spend what little money they have for instant self-gratification. They are stuck squarely in the present; since they perceive little reward from the future, they live for today. It is the only way in which they can perceive themselves as being self-determining. They have an impersonal perceived locus of causality: they perceive themselves to be helpless in affecting their environment. The key to adding quality to our lives in respect to time orientation is to understand the nature of our own motivation so that we can reach a balance, taking full measure of the present while still preparing for the future.

When we are thoroughly familiar with human life-stage theory we have a road-map not of specific direction, but of things we might experience and see along the way. We have the benefit of the knowledge of those who have passed this way before. And since we have some knowledge of what to expect, we have less reason to fear the journey and more time to plan.

CHAPTER SIX

The People Sciences

*For if liberty and equality, as is thought by
some, are chiefly to be found in democracy,
they will be best attained when all persons
alike share in the government to the utmost.*
— Aristotle

The people sciences cover the whole of human relations, from how we relate to one another as neighbors, citizens, and co-workers to the political ideologies for which we are willing to fight and die. This chapter will take a brief look at sociology, management, politics and some of the anxieties they generate. Most of what can be called the people sciences falls under the category of sociology.

Sociology

Simply put, sociology is people synergy (when the sum of the whole is greater than the sum of its parts). It is behavior clash, behavior competition and behavior cooperation. It is culture rubbing against culture. Why study sociology? It is only by studying others that we can put ourselves in perspective.

The United States of America owes its record of achievement to the differences in its people, not their sameness. The friction of culture rubbing against culture (the melting pot theory is an inaccurate metaphor for describing the process) has had a profound synergistic effect, because creativity and innovation grow exponentially. To validate this assertion one has only to study history. Tribal societies have produced little innovation relative to the years of their existence. It is only when they have rubbed against other cultures that they have experienced substantial growth through knowledge and innovation. There are some exceptions, notably the Incas, but for the most part it is easy to see that tribal societies remain static for centuries without significant change.

Sociology is a relatively new field of study in comparison to traditional disciplines. Names you will find associated with the origins of sociology include: Adam Smith, Auguste Comte, Karl Marx, Herbert Spencer, Emile Durkheim, Max Weber, and Talcott Parsons.

In *The Story of Philosophy*, author-philosopher Will Durant quoted Herbert Spencer as he wrote of sociology:

> What biography is to anthropology, history is to sociology. Of course there are a thousand obstacles that the study of society must yet overcome before it can deserve the name of science. The young study is harassed by a multitude of prejudices—personal, educational, theological, economic, political, national, religious; and by the ready omniscience of the uninformed. "There is a story of a Frenchman who, having been three weeks here, proposed to write a book on England; who, after three months, found that he was not quite ready; and who, after three years, concluded that he knew nothing about it." Such a man was ripe to *begin* the study of sociology. Men prepare themselves with life-long study becoming authorities in physics or chemistry or biology; but in the field of social and political affairs every grocer's boy is an expert, knows the solution, and demands to be heard.

The study of sociology logically begins with the study of history, but it's not necessary to start at the beginning in the traditional manner. In fact, I would argue that it's more meaningful to start with the present and work back in time. It is often startling to discover why we behave as we do according to social custom; the reasons are often silly and arbitrary. Unfortunately, the objective study of the past is, at best, difficult. Recorded history is laden with the bias of the recorders, and for that reason it is often difficult to put the past in perspective. For example, traditional American history texts often gloss over facts that do not fit with a desired political ideology. At the time of their great historical endeavor, the American apostles of freedom, the founding fathers who wrote and signed the Constitution, were slave owners. While this is not totally hidden from the student of history, it is usually presented so as not to appear a salient feature. It may not seem important to you, unless of course you are the descendent of slaves.

History is written from perpetually changing points of view; these are easy to identify once you know what you are seeking. For example, the most commonly found perspectives are: authoritative (theological, divine, royal order, or aristocratic), geographical, economic, political, psychological, scientific, and sociological. Written history offers these perspectives in varying degrees and proportions. Learn to recognize and use them and they become keys for greater understanding.

Today we have an incredible array of methodologies available to place society under the microscope. We have polls, computer data, consumer data, surveys, zip code data, aerial photographs, Nielson ratings, magazine subscription data, health records and thousands of other ways of examining the residue of human social interaction. History, on the other hand, is speculation based on artifacts. Every few years we are stunned by a new thesis that offers totally different ways of thinking about the past by reversing earlier assumptions.

For the autodidact the study of history is not a single subject. It is only a perspective with which any subject may be examined. And it must be used with the knowledge that a part of history is lost to us that will never be found. For example, we may read the words written by a soldier during the Civil War. If we put them in context with what we already know about that period, we can feel that we have knowledge about what he has written, but we can never ask him questions. History is thus full of blind spots, because, in the face of questions that they can no longer ask, most cultures interpret the answers to suit themselves. To be truly self-educated is to realize this tendency and avoid making self-serving interpretations.

Management Philosophy

For several years those on the cutting edge of management theory and practice have argued for the urgent need to radically change the way people are treated in organizations. Tom Peters, co-author of *In Search of Excellence*, author of *A Passion for Excellence* and *Thriving on Chaos*, summed it up when he said what we need calls for "a blinding flash of the obvious." Today, almost everyone with expertise in management science argues for management techniques that "humanize" the work place: for ways of treating people as if they really mattered, for empowering people at the lowest level in an organization with the authority to control their immediate work environment, for allowing them to make routine decisions without the often humiliating experience of seeking (parental-like) approval. Allowing people who are affected by decisions to give input into the decision-making process is becoming an accepted part of American management practice. But there is still a long distance to go.

Classical Management

In the Forties and Fifties most management practices in the U.S. were patterned after Frederick W. Taylor's *Scientific Principles of Management*. The practice came to be known as "Classical Management," which assumed that workers were naturally lazy, that work had to be planned by management and performed by workers under tightly controlled, highly supervised conditions.[1] This management style was the foundation of industrial America. In the typical factory, management was unquestionably the pinnacle of authority. In the Sixties, studies based on the work of Fredrick Hertzburg, and on the theories of self-actualization that came out of the humanistic psychology movement, brought a shift in management theory to "human relations." It became fashionable to assume that a happy work force was a productive work force. Efforts to make the work force happy were simply added to existing systems while most of the authoritative practices of classical management were left in place. The process led to confusion and a call for a return to basic management practice (classical management).

Situational Leadership

In the Seventies "situational leadership" offered to save the day by producing leaders able to respond to each employee according to his or her needs. The problem was that such flexible leaders were hard to produce. Managers imprinted in their early years by the authoritative behavior of their bosses found it easier to imitate them than to adjust to situational leadership.

Cultural Assessment

In the Eighties the work of Tom Peters, Robert Waterman, and others led to "cultural assessment": a common-sense approach to management attempting to find out what works and what doesn't. The cultural assessment approach acknowledges that we have learned a lot about human nature in this century, but we have used very little of it. Most attempts at changing management practice amount to adjustments of authority from centralization to decentralization. This phenomenon swings back and forth like a pendulum, first in one direction then the other. It has done so for so long that labor rarely believes anything that management says about proposed change. They take a "wait and see," followed by an "I told you so" attitude.

Organizations and Management

Organizations that lose their sense of mission and atrophy into massive bureaucracies become "black holes" where initiative and innovation are drowned in a vacuum of petty differences between various factions. Managers and those who aspire to management positions in such organizations spend their time scrambling for ways to illuminate whatever supports their position and authority.

Today we talk about flattening the pyramid, removing excess layers of management, turning bosses into facilitators and generally humanizing our organizations. In order to understand our behavior in the workplace, it is necessary to look again at the way we are taught. The behavior that is learned in our educational institutions is often the very same guise we use daily in the workplace.

In Chapter One, I cited how students in grade school learned how to bypass curriculum intent by learning how to respond to the needs of the teacher. These students achieved passing grades by giving the teacher what he or she wanted. I suggest that what has been mistaken in many cases to be a causal relationship between grades and performance is simply learned effectiveness at manipulation and adaptation. The student who misses an education by keeping the teacher happy can use the same practice in the corporation to appease the boss. When this is the case, the boss's perception of the employee's performance is impaired; only the employee's peers and the employee know of his or her organizational ineffectiveness.

Why Study Management?

Why study management if you have no intention of becoming a manager? If you don't know the philosophy of management, how do you know what management expects of you or what you should expect of management? If you are unaware of the philosophy and agenda of management in today's rapidly changing environment, you may as well be at sea with no idea of the destination of the ship on which you are a passenger.

Management is everybody's business. My own efforts at self-education have caused me to conclude that, as humans, we are at our best when we truly try to understand others; we are at our worst when we try to "manage" them.

Paul Hawken, author of *Growing a Business*, said, "You don't ever manage people—you work with them." It is a fundamental truth that is validated by almost everyone's experience, yet we still do not seem to learn from it. We know that nothing in the form of manipulation or coercion will enlist individual performance comparable with what we are capable of when our enthusiasm and cooperation are sought respectfully. Yet, when we become managers we persist in the assumptions that indeed people can and should be managed. Such assumptions assure resistance, resentment and mediocrity in performance.

The difficulty of management is in large part aggravated by the fundamental assertion that we are nurtured without the benefit of acquiring self-knowledge. People with little self-knowledge can hardly be expected to be intuitively wise, or to have the knowledge necessary to effectively deal with others, let alone manage them.

The ancient Greeks, notably Socrates and Plato, had a special contempt for those who saw themselves fit for political office without the benefit of experience or expertise in the matters of government. Then and now many people view themselves to be sufficiently knowledgeable for political office based solely on their experience at living. This phenomenon is even worse in the field of management. Almost everyone sees himself a manager, yet few people possess the talent to be an effective one. They think of themselves as being qualified to manage, not because of what they know about people, but because of what they know about the nature of their own work and what they think needs to be done.

The Enneagram personality topology introduced in Chapter Ten is a useful means for understanding the dynamics of an organization. My own experience is that managers who are personally insecure in their position will shun such efforts as nonsense, primarily because they perceive them to be threatening and because they do not have enough knowledge to control the exercise. Good managers, on the other hand, understand the importance of assessing the dynamics of the personalities within their organization. They know that, like it or not, organizations are personality-driven organisms. The clash or mesh of personalities within an organization provides the subtle sustenance that produces shipwreck or synergy. In Japan organizations seldom assume the personality characteristics of their leaders, but in America it is expected; it goes together like Lee Iacocca and Mustangs. (Lee Iacocca headed the Mustang division at Ford when the Mustang became one of the most popular cars in America.) Divisions and departments in American companies often take on the dominant personality characteristics of their managers. The organization assumes a personarty of its own, reflecting that of its leaders and containing the message of what it takes to succeed in the organization.

Regardless of your position in an organization, an understanding of the general dynamics of personality theory will put you in the driver's seat because you will likely be the only person who has a clear idea of what is going on and why. The key to effective management is a solid understanding of human behavior and the ability to build on an employee's sense of self-worth and accomplishment. Good managers know the secret of successful management philosophy, which is simply that there are no secrets. Good management practice is simply understanding human behavior to such a degree that the people within an organization reach maximum congruence in blending their needs for achievement with the objectives of the business. Good managers know that you gain power in an organization by giving power away, not the reverse. Managing people is a lot like handling ripe fruit: they are easily bruised, quick to spoil, and once the damage is done, the damage is done.

Organizations that offer employees real opportunities for personal growth on the job do so by empowering them to discover what they are best at; this sometimes results in the employee leaving the company to pursue a new career. This may seem like a losing proposition for the employer, but it is not. Both parties win. The employee is able to offer a greater contribution elsewhere, and the employer has a chance to fill the vacant position with someone who will do likewise. But the greatest benefit from this effort is that employees perceive management's interest in them to be genuine— which it is, when unconditional assistance is given. This situation in and of itself is so unusual in large companies that it is likely to result in a willingness on the part of the employees to take a greater interest in the business of the organization.

Finding a New Bottom Line

Strange as it may seem in light of American management style, continued focus solely on the bottom line is a poor way to run a business. It's analogous to the grading system in school: it changes the focus from empowering the student to labeling him. To illustrate this point further, ask yourself this question: What would be the consequences of eliminating the word "education," which has come to have passive implications because of the process, and replacing it with the word "empowerment"? Would teachers and students have a better understanding of what is expected? Would the focus shift from grades to the general well-being of the student?

The "bottom line philosophy" is driven by external motivation— it propels us to act without really knowing why. We sacrifice the present without a clear vision of what to expect from the future. Thus we measure the results by looking where we have been instead of paying attention to where we are going. And when our response is conditioned to the point where it becomes automatic, we almost never ask why.

"Bottom line philosophy" causes people charged with improving quality to focus on defects. The dominant tendency is to look for someone to blame. The guilt and ill feelings produced by this process continually undermine production and morale. We seem incapable of pursuing quality without following pedagogical methods for finding fault. How can you improve quality without focusing on inspection? You do so with a clear definition of what is expected. Instead of focusing on correcting defects in the output stage, you create a vision and design of quality so compelling that it is an obvious waste of time to look for blame. Input is a stage of opportunity. Making changes in the output stage usually means it's too late to do what should have done in the first place.

Our focus on output versus input is conspicuous in our society by the pathogenic way in which we balance the growth of ghettos by building prisons, instead of dismantling the ghettos in the first place by "empowering" the young people who live in them. You don't have to be a police officer to know that a high percentage of crime is committed by drug addicts, yet in many of our major cities addicts must be on a waiting list for months in order to obtain medical assistance. We react to the news of the crimes these people commit with anger and frustration while our politicians use our dependable emotional reactions to enhance their own images by appearing to be "tough on crime." They call for more police and equipment, a clear focus on output. They know that if they advocate the input side of the issue by spending money for medical treatment in order to prevent the crimes in the first place, they will be seen as being "soft on crime." Even if some constituents see value in the input approach, it simply doesn't carry enough emotional weight to sway voters who refuse to think about it except when they are angered enough to respond. My argument is that it is merely a question of when we pay, now or later, and that the input stage is much cheaper in terms of dollars and human suffering (victims and criminals). Critics argue that it is naive to think that addicts who steal to support a drug habit will stop stealing when they are off drugs, and they may be correct. But it is also naive to overlook the significance of drugs as a motivator and the amount of crime necessary to support a drug habit.

Politics

In Chapters One and Two, I stated that the perception of reality is unique to each of us. In this respect our individual perceptions of reality are a lot like conscious "dreams." We have created these versions of reality through the processes of education, cultural values and experience, using our perceptual constructive processes selectively to justify our actions along the way, in the same manner that all societies do. Politics in this context can be thought of as the juncture where dreams collide. It is the process with which we try to persuade others to dream as we do and to shake those awake who do not. Politics is the intellectual substance that both pulls us together and pushes us apart. It is the residue of everything that we believe thrust in a form to perpetuate our dreams, a form which we use to rationalize everything we do. Each of us has a political philosophy regardless of whether we acknowledge it or act upon it. When we share our dreams with others they become political ideologies.

Global politics is a clash of ideologies. Our differences with our allies and our adversaries influence our behavior in ways we do not readily perceive. For example, we clash with the Soviet Union on a continuum concerning freedom and responsibility. Human rights and individual freedom are the heart of our politics, but we damage the heart, because in our zeal to demonstrate to the Soviets our capacity for freedom, we abdicate our responsibility for citizenship by not participating at all. We would likely gravitate to this responsibility ourselves if it were not for the nature of the clash. The Soviets, on the other hand, focus on responsibility to the point where they turn citizens into prisoners. Conflict between individuals or nations has a way of forcing attention on the bottom line result (output) and away from process (input).

Americans grow up with an ethic of freedom that implies that you are UN-AMERICAN if you do not do your own thing. We acknowledge little obligation of citizenship except a halfhearted duty to participate in the election process by voting. We acknowledge little debt to the government or to society except for the specific services we feel we use, i.e., highways, schools, public facilities, postal services, etc. The part of government's existence that keeps us from being a vulnerable, primitive hunter-gatherer society is neither spoken of nor any longer appreciated. Some argue that what we experience today is freedom from responsibility.

Rousseau wrote of the social compact and the social contract that binds us in freedom and obligation. In his thesis, "The Social Contract," he wrote:

> I suppose men to have reached the point at which the obstacles in the way of their preservation in the state of nature show their power of resistance to be greater than the resources at the disposal of each individual for his maintenance in that state. The primitive condition can then subsist no longer; and the human race would perish unless it changed its manner of existence.

But as men cannot engender new forces, but only unite and direct existing ones, they have no other means of preserving themselves than the formation, by aggregation, of a sum of forces great enough to overcome the resistance. These they have to bring into play by means of a single motive power, and cause to act in concert.

This sum of forces can arise only when several persons come together: but, as the force and liberty of each man are the chief instruments of his self-preservation, how can he pledge them without harming his own interests, and neglecting the care he owes to himself? This difficulty, in its bearing on my present subject, may be stated in the following terms:

The problem is to find a form of association which will defend and protect with the whole common force the person and goods of each associate, and in which each, while uniting himself with all, may still obey himself alone, and remain as free as before. This is the fundamental problem of which the Social Contract provides the solution.

I would argue that this association, which is necessary for freedom, requires a legitimate obligation upon the citizenry of any free nation to be knowledgeable about the affairs of his government, as a duty to his country and himself. This is a duty that we preach in America, but do not practice.

After each major election in America we hear self-congratulatory speeches ad nauseam in which politicians try to flatter the electorate by talking about "the great wisdom of the American people." They do this in spite of the fact that every study conducted to determine the political knowledge of the American people shows that such claims are nonsense.

In my own studies I have read the works of Rousseau, Montesquieu, Jefferson, Mason, Locke, Hume, Hobbes, Bacon, Voltaire and a great many others who were once concerned with the nature of government and politics. The study of politics fills the void or distance from philosophy to sociology. I came to an insightful conclusion on my own that freedom is *process*, rather than *experience*. If I had been told this by a teacher in a classroom, it would have probably passed by as just another fact with little significance, but to discover such a truth on my own was a significant learning experience.

In a world where dreams collide and a perpetual struggle exists to change the dreams of others, freedom is a precious doctrine. The nature and character of freedom are so fragile that maintaining balance requires a constant process. In other words, the laws that permit freedom in and of themselves are insufficient to maintain freedom. For example, it is not the stolid nature of the beams and girders that keep a building standing, it is the unobservable pressure that each exerts on the other that enables it to stand firm. The same process applies to freedom. Without clear visions of what we stand for, the Constitution has no more meaning for us than dreams on paper. It is only when we act in the cause and process of freedom that we are truly free. Process forges coalitions in which differences are negotiated into equitable solutions. Simply put, it is the recipe for balance. When we are not engaging in *process* to protect our interests, we can be sure that our interests at some level are being encroached upon. This ranges from local zoning ordinances to matters of international policy. Engaging in the process of freedom is a lot like a game of tug of war in which our rope is entangled with the ropes of everyone else. The game is played by atheists, agnostics, Protestants, Catholics, Jews, Democrats, Republicans, socialists, developers, environmentalists, corporations, entrepreneurs, investment bankers, small businessmen, politicians, scientists, philosophers, Southerners, Northerners, Easterners, Westerners, blacks, whites, Hispanics, Asians and an endless list of others who profess to know how everyone else should live. Pulling on our rope enables each of us to protect our own interests and to keep from being pulled into a chasm where our rights or interests are infringed upon. When we pull on our end of the rope we are engaged in the process of freedom. When we let go, we think we are experiencing freedom, but it is an illusion because the others continue to pull. When only a few participate, only a few rule, thus democracy is replaced by an oligarchy (a system in which only a few have the power to influence). To maintain power, the oligarchy needs only to convince people that the true character of freedom is experience. In other words, be free, do your own thing, while we maintain power.

In America we place an almost sacred value on one's right and duty to vote, but voting is not process, it is merely a symbolic gesture. Voting is output, process is input. When we vote, it is an either-or proposition; the chance to transform the vision has already passed. When we engage in process (pull on our rope) our actions influence the visions to which politicians aspire. In other words, when we understand the issues and articulate our opinions through letters, telephone calls, public and private meetings on a local, state and federal level, we are engaging in process and gaining the power to influence the visions of what should be. There are thousands of such actions which constitute process, and they all emerge from a thorough understanding of our government. When we engage in process with clear ideas about the character of democracy, its foundation is strengthened. Likewise, when we pursue our own narrow interests at the expense of our ideals or because we are ignorant about democracy, we often enter into a mutually corruptive contract with our political representatives. They give us what we want and we allow them to stay in office, but this weakens the foundation of democracy. When we do not understand or care about democracy, we place our wants above our needs, thereby becoming easily manipulated. We don't need strong leadership in America nearly as much as we need "membership." We must all pull on the rope with a clear understanding of the principles upon which democracy is founded so as to create a tension which prevents democracy from stumbling over narrow special interests.

Jefferson thought that the Constitution and all laws should expire with each generation so that we would always have the benefit of responsible applicable government. Indeed, such a practice would demand responsibility of its citizenry. It would ensure active process. Jefferson thought that the requirements of government would continually be in a state of flux and that new approaches must be regularly tried. And who can argue otherwise?

When our present form of government was formed we had an agrarian economy for which a representative democracy was a superb form of government. The principals upon which our government was founded are today basically the same, except that we are no longer a simple agrarian society and we have expanded the definition of "equal" to include everyone. Our society has grown so complex that no single individual, group, committee, or congress can maintain the knowledge necessary to deal effectively with issues. Indeed no single group can understand the complexities of the American economy well enough to explain it to the rest of us, let alone understand and explain how it relates to the global economy. The net result of this inability to determine definite cause and effect in government is that we now have a government that responds to the individual or group who can best afford to purchase the influence of political lobbyists. When we do not participate in the process of democracy, we do not accept responsibility. For example, when a product's beautiful packaging is discarded, decays and poisons our ground water, we say, "It is a manufacturing problem." Since we fail to accept freedom as process, we fail to see our own complicity and we fail to accept responsibility for our actions. So the pollution of the environment continues, and we continue to point our finger at others.

As we learn about the nature of psychology, sociology and philosophy the obligation of citizenship becomes salient. Thomas Jefferson maintained that a nation cannot remain ignorant and remain free. I would add that for a nation to remain free of ignorance, its citizenry must be free of education by indoctrination. Our ability to think critically must protect us from manipulation. The constant threat of manipulation must ensure that we concern ourselves with the principles upon which democracy is founded and that we maintain clear ideas about the character of democracy and thus the nature and essence of freedom. In *The Waning of Humaneness*, Konrad Lorenz, winner of the Nobel prize for medicine/physiology wrote:

> Millions of completely "normal" humans live frictionlessly in a society against which they should, if they were really to stand on their rights as humans, revolt. Although they continue to uphold the illusion of their individuality, they have already actually relinquished a great part of their freedom. Their continued assent to the present social order can only lead imperceptibly to a further loss of individuality.

Politics, Change and Technology

If you apply Nobel laureate Ilya Prigogine's theory of dissipative structures (discussed in Chapter Three) to governments, it is easy to conclude that, when ideas harden, governments begin to decay because they lose the dynamic flexibility necessary to meet change with intelligent response. The growth in media technology that we have already discussed, which is metaphorically an extension of our senses, will inevitably lead to an electronic input system more pervasive than the telephone. It will likely surface from two-way television cable during the Nineties and will represent an opportunity for improved government because of the ability to access information, knowledge and opinion prior to making necessary decisions. But it will also offer avenues for abuse which will further empower the special interest groups that already bend the ear of government to the exclusion of everyone else. Simply put, the new electronic media will offer improved, informed government with a salient temptation for government by referenda, a chance for the majority to vote on the "rights" of minorities. It is not a question of whether this will happen; it is a question of when. And if we are not intellectually prepared to defend democracy we might lose the opportunity to do so.

A knowledge society must balance its technology with a well-educated citizenry in order to continue. As communications technology expands, democracy will demand greater participation. Rapid technological specialization creates a corresponding demand for liberally educated generalists. By nature specialization contributes to action without accountability, because experts routinely overestimate the amount of knowledge in fields outside their own. This means everyone assumes someone else is in charge, when in reality no one is. Silence in a democracy is construed to be consent.

Ironically, the success of our technologies is creating the illusion that the demand exists for a less educated citizenry. The term "dumbing down" has been used frequently to describe the process in which jobs can be simplified so as to be almost mistake-proof — computer checkout price code readers in supermarkets, for example. Technology seems to be relieving us from making difficult decisions, but in actuality, nothing could be further from the truth. Never has there been a greater need for an informed, educated public than exists today. We have become so accustomed to associating the need for education with the demands of the workplace that we do not think of one without the other.

On August 4, 1822, James Madison wrote to Lieutenant Governor Barry of Kentucky, "Knowledge will forever govern ignorance; and a people who mean to be their own governors must arm themselves with the power which knowledge gives." It was an important issue in the summer of 1822, and it is even more important today. In 1822 the ink on the Constitution was only thirty-five years old. Many of the statesmen who signed it were still living. Democracy was in good hands (for those who were not slaves).

In the eighteenth century it was a straightforward proposition for a statesman to represent the interests of constituents in government matters. In those days the representative, by the very nature of his profession, had superior knowledge in almost all issues concerning those he would represent. Today it is inconceivable to expect an individual to be so informed without our continual involvement, yet we pretend as if nothing has changed. Today's issues transcend the boundaries of those represented. They concern the environment, nuclear power and weapons, international trade, human rights, special interests, and economic questions with consequences that we are totally incapable of determining. These kinds of decisions call for the best government democracy has to offer. And if there are any Jeffersons or Madisons among us today, they are awfully hard to recognize.

During this century millions of us have abdicated any sense of duty we might have felt to participate in the affairs of government in favor of the perceived duty to do our own thing. In doing so we have allowed our knowledge of government to dwindle away to the degree that we are terrified of having a constitutional convention. Most of us have no sense of what we might do to improve the Constitution, but we are fearful of what we might lose. Since we cannot formulate an educated opinion, we respond emotionally. Emotion is more powerful than reason in people who are poorly educated or indoctrinated. Similarly, emotion can cloud the judgment of otherwise intelligent and educated people. Their political reality becomes distorted. For example, many of us responded to the Vietnam War emotionally. Vietnam forced us to examine our political ideologies about the morality of war—something we're not used to doing. The result was that we were not willing to apply reason until years afterward.

Citizens of a knowledge society must have clear ideas about the roles and duties of government concerning equality, human rights, civil rights, the pursuit of happiness, the process of consent and dissent, justice, domestic tranquility, national defense, the general welfare and the nature of freedom and democracy. Millions of us have so abdicated our responsibility as citizens that we would be hard pressed to outline and articulate the needs and rights afforded us by the Constitution. If we ourselves do not practice thinking about these ideas and the basic foundations of government, then we subject ourselves to the phenomenon whereby almost any well-thought-out premise by others seems more practical than our own assessments.

We call ourselves liberals or conservatives based on our political "dream" states. If you search the dictionary for the most favorable definition of each, you can eventually find one supporting the argument that a conservative is someone who preserves tradition and a liberal is a person with an open mind. Conservatives preach individualism, but practice conformity. Liberals preach conformity, but practice individualism. Liberals focus on the rights of the individual. Conservatives focus on the responsibility of the individual.

Conservatives accuse liberals of wanting to create a "zoo" society in which everyone is cared for custodially. Liberals accuse conservatives of trying to create a "jungle" society where survival is a desperate struggle. It seems that good sense dictates that each of us would be capable of deducing the best of both. We should start with nothing less than a safe jungle. We should all be capable of having an open mind and we should also have enough self-knowledge—and therefore knowledge of others—to feel a sense of moral virtue, enabling us to recognize and wish to preserve that which is worth preserving. When we adopt a party line (endorse either party carte blanche), it is usually an indication that we have not thought each issue through. In effect, many of us practice citizenship by letting others think for us.

The paradoxical relationship of capitalism and socialism is equally confusing. From a distance they appear similar, but there is a fundamental difference in the way each system identifies with the concept of freedom versus responsibility. In capitalism we gravitate toward freedom. In socialism the polarity is reversed: the focus on responsibility, which in our case is the conservative agenda, becomes the extreme left. In other words, the conservative socialist is to us an extreme liberal. Likewise the liberal socialist appears to us to have a conservative bent.

In theory, the socialist factory is founded on the assertion that the means of production is owned by the people, and thus their labor will not be exploited. But in practice socialist factories are likely to be totalitarian states with rigid control and an autocratic hierarchy.

The capitalist factory, on the other hand, appears to be a totalitarian state, but in fact imitates the socialist idea that the worker is indeed a part owner in the business. Both systems have classes of elites whose rewards bear little relation to their contributions. Capitalism ceases to be a dynamic means of efficiency when those engaged in it can no longer remember their original objective. In the socialist system, on the other hand, the implied objective is always known, but the oppressive process seems to undermine its significance. Human initiative is strongest when it is in alignment with natural reinforcement. Yet the qualities of natural reinforcement seem to have been effectively removed from work in both systems: another result of people building systems with little knowledge of themselves or others.

In nature and society an equilibrium exists that permits conditions to maintain themselves. Change the balance significantly, and conditions will change dramatically. The same premise applies to freedom and democracy. Democracy allows room for its own undoing, and if the disparity of knowledge between factions of Americans becomes great enough, our state of democracy will dissolve.

The hows and whens of technology must be balanced with the whats and whys of reason. Mass technologies and multi-national corporations fused together have enormous power, a power that must be checked with an active, self-educated citizenry. A major premise of this theory of self-education is that we have the power, and indeed the obligation, to use our intelligence for the betterment of society.

Freedom Redefined

Since the end of World War Two, we have been locked in a battle of political ideology with the Soviet Union over the rights of freedom and responsibility for individuals. Freedom is the heart of our value system, but we have let our differences with the Soviets keep us from demanding more of freedom. Without the continual need to defend our way of life, our definition of freedom might have evolved into something much better.

Rousseau said, "Man is born free; and everywhere he is in chains. One thinks himself the master of others, and still remains a greater slave than they."

We have become confused over how we feel versus what we think about America. In defense of our way of life we assert that America is a great country. I would argue instead that America is a good country and our love for America is great. If America were a truly great country, there would be no working poor, no street people, no ghettos, no underclass, no illiterates and no semi-literates. We have allowed ourselves to be culturized to accept as natural that some people work hard all their lives and yet live in a state of poverty. We franchise poverty by expecting little of freedom. If we were truly a great country, anyone who worked hard at a full-time job would earn a decent living. Is it incomprehensible to believe that if a job in the United States is worth doing, its wages are worth a decent living?

In 1910 Theodore Roosevelt delivered a speech in which he said:

> No man can be a good citizen unless he has a wage more than sufficient to cover the bare cost of living and hours of labor short enough so that after his day's work is done he will have time and energy to bear his share in the management of the community, to help in carrying the general load. We keep countless men from being good citizens by the conditions of life with which we surround them.[2]

Might a better definition of freedom include: Freedom from mindless work; freedom from bureaucracies; freedom from activity that we conclude to be a rat race; freedom from being a human robot; and the freedom to fail without catastrophic consequences?[3]

Political Anxiety, Value and Sports

I suspect our unwillingness to participate in the affairs of government is, at least in part, an unacknowledged political protest reflected in our attitude toward sports. This is demonstrated by the irrational way we reward athletes. How else do we explain our willingness to enthusiastically reward sports heroes in astronomical proportion to their contribution to society? Their contribution consists of the enjoyment and amusement we associate with their efforts, but we allow the intellectual efforts of those who teach our children to go begging in comparison. We enjoy sports activities because they release us from stress and, unlike most work tasks, are intrinsically self-reinforcing. In most other areas of society the rewards are not so readily connected to the activity in real time. We are forced to subordinate our natural desire to pursue self-reinforcing activities. In other words, some of us perform non-reinforcing mindless work all week for a paycheck. The paycheck is a reward, but it is not naturally reinforcing because we don't get paid each moment that we perform. The result is intellectual anxiety. It's not like hitting a home run and having the crowd cheer our achievement. But watching someone else hit a home run enables us to share the reward, and that in itself is a self-reinforcing activity, even if by proxy.

We have an innate affection and need for self-reinforcing activities. This affection, combined with the potential equalizing aspects of sports, may shed some light on why we allow people who can perform a simple non-contributing activity to be showered with lavish rewards. The equalizing effect is based on the premise that anyone, regardless of race, creed, sex, education or wealthy parents, can be eminently successful. And even though most of us know we will never be exceptional athletes, we are grateful for the equalizing possibilities of sport. Sports can make education and social advantage seem negligible. Subconsciously we perceive that society is excessively unfair, so the fact that anyone can be a success by kicking, punting, passing, putting, jumpshooting, backhanding, batting or catching an odd assortment of balls makes the unfairness seem less salient. We justify our lavish rewards for sports by arguing that striving for excellence in any type of performance is a noble effort, but the excellence theory does not always apply itself rationally. No matter how many ways you try to make it sound reasonable and logical, it just doesn't make any difference in the scheme of things that some people can hit a small white ball into a hole with fewer attempts than someone else. But it is useless to try to convince rational human beings that these aren't feats worthy of riches. So, we continue to act as if they are. The sad legacy of our relationship with sports is in the message it sends to young people. Millions aspire to a sports career expecting riches when opportunity is severely limited.

The result is a dream out of focus with reality and a sense of disillusionment for young people created by a system they perceive to be unjust, but can't quite figure out why. The message to the ghetto child is clear: the way to success is through sports or drugs.

I am not suggesting that we take steps to control the free market process in which sports salaries are determined. I am saying that political anxiety, combined with the stress of our personal lives and the external spin of our drive to earn a living, set up conditions that make the entertainment aspect of sports irresistible. Entertainment is the antithesis of creativity, it forces our minds to focus on activity versus output. The result is that if we spend a large portion of our time *watching others* improve *their* skills, we retard our own growth. If we placed our need for entertainment in better balance, our diminished need to watch *others* have fun would likely drop sport salaries into a more rational level. Here again I am not suggesting that we avoid entertainment, just that we keep it equitable perspective. We can have more fun becoming involved *ourselves* than by watching others improve themselves.

Pathogenic Policies

Imagine for a moment that a human life is represented as a wooden wagon wheel with a wedge missing from the rim. The missing piece of wheel represents the void of human self-knowledge. The missing piece varies in size according to each individual. If the missing piece is small, the bump caused by the gap will barely be noticed when the wheel turns. If the gap is wide, the wheel will roll smoothly while in contact with the ground, but will crash violently when it reaches the void of self-knowledge (see Figure 3). Western civilization seems to perpetuate the expectation that the missing piece will remain large in proportion to the total circumference of the wheel.

The shock felt each time the wheel turns threatens the stability and structure of the wheel itself, just as the gap caused by the lack of self-knowledge threatens the very being of society in Western civilization. The wagon ride is so stressful that it is pathogenic. In America the amount of money attributed to stress-related illness is incalculable, but even conservative estimations start in the hundreds of billions of dollars per year. Some medical scientists argue persuasively that if we were to cure cancer and heart disease they would soon be replaced by other maladies induced by the stress of a biological life out of sync with its natural state of existence. And so it is that we live in a society that has grown dependent on operating with broken wheels. If you doubt this, consider how we might respond to society if the void of self-knowledge were small. If we were a well-adjusted society made up of secure individuals, we would likely respond differently to a wide range of social problems. For example, if we were secure with ourselves as whole human beings, we would not accept unfulfilling meaningless work as a lifetime occupation. We would not be so threatened by others that we missed seeing the path to security through a higher ratio of cooperation to competition. If we were secure human beings, we would know instinctively that the security of the "haves" is reinforced by the elimination of categories distinguished as "have nots."

The gap of the missing self-knowledge addles us just enough so that we focus on output instead of input. It ensures our affection for bottom lines. It perpetuates our propensity to treat the disease rather than the whole patient. It guarantees that we will seek and continue to engage in occupations to which we are ill suited, but which we are afraid to give up. It guarantees the franchise of mental health professionals whose practices thrive because of our lack of knowledge about ourselves. It ensures the practice of attorneys who profit from our insecurity and our inability to get along with others. It ensures the existence of the worldwide monolithic military complex, which has become an integral part of our economy. Indeed, the process of our being violently tossed about on our wagon ride has brought us near the borders of schizophrenia. Many of us believe that, as a nation, we cannot afford adequate health care because we have to spend the money on nuclear weapons. If peace were to break out everywhere, hundreds of thousands of people would try to convince us that it was only an illusion so that they could remain employed. We have no economic contingencies for genuine peace.

FIGURE 3.
Our pathogenic society tries to run on a broken wheel. The gap is our lack of self-knowledge.

If we used what we know about human nature to work toward world peace, the bias for war would vanish with the election or appointment of women to positions as chief executives in each country in the world. Given the prerogative, women would not send their sons to fight wars when alternatives exist.[4] Alternatives like these might be explored if it weren't for the confusion a patriarchal world dominance generates with regard to pride, honor and the perceived virtue of blood on the battlefield.

If we were comfortable with ourselves as whole beings, we would be less threatened by others. Think of it. If the citizens of each country in the world suddenly fired everyone in a position to make or affect foreign policy, the world would be instantly transformed into a planet of relationships amounting to nothing more in status than that of being "neighbors." This is easily demonstrable by the U.S.-Soviet telecommunication bridges which link us in conference by satellite. When we question each other citizen-to-citizen, each of us comes away with the perspective that we are just plain people with the same hopes and aspirations for the future. Unfortunately, it is much easier to maintain power by elaborating on the potential vile deeds of the perceived enemy than it is to use knowledge of humanity to negotiate perceived differences into manageable relations.

Summary

We use sociology as a means of describing our cultural differences as well as our common aspirations. We must have some understanding of others in order to maintain a perspective of ourselves, just as the reverse is also true. When we examine society from a distance, we see the price we pay with regard to responsibility by our preoccupation with freedom. This is demonstrated by our focus on output versus input. There is hope, however. There are signs that we are moving toward a transformation of holistic values, a time of synthesis and a better management focus on input. These trends may lead to a more valuable definition of freedom. If we substantially increase our self-knowledge, allowing us to better understand others, we cannot help but transform society. By doing so we will redefine ourselves and thus our system.

CHAPTER SEVEN

The Methodology of Inquiry

In the subjects we propose to investigate, our inquiries should be directed, not to what others have thought, nor to what we ourselves conjecture, but to what we can clearly and perspicuously behold and with certainty deduce; for knowledge is not won in any other way. —René Descartes

How do we discover truth? How do we discern fact from fiction? How do we use intuition, common sense, traditional knowledge, and science as a means of inquiry? How do we decide what we need to know? How do we enroll in the continuing body of reason? The subjects that follow are tools to use in your own quest for truth.

Objectivity

If human beings were programed for truth, any time we searched for knowledge, our minds would default in favor of objectivity, regardless of the nature of the inquiry or the feedback that we received. But such is not the case. Instead we seem to have a propensity for finding irresistible any information that adds to our comfort, security or pleasure. We desire a certain condition and then set about to prove what we wish to be true. True objectivity is a rare virtue. The scientific world aims at the truth, but often it settles for delusion. Fundamental assumptions about scientific truths periodically reverse themselves. For example, we have gone from the perception of a flat earth as the center of the universe, to a sphere of insignificant location, and from a decaying universe to one in the act of reaching higher states of order, to yet another, which is perceived by some to be a perpetual state of randomness.

The scientific search for truth is somewhat analogous to driving while intoxicated. The driver never thinks of himself as "under the influence"—he always feels in control. In fact the intoxicating effect of the alcohol deludes him into thinking that he has more control than ever. Likewise, the scientist trying to prove a hypothesis may begin to feel the euphoria of achieving his desired result and become deluded into believing that the evidence bears him out.

The search for truth by individuals is precarious. We seem to have an innate propensity to see what we desire to see. Ten thousand of us can witness a baseball player slide into home plate and see him as being either out or safe, depending upon on which team we hope will win.

The essence of the ability to become self-educated lies in the ability to remain objective. Like a cat's ability to land on its feet each time it falls from a high place, we must be able to appeal to a reliable instinct for truth each time we are confronted with conflict or uncertainty. To sustain an intrinsic motive for truth and objectivity one must intellectually disengage oneself by tempering emotional involvement and viewing events from a distance. Recall from Chapter Three how Schopenhauer defined genius in terms of the completest objectivity and the ability to leave one's own interest out of sight.

Unfortunately, because we are human, we can never really escape from a perception of reality that is not contaminated from the frailties of human experience. The best we can do is pretend we are not involved, or that we have no personal stake in what we trying to be objective about. It helps if you can get into the habit of assuming the temporary identity of an inanimate object when a situation in which you are involved calls for objectivity. It is one step beyond the third person to that of a non-person. Pretend you are a rock, a mountain, a tree, anything with an imaginary non-human perspective of its own. The point is simply to assume a posture which enables you to view the antics of humans with a dispassionate sense of amusement, or a mild sense of curiosity. With practice you will be able to see through the walls we have engineered with narrow beliefs and prejudice to protect and promote our own versions of reality.

The act of attempting to view life from an unconcerned vantage point will quickly render you capable of being comfortable with higher levels of uncertainty and ambiguity. It is a form of mind aerobics, an exercise in learning how to flex your mind into the "open" position. The assumption of a posture of being not involved is the best way I have found to default in favor of objectivity. For example, it is easy to look back in history and observe the dramatic effects the printing press had upon society. But it is not so easy to observe the effects of television because we are so deeply involved in the experience. Stand back and observe humans watching television and you move closer to objectivity.

Dialectics

The search for truth can be an exercise in dialectics, the process in which an argument is put forward as a thesis. This is countered by an antithesis, which in turn reaches a synthesis followed by yet another thesis. It is not a compromise, but a continual argumentative search for the truth. Socrates was a master of dialectics.

The path to an objective search for truth is more direct in the company of those with whom we disagree, and yet most of us continually seek the comfort of being surrounded by people with whom we almost always agree. In fact, most of the reading we do is devoted to material which supports the views we already hold. We sharpen a knife by rubbing it against a stone first on one side and then the other. Why then, do we consider ourselves to be sharp when we only hone one side of our intellect?

Intuition

As we increase our self-knowledge and seek truth, we nurture the reliability of our intuition. Intuition is a visceral flash of knowledge of unknown origin. It is an ally of inquiry. When we develop expertise we can begin to feel some comfort with our intuition. As already discussed in Chapter Three, experts are thought to have developed their knowledge in a particular field to such a degree that they no longer have to remember rules, but instead act intuitively.

Exlectics

The search for truth can be an exercise in exlectics (a method of inquiry based on the search for value without conflict). Exlectics operates on higher principles than compromise and consensus by being so focused on the process of objectivity that ideas are produced in a manner similar to osmosis. Exlectics is a compelling search for truth which might best be characterized by imagining two or more people meeting to solve a problem while being totally oblivious to how the consequences of their decision may affect each of them personally as long as they arrive at an objective solution.[1]

Common Sense

Common sense is a paradoxical phenomenon to begin with because society is changing so fast that what is considered "common" can no longer be taken for granted. Common sense assumptions range from practical bits of knowledge to prejudice based on bigotry and igno-rance. Common sense is often common deception. All cultures have a tendency to explain mysteries by creating new ones. In the search for truth, common sense should never be taken for granted.

Traditional Knowledge

Traditional knowledge comes from the accumulated wisdom of culture and the trust we place in authority. Authority may be sacred, secular, scientific, political or any number of fields or individuals onto which we bestow the tribute of authority. Science, on the the other hand, is systematized knowledge determined by observation.

Before you decide that you are on the fundamental road to truth, you need to anchor your beliefs in a familiarity with ontology (the nature of being), epistemology (the nature of knowledge), metaphysics (the nature of things), the methodology of empiricism (knowledge based on sense experience), and positivism (knowledge based on pure scientific fact). If you do this on your own, you will begin to appreciate the significance of philosophy, and why it is necessary to ground your beliefs in philosophical thought. These subjects are a good way to approach the study of philosophy by examining each until you are intuitively drawn to ideas that hold your interest.

Religion and Inquiry

There are eleven major religions practiced today with hundreds of smaller diverse groups. If only one religion on earth is correct, then a human has only a small chance of being born into it.

It is not my intent to discourage your pursuit of religion, nor is it my intent to offer an opinion as to whether any one religion is more correct than another. The evidence seems overwhelming that, no matter how you feel about religion, man is certainly a spiritual creature by nurture and arguably by nature. But it has been my observation that often religion is to thinking as novocaine is to a toothache. The source of discomfort is still there, it just can't be felt. Likewise with religion—the questions are still there, but there seems to be no legitimacy with which to ask them.

Religion in many cases tends to assume the characteristics of a closed system, allowing no criticism of its doctrine and attacking the motivation of its critics. If your religion is worthy of your faith, it is worth your objective investigation into its assertions through the methods of critical inquiry. You should not rely solely on the basis of the authority of your clergy. If you can inquire critically into all the aspects of your faith and still believe, then you can defend it without feeling threatened by those who do not accept it. Instead of an emotional response based on the authority of someone else, you can offer reason as a defense.

Cognitive Dissonance

In 1957 psychologist Leon Festinger proposed the theory of cognitive dissonance, a theory somewhat similar to Freud's theory of rationalization. This describes the tension experienced when information conflicts with what we perceive to be true. We act either to rationalize the dissonant information, or we are forced to alter our belief. For example, if someone perceives himself to be an excellent golfer and participates in a major tournament, only to come in last, then there is dissonant information that must be reconciled. The golfer has an opinion of his skill level contrasted with the evidence of his performance. Either he adjusts his opinion of his talent, or he rationalizes his poor performance by finding fault with the golf course or by the thought that he was just having a bad day. It is a demonstrable assertion according to dissonance theory that we seek information that protects the nature of our most cherished beliefs.

Dissonance is a blink in a dream, a perceptual puzzle piece that doesn't quite fit, an icy wind whispering through a tear in your tent on a winter camping trip. Some dissonant information is hard to reconcile. It shows you where to begin to examine the nature of your beliefs. Dissonance is an excellent place to plan your first semester curriculum for Self-University.

With some reflection you will find that your life is full of dissonant experiences. Sometimes a significant experience with dissonance can be the result of something that someone says. I remember being insulted by President John F. Kennedy's assertion: "Ask not what your country can do for you, but what you can do for your country." At the time it seemed UN-AMERICAN to me. It was a startling philosophical change in direction, but it created enough dissonance over time to cause me to re-think the duty associated with citizenship.

From my own past I can remember many other examples that stand out. When I was very young, perhaps nine or ten, and growing up in the South, I was particularly puzzled by adults who said that someone was as "lazy as a nigger," and in the next breath stated that someone who was working hard was "working like a nigger." How could black people, I wondered, seem to have the simultaneous virtues of both laziness and industry? It was my first clue that something might be out of adjustment with the thinking ability of adults, at least with reference to people who were different from themselves.

Several years ago, while listening to the national news on the radio, a black female work associate of mine made a comment in reference to a news story about starvation in Africa. She said that the people in Africa would not be starving to death if they were white. When she said it, I resented it. But after I thought about it for a while, I realized she was right.

During the late Sixties I was a police officer for the city of Dallas. I worked for almost three years in the slum or ghetto sections. Like the ancient Greek philosopher Aristotle who mistook the actions of slaves to be a product of their nature instead of nurture, I, too, thought that the people living in the slums were the way they were because of their nature. Then in the late Seventies I was exposed to the work of Morris Massey, author of *The People Puzzle* and the training film, "Who You Are Is Where You Were When." Massey's work demonstrates the effects of cultural conditioning. It shows how we soak up and assume values and conditioning from society and from the environment through the process of socialization.

After studying the work of Massey and many others, I began to realize just how much a product of such conditioning I had become. It was an intensely disturbing realization to think that my own behavior might be so molded as to make my actions predictable to others, yet remain unknown to me. And if I was such a product of cultural and environmental conditioning, then could I not assume the same about people in slums and ghettos? How could they possibly improve their lives without first reaching a personal level of self-determination that is only possible through experiencing a sense of empowerment? In other words, success breeds success, so how do you initiate the process when people have no knowledge of the way to a better life?

If I find it so difficult to change my culturally conditioned behavior *with* the benefit of knowing how to do so, how could anyone do it without such knowledge? This was a big rip in the tent for me. I realized that I had been wrong in thinking that people who had lived in the slums for generations are the way they are because of their nature. They are the way they are by nurture, and unless they have an extraordinary amount of educational assistance, the slums are where they will stay. I believe strongly in personal responsibility, but I also believe that knowledge bears a close relationship to responsibility. This is a self-reinforcing process—people require a certain amount of knowledge to begin with in order to learn how to become responsible.

One curious aspect of human nature is that we seem unable to remember what it is like "not to know" once we have mastered something new. We look at others who do not know what we have learned and view them with contempt. For a person to climb out of the ghetto and step into a better way of life requires that he or she be able to appear as someone who has never lived in a ghetto. In other words, before a person can be a part of a higher economic level he must be viewed by those who have already attained the level as someone who "fits." And in order to fit he must learn the behavior of those who live beyond the slum, even though he can only view them from a distance. People in the ghetto view middle-class society through the medium of television. They perceive their own ability to achieve such living standards as being light-years away. Unfortunately, their whole assessment of what it takes to succeed is based on illusion.

Another constant source of dissonance for me has been the observation that people do not naturally settle into jobs or positions that match their particular contribution. I grew up buying into the "give-get compact" that Daniel Yankelovich writes about in his book *New Rules*. In describing the give-get compact he wrote:

> I give hard work, loyalty and steadfastness. I swallow my frustrations and suppress my impulse to do what I would enjoy, and do what is expected of me instead. I do not put myself first; I put the needs of others ahead of my own. I give a lot, but what I get in return is worth it. I receive an ever-growing standard of living, and a family life with a devoted spouse and decent kids. Our children will take care of us in our old age if we really need it, which thank goodness we will not. I have a nice home, a good job, the respect of my friends and neighbors; a sense of accomplishment at having made something of my life. Last but not least, as an American I am proud to be a citizen of the finest country of the world.

The give-get compact is at the heart of the American Dream. Its message (at least as I grew up to understand it) implies that you will receive your rewards in direct proportion to your contribution. Such an assumption is the foundation of capitalism, but my experience has been full of dissonance. For years I have seen employees in major corporations who detract value from the company rather than add to it. These people do not set out to do a job poorly, but they have a destructive effect because they know little of themselves and nothing at all about how to get along with others. Their negative effect does not lie in the actual work they perform, but in how their actions or attitudes affect others. It was because of this continued dissonance experience that I began to study management, which led naturally to the study of human behavior.

If you have difficulty setting an objective curriculum for your first year at Self-University, spend your first semester patching holes in your tent.

Deciding What You Need to Know

There are five major schools of thought about the continuing education of adults: liberal arts, progressive, behaviorist, radical and humanistic. The liberal arts philosophy of education is the oldest; it includes the study of history, philosophy, literature, logic and the natural sciences. The liberal education is intended to empower the adult with an intellectual understanding of the world and his relationship to it. It is intended to enable its recipient to develop a sense of moral virtue, spirituality, and a perpetual search for truth and aesthetic appreciation.

Progressive adult education is based on scientific reason and education's implied ability to address social problems. It is intended to empower the student with the faculty for responsible citizenship. Progressive adult education leans toward practical applications such as vocational school.

Behaviorist adult education assumes that all behavior is a result of conditioning by life experiences. B.F. Skinner made the famous assertion, "Behavior is a result of its consequences." Period. The behaviorist theory of adult education argues for the need for natural reinforcements in teaching practice and cooperation-based techniques.

Radical adult education assumes that traditional education is an attempt of those in power to remain in power by educating with a doctrine that supports the status quo. It assumes that most of what we receive in traditional educational practice is indoctrination and argues that the process and institutionalism of education should be decentralized.

Humanistic adult education grew out of the liberal arts philosophy, which challenges the assumptions of the behaviorists and argues that man is much more than a product of environmental conditioning. It asserts that man is unique, autonomous, and capable of self-determination and self-actualization. Humanistic adult education assumes that one's view of reality is the basis for one's actions and that reaching into the reality of others is a means and basis for human understanding.

These descriptions are brief, and each theory covers a much larger and more in-depth agenda.[2] The most puzzling aspect of these diverse schools of thought is not in the directions they advocate, but the fact that each philosophy has narrowed into a field that tends to exclude the others. In the process of educating ourselves we must borrow from each school. If we ignore the "Great Books" approach or similar techniques of the liberal arts philosophy—which in essence allows us to enter into a dialog with some of the greatest thinkers who ever lived—we miss a vital part of our human heritage. It is analogous to being cheated out of an estate left to us by our ancestors; the only difference is that the value is intellectual instead of material.

It is silly to assume that we can or should avoid the assertions of the progressive advocates in the need to address social problems and practical educational objectives, including responsible citizenship. And it would be ludicrous to ignore the significance of natural reinforcements in our learning environment as suggested by the behaviorists. Nor can we deny the warnings of the radical school against the dangers of indoctrination. And finally, it seems that to expect anything less of ourselves than the assertions of the humanists is to sell ourselves unnecessarily short.

The utility of an education is like that of a ball with a lead core. If the education is well rounded, the lead will settle in the center and the ball will roll easily in any direction. If, however, an education is without balance, the lead will settle near the surface and, regardless of how the ball is thrown, will revert to the same position. The longer it sits in one position, the less likely it will be able to regain mobility. If we do not continually work toward a whole education, we lose our ability to move in any direction freely and our ability to be self-determining.

Self-education/self-training is a means of achieving personal equilibrium by complementing one with the other. Take charge of your education and your occupational or professional training, and you have taken charge of your life—assuming that you maintain a balance between the two. Traditional education and training assume the passivity of the student. Becoming credentialed in this way does little to imbue the learner with a sense of empowerment. As already discussed, many traditional methods of education resemble thinking by proxy, simply responding to the questions and subsequent answers posed by others. It does not respect what we already know, and therefore does not allow us to follow a natural learning pattern based on the content we already possess.

Learning by self-directed inquiry is a perpetually self-empowering activity. It increases our expectation of personal effectiveness and thus moves us toward an internal perceived locus of causality. We are likely to get what we expect, as long as our perceived competence is reasonably accurate and we have the desire to act. Even if we base our expectations of ourselves on the assessments of others, we are still able to achieve our goals. The difference is that if we default to the expectations of others, we have abdicated control. We are externally motivated. We pedal a Skinner Box constructed by someone else. The long-term effect is that it reinforces the habit of responding to the control of others. If we are to escape the box we have to know how it is constructed, and that takes something you can probably guess by now: Self-knowledge.

Vocational Training

Vocational training without a counter-balancing educational perspective is a sure way to lose the ability to be self-determining. For example, if you are an equipment operator, and you learn how to operate a new piece of equipment but fail to educate yourself regarding its future utility, you may suddenly find yourself out of a job when its usefulness is ended. On the other hand, if you have properly educated yourself in the field of its use, then you will have the time necessary to turn its obsolescence into an advantage, either by learning to operate the equipment that will replace it or by finding another job in anticipation of losing the one you have.

If you are sufficiently educated in your field, you might have the opportunity to inform your company of a state-of-the-art replacement or an alternative cost-effective solution. In such a case your efforts at offsetting your training with an educational perspective would have an added value to your employer, affording you greater control over your life. Regardless of where your job lies within a company, when you trust a part of your life to an organization, you have an obligation to yourself and others to know where that organization is going, what effect its product or service will have on society, and whether or not it is likely to succeed or fail in its mission. Anything less and you offer control over your life to others. Giving away control over one's life is not always a bad thing, as long as one retains the means to get it back, but it is often not an easy thing to do in a rapidly changing work environment.

Using Educational Institutions to Your Advantage

In *Zen and the Art of Motorcycle Maintenance*, author Robert M. Pirsig wrote of the "real University." He said:

The real University has no specific location. It owns no property, pays no salaries and receives no material dues. The real University is a state of mind. It is that great heritage of rational thought that has been brought down to us through the centuries and which does not exist at any specific location. It's a state of mind which is regenerated throughout the centuries by a body of people who traditionally carry the title of professor, but even that title is not part of the real University. The real University is nothing less than the continuing body of reason itself.

In addition to this state of mind "reason," there's a legal entity which is unfortunately called by the same name but which is quite another thing. This is a nonprofit corporation, a branch of the state with a specific address. It owns property, is capable of paying salaries, of receiving money and of responding to legislative pressures in the process.

But this second university, the legal corporation, cannot teach, does not generate new knowledge or evaluate ideas. It is not the real University at all. It is just a church building, the setting, the location at which conditions have been made favorable for the real church to exist.

Confusion continually occurs in people who fail to see this difference, and think that control of the church buildings implies control of the church. They see professors as employees of the second university who should abandon reason when told to and take orders with no backtalk, the same way employees do in other corporations.

They see the second university, but fail to see the first.

With all the negative effects that I have attributed to pedagogy you might expect me to denounce traditional colleges and universities and advise you to avoid them, but I will not. On the contrary, I believe that for today's adults, colleges and universities are fantastic resource centers. When you become genuinely interested in learning for its own sake, colleges and universities become treasure houses filled with never-ending rewards. Each time I walk onto a college or university campus I get a feeling of exhilaration.

How you feel about learning institutions as an adult depends on what you want from them. For the adult interested in self-education, the first university that Robert Pirsig wrote about can be a place of immense reward and satisfaction. It is in fact Self-University. But if you are interested only in seeking credentials, the pleasure of the first university will be eroded by the second, and the reward that you come away with will be only a fraction of what could have been yours.

I would not talk you or anyone out of attending a college or university, especially if it is within your means to do so easily. But I would suggest that you thoroughly examine your reasons and understand them completely before proceeding. In his book *The Three Boxes of Life*, Richard Bolles lists ten likely reasons for returning to school. He calls them "The Ten Purposes of Education." They are:

1. I want to enlarge my mental, emotional, and/or spiritual horizons.
2. I want to learn how to learn and how to think clearly.
3. I want to learn the virtues and the limits of knowledge; what we can know, and what we can not know.
4. I want to learn reading, or writing, or arithmetic.
5. I want to develop myself in relationship to others.
6. I want to learn how to cope with change and with constancy—especially when there is too much or too little of either.
7. I want to find further "food" for
   a. my mind, and/or
   b. my heart, and/or
   c. my will
8. I want to have a chance to meet other people (with similar interests).
9. I want to pick up/polish up the required skills that I need for
   a. a particular field or line of work in which I need accreditation,
   b. a particular job (present, or contemplated),
   c. a particular role that I have, or want to have, in life.
10. I want to develop my philosophy of life.

Now there's good news and bad news. The good news is better than good; it's fantastic. It is simply that nine of these ten purposes of education are very inexpensive. Nine are governed by Robert Pirsig's first university, the continuing body of reason. And the walls of this first university are easily penetrable by anyone. The price of tuition for Self-University is desire. The divisions of subject matter, the narrow thinking that restricts one subject from another, are dying of necessity. The complexity of the Nineties demands synthesis, and synthesis demands objectivity. When we pursue knowledge objectively there are no restrictions on subject matter.

The bad news is that most people choose purpose number nine, to the exclusion of all the others, when making a decision about school. If number nine is your first choice, and you enter college without a genuine desire for knowledge, you can be said to be enrolled in Credential-University instead of Self-University. Credential-University is expensive. A large section of Part Four of this book is devoted to the problems associated with purpose number nine.

Enrollment in Self-University

Pursuit of knowledge from the continuing body of reason is a person-centered enterprise. You are the only one who knows what your learning experience has been to date. Only you know what you perceive that you know. When you decide to push away from the shore and embark on a journey in search of knowledge, remember that you must continually be able to distinguish between belief and understanding in order to keep from getting lost. Many people who begin this journey make the critical mistake of requiring belief to be a condition of understanding.[3] If you do this, your ship will sail in circles and you will never get far from shore. It is a mistake often made when people use religion as a substitute for thinking.

In his book, *Understanding Philosophy*, philosopher James Feibleman wrote, "When belief is first freed from the chains of faith, it runs wild as though drunk with its new liberty. All sorts of beliefs, all kinds of mysticism, are accepted in one quarter or another. But gradually sanity reasserts itself, and a new set of principles is adopted. The new ones this time were to be based on reason and fact."

A good way to begin an objective search for knowledge from Self-University is to consult the studies of human life stages and compare where you are with relation to those who have gone before. For example, if you are approaching middle age, do you feel the pull of "generativity" that Erikson used to describe how middle-aged people begin to concern themselves with the next generation? Do you feel compelled to give something back to society? Ideas about where to begin will occur naturally.

Another key to developing a natural intrinsic personal reward from the process of learning is to recognize the need for background knowledge. E.D. Hirsch Jr. wrote about background knowledge in his book *Cultural Literacy*. Simply put, this is the knowledge and information that those who produce "media" assume the receiver already has. Background knowledge is essential to understanding, but seeking it is not always a self-reinforcing activity. The same is true with learning to read. The reinforcing aspect of reading does not come until one has already learned to read well. Likewise, background knowledge is not always interesting, but in many cases it is necessary for the sake of understanding what is. The book *Cultural Literacy* is a good place to assess the breadth of your own background knowledge, and it is a good guide for deciding which areas you might need to develop. Another good book on this subject is *An Incomplete Education* by Judy Jones and William Wilson.

When you engage in your own efforts at self-education you cannot always count on family and friends for support. You may even be surprized to find some direct opposition. People who are stalled in their own development at a station of relative comfort will often feel threatened when those who are close to them seem to be moving in new directions. My own sense of this causes me to conclude that such people are subconsciously aware that their self-image is dependent upon the feedback they get from others, so they intuitively know, even if not consciously, that if others improve themselves they will be seen as somehow less adequate than before. For this reason, you should realize that is often easier to find people who are already working toward their own improvement than it is to persuade your friends to join you. And it is important to acknowledge that your associates are capable of influencing your actions. As Joseph Campbell, teacher and author said, "Vital people vitalize."

A Time For Synthesis

Western science is based on the principles of Newtonian physics (classical physics according to Isaac Newton) and Cartesian philosophy (the philosophy of Rene Descartes). The Newtonian principle simply stated means that we have a mechanical view of the world, and we assume that all phenomena can be reduced to simple formulae which, when identified, will reveal their basic blueprint, e.g., Newton's theory of gravity. Descartes held the view that mind and body are distinctly separate. These fundamental principles of Western thought are often referred to as mechanistic, reductionist philosophies.

There is an emerging shift in modern thinking that suggests the contrary. It doesn't prove that Western science is wrong, but offers other ways of looking at fundamental questions. This growing consciousness in the West rejects mechanistic reductionism in favor of a view that suggests a holistic connectedness in a universe whose existence is not hierarchical as we have assumed, but is instead a web of cosmic interrelatedness.

In the West we have been culturalized to assume that we grow from a state of dependence as children to an ultimate state of autonomy as adults. Yet, if we examine our lives through the lenses of scientific observation, we cannot help but see the profound nature of our interdependence. If we use this same posture for examining the natural world, we find similar relationships. Human perception based the hierarchical theory of relationships on the premise of human superiority, yet the totality of human existence may still prove to be but a flash in the pan.

Holistic thinking synthesizes Western science with Eastern philosophy and mysticism. It suggests a cultural transformation to repair our pathogenic policies (discussed in Chapter Six) by seeking and acknowledging holistic relationships, and thus eliminating the traditional void of human self-knowledge. In a simplistic sense the process is comparable to the reconciliation of opposites. For example, if we apply the premise to man/woman we are able to elicit the best qualities of each. If we examine heaven and earth, sickness and health, liberal and conservative, love and hate, work and leisure, with such synthesis we begin to gain insight into balance. In doing so we are able to apply E.F. Schumacher's "human face to technology."

At the edge of science there is a concept called "bootstrap physics," which postulates that there are no fundamental blueprints or basic building blocks which we can use to describe all phenomena. But, on the contrary, there is only a dynamic interconnectedness in a cosmos where the consistency of patterns and relationships determines the nature of the whole.

In the preface of his book, *The Tao of Physics*, theoretical physicist and systems theorist, Fritjof Capra, wrote:

> I was sitting by the ocean one late summer afternoon, watching the waves rolling in and feeling the rhythm of my breathing, when I suddenly became aware of my whole environment as being engaged in a gigantic cosmic dance. Being a physicist, I knew the sand, rocks, water, and air around me were made of vibrating molecules and atoms, and that these consisted of particles which interacted with one another by creating and destroying other particles. I knew also that the earth's atmosphere was continually bombarded by showers of "cosmic rays," particles of high energy undergoing multiple collisions as they penetrated

the air. All this was familiar to me from my research in high energy physics, but until that moment I had only experienced it through graphs, diagrams, and mathematical theories. As I sat on that beach my former experiences came to life; I "saw" cascades of energy coming down from outer space, in which particles were created and destroyed in rhythmic pulses; I "saw" the atoms of the elements and those of my body participating in this cosmic dance of energy; I felt its rhythm and I "heard" its sound, and at that moment I knew that this was the Dance of Shiva, the lord of Dancers worshiped by the Hindus.

Through the process of my own self-education I have come to recognize similarities in the works of many authors who seem to be saying the same thing but in different ways and in varying degrees. John Naisbitt (*Megatrends*), Alvin Toffler (*The Third Wave*), Marilyn Ferguson (*The Aquarian Conspiracy*), E.F. Schumacher (*Small Is Beautiful*), Robert M. Pirsig (*Zen and the Art of Motorcycle Maintenance*), Willis Harman (*Global Mind Change*), Buckminster Fuller (*Critical Path*), and Fritjof Capra, again, in *The Turning Point*, though diverse in style and message, seem to be traveling in the same direction—they have each detected if not a paradigm shift, at least a need for one, a cultural transformation, a call for humanistic values and a rise in human consciousness that may allow for a better world.

The rejection of establishment values in the Sixties followed by the self-introspection of the Seventies has, I believe, brought many people to a similar posture of synthesis. I believe it is a natural result for those engaged in the fascination of "self" to eventually discover a genuine connectedness with others and thus the true nature of interdependence.

I am reluctant to associate the authors mentioned above with the term New Age because of the debris the term New Age thinking has picked up in its course, but I feel it is necessary to make a slight connection in order to make sense of current thinking. I quoted James Feibleman earlier where he wrote of belief freed from faith as being drunk with liberty. Such is true today as Western philosophy embraces that of the East. But those who fail to examine their relationship with authority never completely sober up. They trade one form of allegiance for another. They bounce from astrology (which allows for a reality selected by the observer) to channeling (total faith in the pronouncements of self-appointed gurus who claim to be talking through ancient spirits). They do not think and reason for themselves. Their greatest intellectual efforts are not deciding what to believe but whom. There are many seductive theories which differ dramatically with conventional Western beliefs—many worthy of careful consideration—but a major thesis of this book is that to examine new theories does not require abandonment of reason, or a surrender to yet another external authority.

Summary

When we set out to discover truth we have to develop a method for evaluating knowledge. It means we must be able to extract objectivity out of what is culturally accepted as "common sense," but may in fact be cultural bias. When we develop a personal bias for objectivity we lay the foundation necessary to enter the continuing body of reason. In time we learn that self-directed inquiry is a perpetually empowering experience. When we compare Eastern and Western cultures, and reconcile what we discover with our own dissonant experiences, we are able to understand the bona fide nature of global interdependence. If we can remember what it is like "not to know" long enough to forgive others who fail to meet our cultural expectations, we may have the opportunity to help them empower themselves through the vast proliferation of learning media available today.

Finally, if you have the opportunity, the desire and the means to a college education, then you should pursue it with all the energy and enthusiasm you can muster. Enter the Credential-University with a mindset for truth and objectivity, and you will be assured the full measure of the real University. But if you do not have the means or desire to return to full-time formal learning, there is no reason to feel inadequate. If college credentials are not important to you but knowledge is, you can go further and faster by entering the continuing body of reason. The price of tuition for Self-University is desire. Your degree is a better life.

Part III

CHAPTER EIGHT

Understanding Credentialism

Laches. *Well but, Socrates; did you never observe that some persons, who have had no teachers, are more skillful than those who have, in some things?*
Socrates. *Yes, Laches, I have observed that; but you would not be very willing to trust them if they only professed to be masters of their art, unless they could show some proof of their skill or excellence in one or more works.*
—from Plato's Dialogue, "Laches, or Courage"
as Socrates addresses the problem of credentialism

Proof of competence was a problem for the ancients and it is still a problem today. We have made little progress in two thousand years.

The half life of "facts" (the time in which we can depend upon the assertions we perceive to be true) in leading-edge disciplines is falling fast; for some it is less than three years. Why, then, do we allow the demonstration of an ability to use short term memory as primary evidence of competence? Why are we grade motivated instead of knowledge motivated? Why do we allow businesses to use degrees as personnel screening devices when the work to be performed has little to do with the degree? Why is there so little agreement among educators about curriculum? Why do we allow doctors to be tenured for life when knowledge in the field of medicine is doubling every seven years?[1] Is it any wonder that businesses can find little correlation between a worker's academic performance and his work performance? Is it any wonder that college is becoming more like business and businesses more like college?

Establishing credentials should be as easy as proving competence. And proof of competence should consist of more than proof of attendance and the ability to adapt. As already observed, adaptation by some students is achieved by learning how to circumvent the grading system. Theoretically, the credentialing system now in place is supposed to minimize public risk from injury by the incompetent, but more often than not it acts to protect the incompetent. It does so by franchising the professions so that they and their credentialing institutions are free of competition and scrutiny. The rise in medical malpractice suits is just one of the examples of the problems with certification. Some of the lawsuits are frivolous and some are from unscrupulous patients trying to take advantage of unfortunate circumstances, but some are filed as a result of blatant incompetence on the part of the attending physician.

Use and Misuse of Credentials

The wealthy use the credentialing system as a means of maintaining social advantage. A college degree is but a part of the inheritance bestowed on their young to ensure their place in the social hierarchy.[2] A credential from an Ivy League school is an economic asset, regardless of whether or not the recipient learned anything.[3]

We know that grades are not an adequate indicator of future performance, but the student with financial means can use the school's reputation and his grade point average as a way of exhibiting superiority. If he has good grades, so much the better. A "B" average at a school with a "reputation" is thought to be better than an "A" at a lesser-known school. This process reinforces the franchise of the credentialing institution whose success does not depend as much on the quality of a post graduate student's achievement as it does on how many students are in school and how long they stay. If faculty administrators were really concerned about the quality of education that a degree from their institution represented, they would insist that degrees in rapidly changing fields expire automatically if the holder failed to stay current.[4]

The premium society places on degrees denies our practical experience with education. Instead of acknowledging the value of "experience" and "fluid" intelligence and insisting on a return to rationality in adulthood, our silence and continued participation perpetuates the myth that the only real learning takes place in academic institutions. In *Deschooling Society*, Ivan Illich wrote:

> Certification now tends to abridge the freedom of education by converting the civil right to share one's knowledge into the privilege of academic freedom, now conferred only on the employees of a school. To guarantee access to an effective exchange of skills, we need legislation which generalizes academic freedom. The right to teach any skill should come under the protection of freedom of speech. Once restrictions on teaching are removed, they will quickly be removed from learning as well.

We allow a societal structure to exist based, at least in part, on counterfeit credentials. The possession of a degree is not an adequate indicator of superior performance. Indeed, it's not even proof of competence. How many times have you heard people talk about having an opportunity to "use their degree?" Not the knowledge they have gained, but the degree itself, as if it were capable of operating independently. There is even a book titled *Putting Your Degree To Work*. The degree is spoken of not as an intrinsic part of ability derived from the learning experience, but rather something of extrinsic value that has been purchased. Not having a credential implies that a person is somehow inadequate. There are people who would argue that the whole point of learning is to overcome inadequacy by becoming adequate, and they would be correct. But if the process of learning carries a negative conditioning because the external need for a credential is more important than the learning, then it is not self-reinforcing. Where possible, learning should be a self-reinforcing experience worthy for its own sake; otherwise it is not likely to continue.[5]

In a 1986 report by The Carnegie Foundation for the Advancement of Teaching, President Ernest L. Boyer said:

> America's higher education system remains the envy of the world, but the undergraduate college, the very heart of higher learning, is a troubled institution. Driven by careerism and overshadowed by graduate and professional education, many of the nation's colleges and universities are more successful in credentialing than providing a quality education for their students.

In spite of what we know about the ineffectiveness of today's credentialing system, the process of credentialism is growing. At least for the near future credentials are becoming more important as a means of access to opportunity. Today's degrees have no standard meaning. They imply general study in an area for a particular period of time.[6] As the scramble for degrees escalates, there is less to indicate what to expect from the recipient. Business leaders' experience with employees supports their argument that colleges and universities are better at passing out degrees than educating students.

Many degrees are, in fact, counterfeit currency. Forty-three percent of today's undergraduate students say that many students graduate by beating the system.[7] And what happens to these students? Are they exposed in the marketplace and weeded out to make way for someone who is competent? Probably not. They are more likely to use their learned technique at beating the educational system as a tool for surviving in the corporation. The two institutions, after all, are very much alike. The behavior learned in the first is used in the second because it is the substance of survival.

Hundreds of today's jobs require skills that bear no relationship whatsoever to the degree requirements requisite for obtaining them. The result is a hierarchy in the workplace that often makes little sense. In many cases an incredible mismatch exists between job duties and the worker's ability to perform them. We have managers who can't manage, attorneys who can't conduct a law suit well enough to keep themselves from being sued, engineers who design more flaws in structures and systems than quality, and physicians whose patients would have been better off untreated. But they are all "qualified."

There are also major inequities in pay throughout the workplace. People are supposed to be paid in direct relationship to their contribution—at least that's how the theory goes. But being paid according to one's contribution is not nearly as common an occurrence as we have been culturized to believe. How many secretaries and clerks do you know who are better managers than their bosses? Some of them actually run the business, but their contribution is rarely acknowledged and they are seldom compensated commensurate with their effort. If you point out these inequities in an organization, managers will simply laugh and assure you that such appearances are illusionary and do not reflect reality. And besides, the people who you proposed were really running things "are not qualified." In situations where a subordinate is actually running things, managers often maintain superiority by using their position to access privileged information. In other words, they withhold just enough vital information to keep their subordinates off balance, so that they can be seen as wise and savvy in the business world.

In *The Third Wave*, author Alvin Toffler wrote about the importance of the "law of first price" in establishing the price for natural resources in world trade. This would be demonstrated in an instance where a price would be determined for a new commodity, such as oil or coal. In the beginning, because the product was new, there would be no competition; there would not yet be a market and it would likely hold little value in its native land. In many cases the first fixed price for a raw resource would bear no resemblance to its real value relative to its abundance, but would in fact be set arbitrarily low.

The same principle has held for the job market, particularly in the case of women. Many of the jobs held by women today are a result of a demand that began during the war in the early Forties. With the war effort the demand for secretaries and clerical workers increased dramatically. The salaries set for those jobs bore no relationship to the difficulty required to perform them or to the number of women available. They were set in deference to men and society's value judgment as to the role of the male breadwinner, on the assumption that the woman's income would be "supplemental" (questionably valid then, certainly not valid today). The salaries for these jobs bear the same disparity today, even though the complexities and difficulties of many of these jobs surpass those required to perform the bosses' jobs.

Thousands of people in the U.S. workplace hold positions because they are "qualified." Never mind that they cannot perform, they are "qualified." Once identified as such, it's a characteristic that is hard to shake. Most job descriptions are written by people performing yet another job. If we don't know what it takes to perform a job, how do we know how much it should pay? At best these descriptions are an approximation of reality. At worst, they don't even remotely resemble the skills or qualifications required to perform the job described.

The mismatch between job description and the work to be performed gets worse as the job's level of complexity and discretion increases. Only a small portion of jobs in the future are likely to fall in this category because of the nature of technology—even though it is becoming more sophisticated, it actually requires fewer people to participate. But the tendency to upgrade entry-level requirements will escalate because there will be more college graduates requiring jobs than jobs requiring degrees. The result will be a rise in requirements so that colleges continue to act as employment screening agencies. Ronald Dore, author of *The Diploma Disease*, argues that the reason qualifications are allowed to escalate is that those with the authority to hire are victims of the widespread myth that formal education improves people. Hiring educated people implies getting more for one's money.[8] Dore refers to the process as "educational inflation." About qualifications, he writes:

> In the process of qualification . . . the pupil is concerned not with mastery, but with being certified as having mastered. The knowledge that he gains, he gains not for its own sake and not for constant later use in a real life situation—but for the once-and-for-all purpose of reproducing it in an examination. And the learning and reproducing is all just a means to an end—the end of getting a

certificate which is a passport to a coveted job, a status, an income. If education is learning to *do* a job, qualification is a matter of learning in order to *get* a job.

The difference is a difference in what is now fashionably called the "hidden curriculum." What the educator is saying implicitly—and sometimes explicitly—to his pupils is: "learn this or you will not become a good doctor, a skillful carpenter, a fully-developed human being, a good useful citizen; you will not know how to *earn* your living, you will not be able to appreciate the higher pleasures of art or poetry." What the qualifier says to his pupils is: "learn this or you will not get the chance to be a doctor or a carpenter; nobody will *give* you a living." The first appeals to the inner standards of conscience and promises self-achieved fulfillment; the second invokes external arbiters, threatens exclusion, evokes anxiety. The first preserves the teacher-pupil relation as complete in itself; the second makes both dependent on the tyranny of the examiners.

The race for credentials is likely to get worse before technological systems are produced that will help qualify people for jobs on the basis of what they can do, rather than what they have been exposed to. Such an improvement will happen for two reasons. First, technology will make it possible, and second, as can be clearly seen in our society, a great need exists for this change. Currently it is not in the financial interest of educational institutions to quickly empower students; it is, however, in their interest to keep students enrolled for longer and longer periods of time. Once a relationship is established between a school and a profession, the school has an economic interest in protecting it. This situation will also change when technological methods are readily available that demonstrate people's competence versus their exposure to learning.

Objective screening for competence will occur only when it is demanded by a self-educated public. For as long as degrees and certificates are allowed to be used as tickets of admission instead of demonstrated competence, institutions will continue to operate as ticket agents. How rational a process is it when institutions argue about increasing knowledge requirements and yet justify a system which concludes formal education when the student is still a young adult?

In *Deschooling Society*, Ivan Illich wrote:

A degree always leaves its indelible price tag on the curriculum of its consumer. Certified college graduates fit only into a world which puts a price tag on their heads, thereby giving them the power to define the level of expectations in their society. In each country the amount of consumption by the college graduate sets the standard for all others; if they would be civilized people on or off the job, they will aspire to the style of life of college graduates.

The university thus has the effect of imposing consumer standards at work and at home, and it does so in every part of the world and under every political system.

Cooperation and Competition

In primitive societies the survival of the community was dependent upon cooperation. This fact may contribute to the seemingly natural attraction some people have for communism, because we can all trace our ancestral roots to a form of communism if we go back far enough. Communism is an adequate system for a survival society, but it takes the dynamics of individual initiative to reach beyond survival. For society to flourish we need both cooperation and competition. Today we grossly misunderstand the respective utility of each.

In nineteenth-century America, Darwin's *Origin of the Species*, interpreted by Herbert Spencer and William James, justified practically every human endeavor on the basis of competition and survival of the fittest. Spencer interpreted Darwin to claim that the strongest individuals were best fit for survival. Darwin, however, meant species, not individuals. This misinterpretation of Darwin resulted in what has come to be known as "social Darwinism": "Might makes right," or it is OK for the strong to use force in the subordination of the weak. Darwin's *Origin of the Species* is a good example of how cultures bend perception to suit their own version of reality. Darwin's book, as interpreted by the German philosopher Hegel, laid the groundwork for Nazism, while Karl Marx used it to support his views for dialectic materialism (communism). So in effect, Darwin's work has provided justification for capitalism, Nazism, and communism.[9] With the advent of industrialization, we modeled our schools after our factories, using the capitalist philosophy and letting the struggle of classroom competition substitute for teaching excellence.

Imagine what society would be like today if the learning experience were based on cooperation instead of competition and isolation. Formal education would be radically different. Learning would be an enjoyable experience, but more importantly it would be the foundation of positive socialization.

Researchers have a large body of evidence suggesting that

learning based on cooperation is far superior to competitive-based learning.[10] We appear to have accepted the effectiveness of competitive education on the basis of authority. Intuitively we should have known better. Sibling rivalry is adequate evidence that the very young will compete for attention and acceptance, but we know that the success of the family is more effectively based on cooperation than competition.

Learning is an individual experience. In a competitive environment the individual is sacrificed as an expense necessary for the good of the group. But if learning is based on cooperation, the individual can be empowered at the pleasure of the group. Cooperative learning is pure synergy. Effective teaching can turn rivalry into cooperation. With cooperative learning there are no defensive barriers to overcome. Everyone benefits. The students who catch on quickly can reinforce their own learning by helping others. Teachers are the first to admit that the process of teaching increases their own knowledge by raising their understanding to more sophisticated levels. Students having difficulty can catch on much faster without the added stress of feeling inferior. Students would learn group problem solving as a routine behavior. This one practice incorporated into the workplace would be revolutionary. Seeking input from associates in the decision-making process would be an entirely natural thing to do. Think of the synergistic effect within a corporation if everyone openly cooperated instead of jockeying for personal advantage and position. Such an organization would be truly dynamic. If cooperative learning were a natural method of socialization, people would not try to hide their lack of knowledge from others, as is the norm in today's organizations. Nor would they try to bluff their way through areas in which they have little knowledge—often with catastropic results.

If we studied today's organizations as though they were football teams, we could observe the lack of cooperation that actually exists. We would see that linemen routinely step aside so their own quarterback can be sacked; we would also see the linemen tripping their own ball carriers. And sometimes, believe it or not, the quarterback in today's corporation, even passes the ball so that it cannot be caught. All these acts stem from the fact that in the workplace we preach teamwork and practice individuality. Competition between companies is a great way to produce better products and services, but if competition causes sabotage within each company then we are not getting our money's worth.

Learning based on cooperation would in some ways approximate today's adult practice of networking, which is proving its effectiveness. Yet it's ironic that, because we have been taught the necessity of competition, we regard cooperative learning as a means of cheating.[11]

In order to be effective in a credentialed society, it is necessary to thoroughly understand the way we evaluate ourselves for evidence of competence. We live in a credential-motivated society; many students who manage to receive "A's" inevitably face boredom and disgust with the process that is said to be learning. It cannot be helped. Since each exercise is merely a means to get to the next, the journey cannot in most cases be enjoyed for its own sake.[12] There is not time to take learning paths that look promising purely for the sake of curiosity or exploration.

Some students receive low grades not because they are unintelligent, but because they have a low threshold for boredom. Disgusted with "learning" they begin to follow the path of least resistance. Without the ability to be self-determining, the student learns not to care. Learning loses its intrinsic value.

Robert M. Pirsig wrote of a hypothetical "degreeless" society in *Zen and the Art of Motorcycle Maintenance*. He used an example of a student working for a while in a mechanical shop before returning to school. He wrote:

> So he would come back to our degreeless and gradeless school, but with a difference. He'd no longer be a grade-motivated person. He'd be a knowledge-motivated person. He would need no external pushing to learn. His push would come from inside. He'd be a free man. He wouldn't need a lot of discipline to shape him up. In fact, if the instructors assigned him were slacking on the job he would be likely to shape them up by asking rude questions. He'd be there to learn something, would be paying to learn something and they'd better come up with it.
>
> Motivation of this sort once it catches hold, is a ferocious force, and in the gradeless, degreeless institution where our student would find himself, he wouldn't stop with rote engineering information.

Grades and Testing

Albert Einstein was not an "A" student. His theory of relativity which revolutionized modern science was not an academic project, but the product of self-directed inquiry. Einstein refused to subordinate his natural curiosity for an identity associated with a letter grade. One of the most harmful effects of the grading system is that it discourages the search for self-knowledge. Students are so insecure in their struggle to compete that they hesitate to seek any knowledge about themselves that doesn't support an inflated ego.[13] Self-knowledge is essential to effective learning and the ability to affect one's environment. Imagine how different our experience in school would have been if a reverse grading system had been used to assess the effectiveness of teachers based on the scores attained by students. For example, if tests were used only as a means of determining what remained to be taught, thus evaluating the teacher and not the student.

Tests can be a valuable aid in determining what remains to be taught or what may have been misunderstood, but they are inadequate as an indicator of the student's future ability. We are so grade oriented that in many cases we never look back after the tests to see what we may have failed to understand. After all, the whole purpose of the exercise was to receive a grade. How can we possibly assume that we are becoming competent if we proceed from simple to more complex problems (which is not necessarily the way we learn) with a false sense of understanding? It's possible to answer 90 percent of the questions on a test correctly and still misunderstand the subject totally, as reflected by the nature of the questions that we missed. (In all my experience with traditional educational methods, I can only recall a couple of incidents where a teacher seemed genuinely concerned and reviewed the tests we had taken with sufficient care to clear up any misunderstandings we might have incurred from the incorrect answers.)

Much of the self-help material on the market today promising to help students prepare for tests devotes entire sections to "guessing" the right answers. A competence-based society guessing right answers is the ultimate insult to human intelligence and objectivity. Air Force training for key-turners in missile silos has been documented on film. In that film the instructor coaches trainees to make "educated guesses" on tests by offering psychological insight into the people who write the questions. Wouldn't it be better if these people were qualified for their jobs because of what they knew instead of their ability to guess?

Testing in today's system of forced ranking produces anxiety similar to the "fight or flight" response. Stress has been shown to have a negative effect on the learning process; as stress increases, the learning system is in favor of shutting down.[14] The pressure to get good grades diminishes the enthusiasm for learning. Being condemned on the basis of a grade point has the effect of hammering one's self-esteem into an admission of diminished capacity to function in society. Add contemptible controlling rewards like gold stars, and the student begins to see himself as limited; he becomes humiliated about his capacity to affect his environment. Being measured by such standards causes the student to adopt the same standards for measuring himself and others. Soon he believes that if something can't be measured it's not considered to be important. Ivan Illich, author of *Deschooling Society*, described the term for the experience as "being schooled down to size."

Educators have found that students taking the S.A.T. tests often score higher than their grade history would suggest they should. Some say this is evidence that the students learned more than was perceived, but got poor grades because the information was not well presented. Perhaps the most important message gleaned from our experience with testing and being tested is that the whole purpose of education is nothing more than the preparation for the taking of yet more tests.

Testing is a natural human quality we seek intuitively, as long as we have not been adversely affected by the process in an external sense. We test our physical abilities constantly when we are young, and our desire to test our emotional limits is demonstrated by the fact that we are the only species on earth to scare itself on purpose. But many of us are so adversely affected by the process of being tested in the traditional sense that we do our best to avoid being tested. I believe that many people who express a fear of computers are really afraid of being tested and not measuring up. Imagining themselves sitting in front of a computer and puzzling over what to do next, they subconsciously perceive that their lack of speed in using the computer will betray their lack of intelligence and that they will be judged as having failed the test.

The process of self-education is free of grades and tests. It is based on cooperation. But we are still faced with offering proof of our competence if we expect to use the knowledge we have acquired in the workplace.

The Promotability Factor

Sometimes the greatest problem of credentialing occurs at the place where you work. The difficulty is demonstrating that you should be promoted. Organizations that continually fail to promote from within their own ranks often do so because of what I call the "white knight theory." Management in such organizations is usually fully aware of the talent they have on board and may even be highly impressed by it. But they hold a visceral belief that out there somewhere exists a "white knight," who if hired, will at once solve most of their problems. So they ignore the known talent already working for less within the company and gamble on the unknown. They are often disappointed. The new hire's armor is quickly pierced, and the white knight turns out to be just another soldier. But now there is a new problem, because the employees who were already on board perceive management to be unfair, incompetent, or both.

Management's role in assessing performance is by no means an easy task, and managers are fully aware that no matter what they do with respect to giving recognition by promotion they will be criticized. It has long been my observation that people within an organization expect that anyone who is promoted to a higher level should first be able to perform all subordinate tasks well. This, I would argue, is an assumption we picked up in school; that everything must be accomplished in linear fashion. This is often an unrealistic expectation. I would call this expectation a subliminal assessment that we make as managers without realizing it. We believe that there is no one on board who meets such standards, nor will there likely be anyone in the future who does, but we continue to search. The net result is that few people are promoted from within.

Consider the white knight theory in terms of cognitive dissonance and what its effect might be regarding job promotions and qualifications. Take, for example, the man who has gone to a great deal of expense and difficulty to obtain a college degree. When he is charged with naming the qualifications for a position similar to one that he himself holds (or has held in the past) and must choose between an entry-level hire or an internal promotion, he is faced with a dissonant decision. If he concludes that the type of educational experience that he himself has is unnecessary for the job, then he must consider that his own efforts at obtaining his degree were unnecessary. In such an instance it is easy to see how one can rationalize requirements that are out of line with reality.

Promotability is a word often used to justify promoting someone of lesser ability with credentials ahead of someone who has exceptional ability but lacks credentials. The rationale is, "Yes, we know that A is eminently qualified for this job, but B has credentials. Therefore B has the potential to rise higher in the organization; therefore B has promotability." If this is common practice in your organization, you may be better off somewhere else. It is a difficult mentality to combat. Such is often the rationale in organizations where people feel a strong need for protecting and justifying their actions (covering their behind). Promotability may, in fact, be a valid argument for survival in such organizations, because whoever promotes A does so at his own risk. If A blunders and is discovered to be without credentials, you can guess what happens to the person who authorized A's promotion. Promotability can become a self-fulfilling prophecy based solely on the assumption that there are people high on the ladder who will focus more on credentials than on the competence of those who are being considered for promotion. The psychology of promotability is strongest in rigid bureaucracies, and to fight it you must understand it. If you lack credentials in such an organization you must provide compelling evidence of your competence so as to lessen the risk to those who are willing to take a chance on you. In cases where the phenomenon of promotability is an ingrained part of corporate culture, it may be wise to recognize promotability as an opportunity to market your skills elsewhere, in which case your goal is simply to find a dynamic organization where competence is sought for its own sake.

To what degree this failure to promote competent people within their own organization affects the American work force would be hard to assess, but my guess is that there is an enormous negative effect in terms of cost and productivity. Thousands upon thousands of American workers perceive that their contribution will not be adequately rewarded because of their company's history of promotional practice. As a result, their best efforts are often reserved for a hobby or an off-work activity in which they perceive an internal locus of causality and feel a sense of self-determination.

My early work experience in the U.S. Marine Corps enabled me to witness firsthand many people who did not seem to be candidates for promotion, but who would, when promoted, surprise everyone and rise to the occasion of their new assignment. Imagine what the morale would be in the Marine Corps if, when it came time for promotions, Army and Navy personnel were brought in and awarded the positions.

If you have such a problem, it is often extremely difficult to keep the reality of the situation in perspective, because credentials, or the lack of them, can be used to justify almost anything. It has been my experience that whenever people are passed over for promotion, and someone else is supposedly more qualified, they almost always blame themselves for being underqualified. They are in effect using Ivan Illich's pedagogical ruler on themselves, once again, as they have learned to do.

If you are passed over for promotion when being promoted is

important to you, do everything you can to find out why. This is a very difficult assessment, and, in spite of your best efforts to discover the reason, you may be forced to guess. You may never learn the truth about why you were passed over, but you cannot deal effectively with problems you don't know about. Most managers will not even acknowledge that a "white knight" syndrome exists, let alone the possibility that they might be a victim of the phenomenon. And there might be other reasons to consider why you were passed over. Your work may be perceived as inadequate. You may in fact be incompetent. You may be the victim of a personality clash. Perhaps evidence of your talent is not known and management takes no responsibility for finding out.

Sometimes job qualifications for positions are written not because of what needs to be done, but to provide expertise in an area where the boss feels inadequate. You may have reason to suspect this, if you and others who perform similar jobs continually have great difficulty seeing the connection between the posted requirements for a job and what you perceive needs to be done.

It is not my intent to try to resolve all these problems here. Such a task would require a book in itself. You may be treated unfairly in the workplace in spite of anything you can do to prevent it, but on the other hand, you may be treated extremely well. The task here is to establish proof of competence, to document credentials which will be difficult to ignore, and thus improve your chances for equitable treatment in the future. (See Chapter Eleven: Creating Your Own Credentials.)

Opportunities

Today there is a crack in the armor of credentialism, and it appears that this vulnerability will be present through the turn of the century. This crack presents clear windows of opportunity for competent but uncredentialed people who recognize them as such. There are three major contributing factors. The first is the gap of technical know-how. Today many people are on the cutting edge of technological development simply because they are highly interested in the subjects in which they are engaged. They are self-taught. They are the people who took to computers like kids to McDonald's. Schools cannot keep up with people who are so engrossed and enthusiastic about their work. Managers are in many cases desperate for such people who have such an insatiable interest in their work that they literally exude solutions. I have even read of cases where managers of major computer manufacturing companies have talked some of their brightest young employees out of going to college in favor of on-the-job learning and development.

The second contributing factor is in the area of demographic considerations. Due to the low birth rate from 1965 to 1980, there are fewer young people available to enter the workplace at the entry level of employment. You may have heard it referred to as the "baby bust," and we will feel its effects in the workplace until the turn of the century. On the other end of the demographic scale we have the "baby boomers," those people born between 1946 and 1964. There are so many baby boomers, the competition is heating up for jobs in middle and upper management. Thus there are too few people at the entry level and too many near the top. The Nineties will be an interesting decade. Change will be rampant. Life for those in the fast lane will be chaotic. It will be a decade of both growth and disillusionment.

The third factor that offers opportunity for competent people without credentials is the fact that America's schools continue to turn out graduates who are, for all practical purposes, unemployable. They seriously lack the basic skills that enable a person to function in the workplace.

Ideally the Nineties could be a time when we "rethink" and "re-reason" work into a more rational, equitable perspective with the aid of the external forces of social demographics. The high demand for entry-level workers could push wages up for lower-level jobs, while the competition for jobs near the top could push wages down, making lower-level jobs more attractive for baby boomers. The result could be a more equitable method of compensation. People might gravitate toward positions for which they are best suited. We could design work to be more naturally self-reinforcing.

Just think for a moment: What jobs would you choose if money were not such a powerful consideration? Abraham Maslow argued that we are capable of making our most valuable contribution at the point where we are being the most selfish, but I would observe that most of us never get the chance, primarily because we are afraid to take it. We spend our lives jockeying for position in jobs that we are not suited for, because they afford a level of financial security that we are terrified to lose. The reason for understanding our needs, such as the "getting your ducks in a row" exercise in Chapter Four, is not to create a state of perpetual giddiness and happiness based on personal need gratification. Rather it is to become less intimidated by our perceived needs through understanding how they affect our behavior. If our tendency to avoid risk is dominated by an unnatural fear based on our need for security, then we have lost the ability to be self-determining. Most of us conduct our work lives as if we were walking a high wire far above the ground. When we gain our balance, we are afraid to move.

Matching Qualifications, People and Jobs

The process of finding the person best suited for a particular job mirrors our failure to establish enough cause and effect in the hiring process to approach the problem rationally. For example, when filling the position of school superintendent every community that I have ever lived in has made it a practice to pull out all stops in the search for the perfect candidate. The school board members meet and decide unanimously to search the "earth" for a new school superintendent. Magazine and newspaper ads are placed. Letters are sent out to prospective candidates and to educators who might know of the perfect applicant. Applications pour in, and in a frenzy of enthusiasm the school board members pounce upon the pile of resumes looking for Mr. or (rarely) Ms. Education. The candidates with the slickest resumes are called in for an interview, and with much ado a selection is made.

I have witnessed this exercise enough to know that it is a common practice all over America. This process results in mediocre schools. Common sense would suggest that we reverse the process. If such a fuss occurred when teachers were hired, emphasis would be where it should be—in the classroom, or as a boss of mine used to say "where the tire meets the pavement." Competition by school districts to get the best teachers would ensure that teacher salaries reach professional income status where they belong. If we were intelligent enough to place emphasis correctly, the job of school superintendent could be handled by any competent administrator. How often are students routinely inspired by the school superintendent? We know that the single greatest turnoff to great teachers is school administration, but we still allow our school systems to develop into hierarchical bureaucracies with the vague notion that great teaching can be motivated by a charismatic leader.

My intention here is not to rehash the problems of the educational system. My point is simply that even if our understanding of cause and effect were not so muddled, our process of selection is. At least two of the school superintendent pageants that I have observed have culminated in the firing of the individuals hired because it soon became obvious they were really inept. Not to be confused with educational reformers, these people were simply not what they seemed to be at all. One might be tempted to conclude that to stand out among credentialers, a top credentialer might have to be a master of disguise.

In his book, *Hold On, Mr. President*, White House news correspondent Sam Donaldson recounted an experience he once had with the late billionaire H.L. Hunt. Donaldson applied for a job with Hunt and was told by someone on Hunt's staff that he was a front runner for the position. During his interview with Hunt, Sam was asked how cheap he would work. Donaldson, trying to be accommodating, indicated that he would settle for what the job paid in order to get the opportunity. Hunt took the answer to mean that Donaldson had no sense of what he was worth and was therefore not likely to be worth much to his company. Donaldson didn't get the job. But I would argue that the loss wasn't his; it was Hunt's. Regardless of Sam Donaldson's reputation as a reporter, the continual attacks by his critics are testimony to the fact that he is a hard-working individual.

The ability of people to select other people for jobs is little more than a guessing game based on the education, experience, and values of the person doing the guessing. The perceived ability of many people to size up others with a simple one-hour interview loaded with one-liner hook questions is an exercise in personal delusion. There is no doubt that H.L. Hunt had keen insights and was indeed a shrewd businessman, but he was not an expert in the assessment of the potential of others. Not many of us are. Yet our whole system of hiring is based on the premise that the ritual of a simple interview is sufficient to find the right person for the right job.

The burden of finding what we are best at is ours and ours alone. It is not the responsibility of a personnel director or a boss, yet so many of us stumble about as if we are waiting for our talents to be discovered. Asked what we would really like to do with our lives we respond with a look of puzzlement and mild amusement as if we are being asked a question that has no determinable answer.

Consider the question of self-discovery for the purpose of livelihood in a political context. Regardless of whether we see ourselves as liberal or conservative, do we not have an obligation to put forth our best effort? Does not capitalism demand our best? Does our purpose matter? If we can make our ultimate contribution, as Maslow argued, only when we reach the point of maximum selfishness, then do we not have an obligation to find out what that is?

Self-University and the Workplace

Socrates, Freud, and Maslow were all strong advocates of the need to develop self-knowledge. And nowhere is the need for self-knowledge more obvious than in preparation for the workplace. In his book, *The Farther Reaches of Human Nature*, Maslow wrote:

> The ideal college would be a kind of educational retreat in which you could try to find yourself; find out what you like and want; what you are and are not good at. People would take various subjects, attend various seminars, not quite sure of where they were going, but moving toward the discovery of vocation, and *once they found it*, they could then make good use of technological education. The chief goals of the ideal college, in other words, would be the *discovery of identity*, and with it, the *discovery of vocation*.

Such a college is the fundamental idea for Self-University. Self-University is an attitude based on intelligent self-discovery and objectivity, an attitude that will serve you in coping with and conquering the frequent lack of objectivity at Credential-University. Never forget that the purpose of your education is to learn, even if you are forced into a credentialing process that considers actual learning unimportant. When you reach the genuine and natural level of objectivity that accompanies self-education, it becomes a part of your personality. There will be a perceptible difference in your resume. It comes across in a personnel interview. It is an internal perceived locus of causality. It is confidence.

There are many good methods for finding out where your strengths lie, where your skills are and what type of occupation you are best suited for (see Part Four.) However, your skills are not nearly as important as the attitude you take toward the process itself. Self-education/self-discovery is a life-centering, lifelong activity. It is the means for self-management. What better attribute can you offer an employer in addition to your obvious skills than the assurance that you are a self-managed individual?

In his book, *Managing The New Careerists*, author C. Brooklyn Derr identified five character traits that describe the salient desires of today's work force. They are: getting ahead, getting secure, getting free, getting high, and getting balanced. Getting ahead means moving up, climbing the ladder, making your mark. Getting secure means financial security and the recognition and respect of peers. Getting free means maximum control, autonomy, the ability to call your own shots. Getting high means high adventure and creativity, it means that you have acknowledged your need for novelty. Getting balanced, as it implies, is a means of obtaining and maintaining an equitable relationship among the first four. Which characteristic is the most important to you? How does the priority of these desires compare with "getting your ducks in a row"? Do you feel confident that your assessment would match the results of Brooklyn's test designed to reveal your preferences? If not, it might prove worthwhile to get the book and take the test.[15]

If you use self-education as a life-centering method by offsetting your vocational education with a liberal education, and by keeping your career and your role as a citizen in an equitable balance, then you will always maintain the empowerment for a degree of self-determination. Millions of us receive the measure of our worth as human beings almost solely from the feedback of our performance at work. We are what we do. We have taken the ruler with which we measured our perceived progress in school with us to the job. In doing so we diminish our ability to make a contribution because we are not sufficiently well-rounded to maintain a balanced perspective. We need the ability to view our work from points of view other that those related to the work itself. We also need to become comfortable with the fact that people have value as human beings totally independent of career.

As you pursue your vocation, remember the words of Buckminster Fuller in *Critical Path*:

> All of those who have attained high scholarly capability assure us that the only real education is self-education. They also say that this self-disciplining is most often inspired by great teachers who make it seem apparent that it will be excitingly worthwhile to take the trouble to bring oneself to apprehend and then comprehend variously pertinent data, phenomena, and derived principles. The intimate manuscript records of all the great self-educated individuals show that they discern intuitively when and what it is that they want to learn. Thereafter they arrange to do so by four main strategies. The first is by self-conducted experiments, if they are scientists. The second is by going to those live humans who have educated themselves from direct experiences. The third is to contact through books those who have discovered and learned but are now dead. Fourth, they sometimes have recourse to the esoteric and often exquisitely valuable information contained within the word-of-mouth information system relayed almost exclusively from generation to generation by the craftsman-artists.

We know intuitively that these methods of discovery are legitimate because we rely on them without giving them a second thought, yet they fall outside of the formal educational certification process. And because this is so, we come to view the process of certification as suspect without realizing why.

Summary

Establishing proof of competence in a reasonable manner has always been a problem. Educational certifications are sufficient grounds to only suspect competence, but not to expect it absolutely. There are many people with impressive credentials whose competence is also impressive, but there are also enough incompetents with credentials to render the credentialing process as suspect. This fact, combined with rapid change and intense competition, is an opportunity for the competent uncredentialed person to enter areas that have traditionally been off limits. To take advantage of the opportunity requires an understanding of the credentialing process, testing methodology, the employment scene, competition versus cooperation, and the imagination and creativity to offer compelling proof of your ability.

But most important is that you understand the credentialing process so as not to inhibit your own personal development. What would you want to do with your life if money were not such a pervasive consideration? If you become financially successful, must you stop learning?

CHAPTER NINE

The Possibilities of Tomorrow

*We are made wise not by the recollections
of our past but by the responsibility for our
future.*
— George Bernard Shaw

The implications of today's expanding technologies are underrated, overrated, misunderstood, maligned and, for the most part, ignored by Americans from every walk of life. Technology will not solve all the problems associated with being human. But it is short-sighted not to be excited about the possibilities of the future. Technology offers a multitude of scenarios. The fundamental principal that will ultimately prove our success or failure is the objective use of our collective intelligence. If we do not increase the education and reasoning ability of the average citizen substantially then we are in danger of being unable to sustain a democracy. We have begun to call ourselves a knowledge society, yet we hesitate to act like one.[1]

As our technological knowledge implodes and explodes exponentially, the responsibility that goes with its use increases likewise. We subscribe to the simple principle that we are a self-governing people, but the distance is growing at an alarming rate between science and the ability of the average citizen to understand its consequences. The results of our collective ignorance are becoming salient global issues. We have the precarious state of the ozone layer in the atmosphere, the rapid depletion of topsoil worldwide, the loss of tropical forests, the growing disparity between developed and underdeveloped countries, acid rain, poisoned ground water, and the general expeditious pollution of the environment. That we have responsibility for our actions is clear, but whether or not we will own up to such responsibility is not.

The ancient Greek philosophers who lived in a simple nontechnological world had a special contempt for the idea of participatory democracy. They believed that the ruling class should consist of an informed, educated aristocracy. They argued correctly that the ability to govern requires expertise, just as does any other profession. But the ancient Greeks were about as curious a group of people as have ever lived. They were driven by reason, truth and wisdom. Mistaking nature for nurture they believed some people were born to be slaves; slaves performed the work while the aristocracy contemplated.

We, on the other hand, live in a technologically complicated society where a few representatives cannot hope to govern intelligently without the participation of an informed electorate. Yet we seem to believe that everyone has a right to an opinion, no matter how uninformed. Only a minority of us maintain a sense of curiosity relative to the complexity of our environment. And, like the ancient Greeks, we have been fooled into thinking that by nature and not nurture some people are better than others. If this were not true, then we would not stand by and watch others die of starvation. We would like to think of ourselves as a more morally virtuous people than the ancients, but upon reflection it appears only that we have failed to achieve wisdom. We build machines and then become slaves to them ourselves, for unlike the ancients who lived in a simple world, we do not perceive ourselves to be "thinkers." Paradoxically, we live in an incredibly complex world and see ourselves as "doers."

Our technological future will be influenced in large part by demographics and geographical considerations. Values and societal orientations toward the future tend to follow characteristics such as age, education, experience, wealth, and ideology. Numerous scenarios about the near future will be based on the values and expectations of today's aging "baby boomers." This group of over 76 million will have a tremendous influence on the direction of the future, simply because they make up such a large part of the population, combined with the fact that they share common values and expectations. The study of "like" groups identified by demographic similarities (such as the VALS profiles described in Chapter Two), will become more focused in the future, as businesses speculate about group buying habits and as political groups look for the collective nerve centers of group motivation to learn how to exploit them. Matching current technological capability with the desires and expectations of a given population is a useful method of obtaining insightful glimpses of the future. It can also be a means for manipulation, if the process is not safeguarded by a self-educated citizenry.

Impact of Technology

Time and distance are continually being compromised. The electronic world is getting smaller. The price of telecommunications hardware is falling rapidly. Communications and information will soon replace natural fuels as the driving forces in the U.S. economy.

We will assume a relationship to information similar to that of our highways. We will use it, as we do our highways, without the necessity of owning them.

Man creates an artificial environment and then has to adapt to what he has built. If we are to increase our human potential commensurate with our technical ability, a monolithic intellectual utility will emerge from growth in the communications industry. If it does not, then we are likely to become a country sharply divided between the informed and the uninformed. In either case, the influence of technology demands a constant vigilance to determine who is master of whom or what. An introspective cultural assessment of human values must keep pace with technological change. Continual re-evaluation of technology should allow the emergence of a form of technology that's in concert with human dignity.

An electronically wired, sophisticated society will resist being understood by its creators, just as the national or world economy resists being understood by economists. It is a peculiarity of synergistic relationships that causes and effects are difficult or impossible to pin down.

Rapid technological change has an intensifying effect on the present. Intensification of the present translates to higher stress, which increases the likelihood that we will respond emotionally rather than rationally to impending change. To maintain equilibrium during such times, it is necessary to offset the destabilizing effects of change by developing a philosophical approach to the future. Developing a philosophy is merely the shaping of knowledge into a system for examination. Philosophy is the key to counterbalancing technology because it demands the freedom of inquiry. Technologists have a propensity for reducing all human activity to numeric value so that its worthiness can be measured. Philosophy assesses the methodology and objectivity of those who seek to measure.

Education and Technology

The prices of computer hardware and interactive learning equipment will be less expensive than transporting students to and from school and many adults to and from work. This new method of interaction will require a significant initial capital investment by the school systems, but it will be followed by a corresponding dramatic reduction in the cost of formal education and transportation costs.

At some point we will realize that we already have enough physical school facilities in place and that the use of telecommunications and the sharing of facilities will allow for high school during the day, college at night and student-faculty interaction twenty-four hours a day. If teachers or students are not available at the same time, assignments or communication can simply be stored for when that person "logs on" to the computer. In other words, there is no need to play telephone tag. It is inevitable that a monolithic electronic educational utility will evolve. Libraries will link up with educational institutions and become appendage learning centers. They may even become a source of accreditation. College and university enrollments will soar as the electronic campus emerges. Universities with a hundred thousand registrants will be common.

Local institutions will become national. National institutions will become global. The computer fused with CD ROM and CD interactive technology will cause the demise of pedagogy and the rise of self-directed learning. These developments will revolutionize learning, and the educational system will transform society.

Teachers will be celebrated and supported by technology, not replaced. Some educators argue that the personal equation (having a live teacher) is superior to the electronic media in education. But, as Buckminster Fuller said in *Critical Path*,

> What I've long observed in the moving picture world is millions and millions of human beings falling in love with female heroines or male heroes, though knowing only their photographic images cast upon a blank wall. All the "personal equation" was, and as yet is, transmitted probably a little more poignantly by electronics than would ever be feasible in ordinary, personal-contact life.

The professors and actors with great oratory skills and media presence will be a tool of the ordinary teacher, not a replacement. The proliferation of technological tools and sources of classroom learning aids will enable teachers to use their creativity and independence as never before. The power of the individual teacher, enhanced through technological assistance, will amount to the largest increase in productivity in decades. Teachers will be able to eliminate the negative effects of pedagogy through the use of interactive technology. Computers will allow the teacher to match the method of learning to the "need" of the student. Curriculum will be continually restructured and customized to cater to individual needs and rates of learning. Teacher boredom will be drastically reduced. The continual personal growth of teachers through the use of technologies will match the continual growth and sense of achievement of students. Teachers will live on the cutting edge of inquiry. Indeed, teachers and managers have an opportunity to revitalize the present by re-examining their roles in society.

In this environment, students will not be so severely affected by incompetent teachers because the tools of technology will offset the negative impact. Students will learn at their own pace, with their own learning style and on their own schedule. Student autonomy will reinforce the desire for self-directed inquiry and self-discovery. Paradoxically this ability to work autonomously ensures a natural tendency to participate in cooperative learning without any stigma associated with cheating. Students will be able to demonstrate their competence without being passed through mandatory time periods of initiation. The grade barriers will dissolve, so that students who can do higher level work than their corresponding age group will be allowed to do so. Credentials will expire, but the means to re-activate them will be swift in comparison with today's methods. The instant availability of data and the manipulative nature of word processing will likely lead to an increase in the use of verbalization as a means of testing and demonstrating knowledge. The ability to use synthesis, creativity and innovation will replace the demonstration of the ability to regurgitate trivial facts. Methods to review material studied in earlier years will be instantly available.

Educators and psychological health professionals face the monumental task of creating learning experiences that will compete with, or perhaps transcend entertainment. We refer to television as the entertainment industry and indeed, we make a conscious decision to be entertained, but we have not yet learned how to reach media equilibrium. The pervasiveness of television demands that we learn how. Television can be a source of information and learning, just as it can be a mind-numbing experience. It will become increasingly easier to compete and to cooperate with television as the level of literacy begins to show signs of significant improvement. The acquisition of knowledge increases the desire to know, especially when it can be done without the damaging side effects of pedagogy. A positive future will be a continuum ranging from the desire to know, to the rage to know.

The Next Big Bang

When writing was invented some scholars of the day, including Socrates, assumed it would lead to the ruination of human memory. Writing did indeed have a profound effect on how we use memory, but it gave us the option of vastly increasing the use of memory by creating more to remember. Writing also affected the way we assimilate and disseminate our knowledge—most notably, it led to the demise of oratory skills. For example, philosopher Herbert Spencer seldom consented to an interview because he felt that no man was "in person" equal to his book. But during the time of Socrates, Plato and Aristotle, the nature of discourse in education ensured that each person was in fact his own book. The process of writing led to the invention of the Gutenburg press and to the proliferation of books. Books became external memories that grew into libraries. The result was the "big bang" of knowledge, an explosion of media and an extension of human senses that continually gains force. With the arrival of the computer we now have a semblance of external minds at our fingertips. At some point in the future the contents of the world's libraries will be connected with the computer and the problems of copyright for intellectual property will be solved. This will be another "big bang," perhaps even more resounding than the first.

When the entire world is "on line" and the totality of human intellectual experience is accessible by a process as simple as a key word search, perhaps people will feel a sense of connectedness so acute that the concept of "bootstrap physics" discussed in Chapter Seven will be a foregone conclusion. When we reach such technological capability, the nature of our relationship with "news" will change. We will in effect become our own publishers by setting the specifications for what we wish to receive in the form of media news. Complaints about news media coverage will disappear as the control of viewing tips in favor of the viewer's selected interests.

Technology will permit us to live our lives in an intelligent environment, an environment to which we are physically and emotionally suited—one that supports our efforts to synthesize education, work, and leisure into parallel instead of linear or vertical activities. Communication technology will continually enhance the ability of individuals to be self-directing and to control their environments.

Networking and Empowerment

At the heart of a balance of power in a literate society is the potential power of networking. Networking through the use of mass telecommunications is, simply, self-directed people power: people connecting with people, similar and dissimilar interests sharing information and adding value. It is dynamically synergistic. Through the use of networks, individuals and groups can smash the hierarchical pyramids of bureaucracy in favor of instant, informed action. Each member of a network is a part of the whole as well as a part of the sum.

Each is part of the center, but the whole is not dependent upon the center, nor is any part indispensable to the whole. Networks contract and expand spontaneously, and are likely to be the greatest source of social transformation in the future. Marilyn Ferguson, author of the *Aquarian Conspiracy*, said, "Networks are the strategy by which small groups can transform an entire society."

Networking is decentralization by nature and empowerment by action. Networking encourages dissonance and debate. Networking inspires creativity and innovation. It is a natural human means of reaching for truth. Networking will shatter the preconceived notions of personal limitations with which we have become comfortable. Therefore, as a protection of democracy it is an absolute necessity that electronic communication not contribute to a worsening of the information gap between the informed and the uninformed. We must insist that the new technologies are made available to everyone. Indeed, communication technology should be a tool for closing the literacy gap. It will be necessary to parallel or replace the "right to work ethic" with a "right to know ethic." Paradoxically, technology has brought us to serious discussions about the possibility of downloading the human brain into a machine before most of us have learned to use it.

Robert E. Kelly, author of *The Gold Collar Worker*, wrote, "Knowledge management will be to the Nineties what energy management was to the Seventies." The massive manipulation of information in an electronically wired society will bring about profound changes in lifestyle. Changes for the better are possible, as are changes for the worse, but it is a mistake to expect that technology will wash away our problems in a wave of technological solutions. The future portends an increase in stress, competition and high risk for individuals and society that will threaten the very survival of democracy. To help people cope with stress induced by rapid technological change, technology must not only be user friendly, it must also be "psychologically friendly." Societal consequences must be weighed as the ability to induce rapid change increases exponentially. Computer technology has produced "computerphobia," a fear of the loss of control over the individual's life by machines. A psychologically friendly approach to technology will ensure that this fear of control is reversed in favor of a feeling of more control over one's life, not less.

Value Versus Activity

The same telecommunications system that offers a continuing education will revolutionize the way we work. A global business utility will offer the capability for forming electronic associations which are job-specific, and which dissolve when the job is completed. For example, an engineering firm may accept a design project through an electronic bidding process and then solicit subcontractors electronically. The process may be completed from bidding to final payment without the need for the parties to meet except via telecommunications.

Microelectronics adds an intelligence quotient to every type of product imaginable, or as Paul Hawken, author of *The Next Economy,* stated, the relationship of information to mass is increasing. The result is that we are continually doing more with less. We will apply the same ratio of technology to manufacturing that we did to agriculture. The result was not the destruction of farming, but the ability to feed the nation with less than two percent of the workforce.

The assumption of menial tasks by machines will eliminate some of the drudgery and dangers of work. Training for specific skills will be easy to access because it will be more economical than the alternative of unemployment. It is inconceivable that technologies capable of continually enhancing the quality of life will result in the destruction of society, unless we passively allow it to happen. Millions of us have boring, de-humanizing jobs. We should celebrate the opportunity to assume more meaningful work, and we would, if we knew what to look for. The only way to avoid the progression to more meaningful work is to deny that there is anything more meaningful to do.

Given the current state of the environment, public health, general welfare and quality of life in today's society, it's absurd to assume that humans don't have better things to do than perform the mindless work of machines. Paradoxically, jobs that permit a form of congruence with the natural environment, jobs that are cyclic, jobs that provide natural reinforcement and a sense of human connectedness with the earth offer little monetary reward, while jobs that have a long-term negative effect on the environment pay very well and are positions that command the respect of most people. Many of the so-called "service sector" jobs fall into the former category, the jobs in which people prepare and serve our food, clean our streets, carry off the garbage, nurse us back to health, teach our children, harvest our crops and a myriad of similar functions that make life livable. If these services were not performed, their importance would blind us to everything else. Yet many of these jobs do not command a living wage. If that were not bad enough, we have a propensity to use punitive measures when the people performing these functions ask for human considerations such as flexible hours to accommodate child care. In other words, we punish people in the workplace (women in particular) for possessing the very qualities we admire. We say things like, "By God, I never got any special treatment when I was doing that job and neither should she." Never mind that the change in hours is nothing more than a change in hours and does not adversely affect the business at hand. If the special considerations requested go against our "shoulds," we think no further.

Patriotism and Perspective

We have reached a "crisis" in what we "value" as human beings. We reward those with unimaginable riches who can hit, kick, pass, or putt an assortment of balls through hoops, over goal posts and into holes, while we allow those individuals who use their minds for research and teaching our children to receive less than adequate compensation. Each generation has been taught from birth that we are part of a great country. We believe it viscerally, to the extent that too many of us assume there is nothing we can do to make it better.

I would argue that in some areas our greatness has faded, if indeed it ever existed. Our sense of patriotism obscures our ability to see things as they are. We share a fault with the Soviets: when we are attacked for our beliefs in the American system we become outraged. We defend ourselves as they do. We reinforce our convictions. We deny the charges which we would otherwise concentrate on correcting, if we were not so defensive. We have become so accustomed to being limited in potential and secure with de-humanizing work that we insist on having a right to do it. Who would want to replace the backhoe with men armed with shovels? There are people who would argue that at least the men would have jobs, but at what price, what value? Would it not be better to save their backs and use part of that savings in the efficiency of the technology to raise their potential worth and quality of life? Using human muscle power to dig a ditch is like using a supercomputer to play games. It is a waste of potential. Philosopher James Feibleman characterized a machine as a man with a single idea. Microelectronics is producing machines with multiple ideas. In order to keep technology in perspective we need to build machines that will free and outperform the body while enhancing the use of our minds.

Scientists argue continually about the influence of genetics versus environmental stimulation. Some argue that our potential is genetically predetermined, while others assert that our potential depends on the stimulation we receive. Finding the ultimate answer will be of value, there is no doubt, but all of us live our lives so far from utilizing our full potential that genetics or environment hardly seems to be as much of an issue as our willingness to embrace "lowly expectations."

We have developed the technology to go to the moon, yet most of us live our whole lives as partially developed, earth-bound organisms. We use less than 10 percent of the capacity of our brains. We are accustomed to expecting very little of ourselves as a society. We have little difficulty accepting as normal a trip to the moon, 60 million semi-literate citizens, great prosperity, and a permanent class of working poor.

When we compare human potential with its application, it is easy to conclude that as a learned society, we are barely awake. To use the computer-human analogy, we are a nation of some 250 million mainframes, hard wired with software appropriate for toy computers. A majority of us act as if technologies were the enemy. Yet even a cursory review of history should make it clear that the exponential growth of the human race is the product of advancing technology. Human brain development occurred in congruence with the use of tools. Philosopher James K. Feibleman used the phrase "man the tool maker" or "tools the man-maker" to assert his thesis that we are here because of tools and not in spite of them.

Social Responsibility

If the optimistic view of the future is to prevail, it will occur not because of technology by itself, but because we have learned to balance human needs with technology. To accomplish this end we desperately need a citizenry with an education balanced between practical business application and the intellectual reasoning necessary for the preservation of political freedom. The desire for freedom by society's disenfranchised citizens is subordinate to their desire for "equality." In an electronically driven society, a disenfranchised electorate will be easily manipulated by those who know how to incite an emotional response. Adolf Hitler seized power in Germany by appealing to the emotions of a "panicked" middle class. We should never forget that democracy allows room for its own undoing. In America the "haves" have a vested critical interest in the well-being of the "have nots." If we were all well educated in the matters of human nature and nurture, we would know that the role of nurture has to be broken in order to change behavior. To do this means we must take the initiative to help people help themselves out of the ghettos. And, perhaps more importantly, it means we must set prejudice aside to allow them to do so.

In an environment conducive to instant change, political decisions should be based on intellectual reason, not on an emotional response from a lack of knowledge and understanding about others. To be an intellectual is merely to possess the powers of reason, provided that one can see beyond the power of destructive persuasion, self-delusion and prejudice.

Is it unreasonable to assume that ordinary people can aspire to greater achievements than those of assembly line workers? The ancient Greeks enlisted slaves to perform menial tasks while they developed intellectually to the extent that we are in awe of them even to this day. Two thousand years later the majority of us are incapable of thinking on their intellectual level. Is it any wonder that we demand the right to perform the work of slaves? Or that we cannot reach a consensus as to the need to replace undignified work with jobs that add to human dignity?

Toward a Human-Centered Technology

A liberal education in a high-tech society is "human software" sufficiently powerful to keep technology and the human condition in perspective. If we insist on a "human-centered" perspective for technology, we will ensure that we do not become slaves of a technically driven society dominated by the agenda of narrow interests. By human-centered I mean technological development dedicated to the protection of freedom and human dignity.

All organizations and institutions, public or private, have an agenda. With time this agenda almost always becomes survival before objective. If the organization is efficiently and effectively meeting a normative objective, the organization can be said to be synergistic. If the organization loses sight of its objective, it is likely to become bureaucratic, which is an anathema to synergy. Synergy occurs when the whole is greater than the sum of its parts. In a bureaucracy, the sum of its parts is always greater than the whole. Another major point is that organizations are anti-democratic by nature and hierarchical by design. This is hardly news, but we often try to change organizations by acting as if they are something else.

Change is stimulating, unsettling and beset with dissonant experiences. In a dynamic, rapidly changing technological society the struggle of public and private organizations for their very existence requires that they seek power and control. Did you ever see a government agency that failed to grow or that, in growing, did not become further removed from its original objective? The appetite for power by special interest groups is growing stronger. The potential exists for great technological change that will not be progress, but the manipulation of the majority.

Confronting Change

Changing technology requires continual training and retraining. Robert Hillard, educational specialist for the FCC, put this training dilemma in perspective when he said that by the time a child born today graduates from college the knowledge in the world will be four times as great. By the time he is fifty years old it will be thirty-two times as great. In other words, 97 percent of everything known will have been learned in his lifetime.

It is dangerous to confuse education with training. Education is the control mechanism of the individual, while training is the control mechanism for business. What kind of training will prepare an individual for a lifetime of work in a dynamic environment? A liberal education, regardless of how it is obtained, offers the individual intrinsic utility. In contrast, the nature of training is that it is used for an extrinsic end. Without a liberal education as a counterbalance, training offers a fleeting, temporary solution.

In times of rapid change the need for training is perpetual. People who are self-educated and self-directed can take charge of their own training. The confidence afforded by the ability to be self-determining is the catalyst for an optimistic view of the future. Such a view leads to a welcoming of change. People who must rely on others for training for future jobs resist change. Their inability to be self-determining translates to a fear of the future.

In a few years, if we manage a human-centered approach to technology, knowledge will be available to everyone through the use of telecommunications. But the ability to determine whether or not we are the targets of manipulation by special interest groups will become increasingly difficult. It can be checked only by a literate citizenry capable of detecting a hidden bias in the kind of information and data that is available.

The growth of telecommunications and the decentralizing effects it brings will allow millions of information employees to work at, or near home. Moving the work force to and from work each day over long distances is an incredibly unproductive, unintelligent exercise. It wastes time, fossil fuel, and pollutes the atmosphere. Imagine the dramatic effect telecommuting will have on real estate values and major city development if even a modest percentage of the work force stops traveling long distances to work. It's likely that telecommuting will grow in incremental leaps as we face future fuel shortages, experience gridlock (traffic problems) from too many automobiles, and try to protect the environment from automobile emissions.

A human-centered approach to technology requires that we allow for the fact that humans will be relieved of thousands of jobs by machines. It can be either a cause for celebration or despair. Living standards will be under intense pressure. High stress and frustration will be a part of all our lives during rapid change, but stress will dominate the lives of the under class. Over 60 million Americans make up the semi-literate under class. Sixty million disenfranchised Americans threaten the very existence of democracy.

Scientists conducting research in bio-technology are promising to revolutionize food production before the turn of the century. A human-centered approach will ensure that there is adequate topsoil available so that the products of bio-technology will be used to lessen world tension by empowering third world countries to feed themselves.

The subtitle of E.F. Schumacher's book *Small Is Beautiful* is "Economics As If People Really Mattered." This is a premise we need to use to examine our whole society because of the logical conclusions that naturally follow. For example, if our system of health care provided medicine as if people really mattered, people would not die from the lack of an operation because they didn't have enough money to pay for it. Elderly people would not be given multiple prescriptions from several different doctors that counteract each other to the detriment of the patient. Doctors would treat the whole patient. Indeed, if medicine were practiced as if people really mattered, the terminally ill would be allowed to die with dignity instead of being kept alive as an association of treatable parts. This subtitle, as if people really mattered, needs to be added to every facet of our social, economic, and governmental agendas.

Questions of Morality

As stewards of the planet earth we have great moral questions that must be addressed. For example, our economy is based upon the principle of continued mass consumption, even though it is clear that there are not enough natural resources to allow us to live so wastefully. We pretend that there is a high degree of moral virtue in the nature of our productivity, while the state of the environment clearly suggests that much of what we do in the name of industry would be better left undone. We are faced with the ultimate dilemma defining progress. If world resources are finite, does using more than our share mean that we are better people? What must we do to adjust our economic system to the inevitable possibility that people are going to start living substantially longer lives? Might we use the expertise of the old as a means of empowering the young? Might we charge our local schools with solving real problems and, in so doing graduate students with a sense of responsibility and an appreciation for a direct causal relationship between education and practical experience? Might we redefine work in congruence with human dignity so that the quality of human life is considered a matter of greater importance than the busyness of activities that destroy the environment? What do we ask, or rather what should we demand, from a technological future that simultaneously offers to increase the opportunity for choices in our personal lives while threatening to limit our choices in employment? Are we not smart enough to produce a method of demonstrating competence that will protect us from incompetent practitioners, while still allowing the practice of competence regardless of how it was obtained?

Such questions must be addressed by a citizenry who can see through the effects of cultural conditioning and who can articulate their visions for democracy with at least as much zeal as they would normally express their career plans. History tells us that great nations die from an overindulgence in their fundamental principle. I would argue that America's undoing may result from a basic misunderstanding of ours. Failure to understand that the essence of freedom is process and not experience is the means by which we produce our excess of the basic premise of freedom. We do so by abdication.

The Danger of a Pleasant Existence

Society tends to view the necessity or propensity for change according to its position of relative comfort. Eric Hoffer, author of *The True Believer,* wrote:

> A pleasant existence blinds us to the possibilities of drastic change. We cling to what we call our common sense, our practical point of view. Actually, these are but names for an all-absorbing familiarity with things as they are. The tangibility of a pleasant and secure existence is such that it makes other realities, however imminent, seem vague and visionary. Thus it happens that when the times become unhinged, it is the practical people who are caught unaware and are made to look like visionaries who cling to things that do not exist.
>
> On the other hand, those who reject the present and fix their eyes and hearts on the things to come have a

faculty for detecting the embryo of future danger or advantage in the ripeness of their times. Hence the frustrated individual and the true believer make better prognosticators than those who have reason to want the preservation of the status quo.

Of fear or faith in the future, Hoffer said:

> Thus the differences between the conservative and the radical seem to spring mainly from their attitude toward the future. Fear of the future causes us to lean against and cling to the present, while faith in the future renders us receptive to change. Both the rich and the poor, the strong and the weak, they who have achieved much or little can be afraid of the future. When the present seems so perfect that the most we can expect is its even continuation in the future, change can only mean deterioration. Hence men of outstanding achievement and those who live full, happy lives usually set their faces against drastic innovation. The conservatism of invalids and people past middle age stems, too, from fear of the future. They are on the lookout for signs of decay, and feel that any change is more likely to be for the worse than for the better. The abjectly poor are also without faith in the future. The future seems to them a booby trap buried on the road ahead. One must step gingerly. To change things is to ask for trouble.

I would argue that, for better or worse, we will inherit the future that we deserve. Whether it is idealistic or laden with doom will depend more on our intelligence and our political fortitude than our technical ability.

John Naisbitt asserted in *Megatrends*, "It is truly an exciting time to be alive." I believe that for people who have constructed their own Self-University it has always been and will always be an exciting time to be alive. We have to proceed on the assumption that a positive view of the future will prevail. To do otherwise would have a negative prophetic effect.

Summary

In summary, we are due for near- and long-term profound changes because of the proliferation of technology. It will happen whether we welcome it or not. If we harness and humanize it, we can reach for the highest quality of life that man has ever known—not because of gadgetry, but because of freedom from mindless work and the technological wherewithal to develop our minds and reach our potential as fully-developed organisms. The alternative is a technologically driven society with groups of people separated by divisive categories of social class. The division will exist between the informed and the uninformed: the "knows" and the "know nots." Manipulation will lead to unrest. If we cannot manage our own society on a equitable basis, there is little hope that we will be able to use our technological capability to avoid war with others.

There are many ways to look at the human sociological condition. We have examined ourselves as a nation with categories such as: poor, middle-income, rich, conservatives, liberals, moderates, traditionalists, in-betweeners, rejectionists, synthesizers, lower-class, middle-class, upper-class, survivors, sustainers, belongers, emulators, achievers, integrateds, organization men, jungle fighters, craftsmen, gamesmen, warriors, intellectuals, acquisitors, and laborers. These are useful, insightful, thought-provoking ways of looking at social interaction. Economic necessity suggests that we play different roles, but these roles should not prevent any one of us from possessing the intellectual properties of literacy and reason. Technology used intelligently can be used to empower everyone.

Self-education is a journey, not a destination. In the same manner that "the medium is the message" rather than the content, "the desire for truth" is more important than what temporarily poses as fact. Self-education is a journey whose admitted purpose is self-knowledge and self-discovery, but it is not an exercise in self-indulgence. In fact, it is precisely the opposite. Self-indulgence is a result of narrow focus. I would argue that we have become self-indulgent because we have not gained enough self-knowledge to understand how to separate what we need from what we want. In other words, we are self-indulgent because we do not know any better. The social ethic of self-denial is a glitch in the program of human intelligence. The adoption of the ethic of self-denial in early American society, though intended as an act of moral virtue, was also a means of avoiding self-knowldege. Because so little was known about human behavior, investigation of it was better avoided.

We have so persistently and consistently overlooked the need to understand ourselves and others that most people are at a loss even to describe self-knowledge. Psychology and sociology are split apart, as though one could exist without the other. Even more important is the well-accepted, though fallacious, premise that mastery of human behavior is necessary for only a few of us, who will in turn act as human mechanics for the rest. This propensity to ignore what is most important to all of us affects us just as if we had all been put into a giant steel drum, shaken up, and then pounded upon with a giant steel hammer. The result is that we stumble through life a bit addled with the sound of the pounding ringing in our ears.

Self-education as a means of self-discovery encompasses learning about human needs, feelings, personalities, interpersonal relationships, family relationships, human rights, human dignity, and human spirituality. It is only through this that we can conduct rational, reasonable government and reach a social equilibrium both locally and globally. Our future depends upon humans understanding humans. Every person on earth is not more than thirty minutes away from possible nuclear annihilation. We are protected only by those whom we choose to manage our social affairs. And if history tells us nothing else, it literally screams about our inability to trust our future to managers with carte blanche. In a knowledge society such as ours, and with explosive technological development, the price of citizenship continually becomes higher. The obligation of citizenship becomes salient to those with a thirst for knowledge. Responsible citizenship cannot be forced—it has to be felt.

We place our hope for the future in the power of human reason, and while reason is one of our most powerful human qualities, it is not always a superior avenue to truth, any more than human emotion is. Indeed, the ultimate act of human intelligence would be a synthesis of reason and emotion. If we were able to achieve this end, we might survive long enough to stop worrying about our lack of natural resources and find their replacements among the stars.

Part IV

CHAPTER TEN

Practicum

Much learning does not teach understanding.
—Heraclitus

Your Self-University campus begins and ends where you say it does. You are in charge. What follows is practical advice on where you go from here. Up to now we have been mostly concerned with rationale. This section is practicum, which includes methods for creating your own Self-University and finding your way around campus. This chapter sheds light on the changing nature of self-reliance, understanding personality theories, tips for improving your memory, learning through media, language, writing, books and where to find what you need.

The Changing Role of Self-Reliance

Self-reliance is part of the American Dream, but what we define as self-reliance and how we develop it change with the times we live in. America grew out of an agrarian society in which it was common place for people to do almost everything for themselves. They raised their own food, bred and slaughtered animals, tanned their own leather, concocted their own medicine, made their own clothing, and built with their own hands whatever needed building .

Industrialization changed the nature of self-reliance dramatically, because it meant specialization. Self-reliant people in industrialized, specialized America were self-reliant not so much because of what they did for themselves but because they earned enough money through a specialized skill to maintain independence. As people lost the ability to do for themselves, they began to hire other specialists to do for them.

Today society is changing so fast, and the nature of information is so volatile, that self-reliance for some is giving way to a desperate struggle for survival. In an agrarian society, self-reliance was necessary because of the nature of the environment. When the majority of people in America lived on farms, almost everything that was needed for livelihood was accessible within easy walking distance. Once the farm was established, everything that was needed was at hand. It was a time in which specialization was achieved on the assumption that everyone was, in fact, a generalist.

It is happening again today, but it is not because we have come full circle, as the saying goes, or because the pendulum has swung in the other direction. It is because we have become an information-focused economy, and for many people almost everything needed to participate is obtainable within easy walking distance of where we live. The physical nature of the farm and factory is giving way to electronic telecommunications. It's almost as if we are beginning to share the same farm. From now through the turn of the century, self-reliance is going to assume a new definition. The availability of electronic information and its explosive growth is about to affect us so profoundly that the next two decades will likely resemble a century of change.

A rich, responsive electronic information environment has the potential to tear away the walls that have long prevented many people from getting a first class education. Such an environment has the potential to radically alter a society based on credentials to one based on demonstrated competence. It's already happening in the sense that people don't care about the formal educational level of the person who has written the software that they use—as long as it works.

Self-help and self-education are what's needed to deal with a future sure to bring traumatic change. Unfortunately, the term education has in many instances come to mean something passive. When we use the word education, we seem to imply that it is done to us or someone else, a process which we endure through time and which is measured by attendance and an occasional dipstick assessment by testing our attentiveness. A better word to use for the process of self-help and self-education is "empowerment." Add the desire for knowledge and self-understanding to the following subjects and you have empowerment.

The Study of Personality Theories

One way to develop self-knowledge is through the study of personality types. This is less threatening to belief systems than psychological theories in a philosophical sense, although, unfortunately, it still has not made its way into the educational system early enough. Can you imagine anything that high school students would be more interested in studying than "themselves"?

The Enneagram

One of the best systems I know of is described in the book *Personality Types: Using the Enneagram for Self-Discovery* by Don Richard Riso.

He categorizes personality types by numbers for identification purposes only. They are:

One: *The Reformer*—principled, orderly, perfectionistic. Key motivation: Wants to be right, to strive higher and improve others, to justify his or her own position, to be beyond criticism so as not to be condemned by anyone.

Two: *The Helper*—caring, possessive, manipulative. Key motivation: Wants to be loved, to express his or her feelings for others, to be needed and appreciated, to coerce others into responding to him, to vindicate his claims about himself.

Three: *The Status Seeker*—self-assured, narcissistic, hostile. Key motivation: Wants to be affirmed, to distinguish himself from others, to receive attention, to be admired, and to impress others.

Four: *The Artist*—creative, intuitive, depressive. Key motivations: Wants to understand himself or herself, to express himself in something beautiful, to withdraw to protect his feelings, to take care of emotional needs before attending to anything else.

Five: *The Thinker*—perceptive, analytic, eccentric. Key motivation: Wants to understand the environment, to gain more knowledge, to interpret everything as a way of defending the self from threats from the environment.

Six: *The Loyalist*—likable, dutiful, dependent, masochistic. Key motivations: Wants security, to be liked and the approval of others, to test the attitudes of others toward him, to fight against anxiety and insecurity.

Seven: *The Generalist*—accomplished, impulsive, manic. Key motivations: Wants to be happy, to have fun and amuse himself, to do and have more of everything, to escape anxiety.

Eight: *The Leader*—self-confident, forceful, combative. Key motivations: Wants to be self-reliant, to act in his own self-interest, to have an impact on the environment, to prevail over others.

Nine: *The Peacemaker*—reassuring, passive, neglectful. Key motivations: Wants union with the other, to preserve things as they are, to avoid conflicts and tension, to ignore whatever would upset him or her, to preserve his peace at any price.

These descriptions are limited and there may not be enough information for you to discern your style, but the book offers a wealth of insightful information that makes it easy to discover your own style as well as that of your friends. The enneagram (pronounced "Any-a-gram") not only enables you to better understand yourself and others, it also points to the natural path by which you can improve your own behavior. The brief descriptions above are only a snapshot of the nine different personality types. The book offers a complete profile that examines each on a continuum from healthy to unhealthy behavioral traits.

Humans should understand the general mechanics of human personality at least as well as the multiplication tables. From my own experience I would guess that, depending on your style, you might have responded to this book as follows:

If you are a *reformer*, you may be concerned with my facts, especially if they do not match yours. You may resent my arguments directed toward authority because you are likely to be uncomfortable with ambiguity. Indeed, many reformers are not likely to read this far.

If you are a *helper*, you may be genuinely interested in learning about any methods which you can use to improve your relations with others. Your intentions are good, but you may be reluctant to accept views of reality that differ with your own.

If you are a *status seeker*, your response at this point may be ambivalent. You may seek information that will enable you to become more inner-directed, but you are likely to resist information which suggests that you are not already so. If you are in search of sizzle, you will likely resist that which leads to fizzle.

If you are an *artist*, this book may have given you something to think about, something to ponder. You may be either excited or depressed about it.

If you are a *thinker*, you may have truly enjoyed the book so far. If you disagree with it, so much the better, because now you have something to synthesize with your own experience. You may also resent the fact that there is any type of formula that can predict your reaction with any degree of dependability (as I can attest, being in category five myself).

If you are a *loyalist*, you may be uncomfortable with challenges directed at traditional authority or ideas that seem to threaten your security, but you may respond with a resounding, "So what?"

If you are a *generalist*, you will likely synthesize what you find useful and then move quickly ahead so that you can get on with it.

If you are a *leader*, you will probably want to discuss *Self-University* with me in person so that you can persuade me to change something. And you may be correct. After I make the change you may use the better version to influence someone else.

If you are a *peacemaker*, you may have glossed over differences without wanting to get too deeply involved, especially if the ideas presented in *Self-University* might conflict with others' opinions; on the other hand, you may have found information useful to affect future relations.

Another exceptional method of gaining insight into your own personality type and that of others is in the book, *Please Understand Me: Character & Temperament Types* by David Keirsey and Marilyn Bates. Expanding on the four temperaments of Hippocrates and the works of contemporary psychologists, the authors provide a simple test to narrow your personality style down to one of sixteen basic temperament types.[1] Key words are used to broadly describe each type: architect, inventor, scientist, fieldmarshal, questor, journalist, author, pedagogue, seller, conservator, entertainer, artist, administrator, trustee, promoter, and artisan. This is a highly illuminating exercise, and is especially useful for better understanding close relationships by comparing your test results with those of friends and family.

Ego States

Transactional analysis is an excellent method of developing self-understanding. Developed by Eric Berne in the Sixties and made popular by the book *I'm OK—You're OK* by Dr. Thomas A. Harris, transactional analysis describes our personalities as consisting of three postures which we use for interacting with the world around us: Parent, Adult and Child. The Parent is the residue of nurture that became a part of our personality. It is the "shoulds" and "musts" echoed by our parents. The Adult is the part of us that learns to make independent decisions and rational judgments. The Child is the emotional makeup which developed during our actual childhood which is still a part of us. Each time we interact with others we assume one of these three postures, sometimes changing in mid-sentence. For example, if I say, "I knew precisely where I was going; I shouldn't have gone; but I just felt like going," then I have changed from Adult to Parent to Child. Transactional analysis is easily learned and is an outstanding method of developing insight and self-understanding.

The point of these exercises is to develop enough self-knowledge so that we are no longer surprised with the results when we take tests designed to reveal ourselves. When we have reached this degree of personal expertise, we don't need to take tests to find out what we want to do with our lives. We know.

Avenues to Learning

Part of the enjoyment of self-directed inquiry is discovering your own unique methods of turning information into knowledge. But it is equally rewarding to learn of a new technique, try it and find that it works immediately. Some of the methods I use are listed under the sub-categories that follow.

Techniques for a Better Memory

Most of us are confused about how best to use our memories. Our capacity for remembering is practically limitless, yet we seem to have a fear of overloading. Short-term memory is limited to how much information can be handled at one time, but there is virtually no limit for the capacity of long-term memory. We are confused about how to use memory, primarily because of our experience with formal education. The emphasis placed on memory in school has more to do with the demonstration of the ability to use short-term memory than long-term.

In the beginning of civilized education, however, it was the reverse. Everything learned was placed into long-term memory. Students had to depend on the storage utility of memory because there were no books. Law and tradition were passed from the memory of one generation to the next, and memory was thought to be a virtue. With the invention of writing, the publishing of books, and finally the alphabetical indexing of books, attitudes about the use of memory took a dramatic turn. One had only to memorize the alphabet which could then be used as a key for finding information. Memory as a virtue began to be ridiculed. In 1580 Montaigne said that "a good memory is generally joined to a weak judgment." In the twentieth century, Albert Einstein often scoffed at the suggestion of cluttering his mind with anything that he could simply look up in a reference book.

Today an informed, intelligent use of memory can allow you to become an expert on almost any subject in noticeably less time than those who do not use their memory effectively. With external memories available in books and computer files, today's emphasis is on the ability to reason and to form critical judgments. But before you can reason or make critical judgments you have to know something to be critical about. We learn best by adding new information to something already known. If you want to acquire knowledge in a new field, the fastest, most effective way is to make a preliminary investigation and outline the information into categories. Then memorize enough information to establish a memory file. Once that's established and committed to long-term, you need only compare new information to what is already in memory and have enough knowledge to mesh meaning into memory. It sounds simple, and it is. When I was very young I became interested in astronomy. I began to read everything I could find on the subject, only to find that I wasn't making very much progress. Even though I was interested in the subject, the new information just didn't seem to stick. So I committed to memory the locations, descriptions and the salient characteristics of all of the known planets, their moons, the largest asteroids, the nearest stars and many other celestial objects. With these bits of information my memory files were established. Thereafter, adding information that I could retain at will was easy.

Memory is the most powerful force we have for learning, yet most of us use it begrudgingly and almost never objectively. It is an incredible paradox that we judge intelligence by the demonstration of memory, but we drag our feet when it comes to practicing it. Perhaps it's because when we were forced to use our memory in school we knew that we would only be required to remember for a short time. If we encountered the same material again in the future, we knew we would be able to review it before being tested, and this allowed us once again to use short-term memory instead of long-term.

One of the greatest aspects of self-education is that it becomes a tremendous source of intrinsic satisfaction. It is a way to be totally self-determining. A feeling of empowerment begins to develop once you see how easy it is to learn something when you really want to know. You are in charge all the way. It is a self-reinforcing experience that continually becomes stronger. Set out to develop knowledge in a particular field, commit an outline of the basics to memory, continually follow up by studying new material and you will find the results amazing. Memory by association is superior to sheer memorization, but like knitting, you must have something to begin with so you can continually add to it.

The ancient Greeks and Romans developed a mnemonic process of memorization by association known as the loci system (loci is a Greek word meaning locations).[2] It is a simple memory-by-association method. It was developed by orators so they could give long speeches without having to use notes. First, they would memorize the image of a number of locations in a sequence that they were comfortable with. Next, they associated the material to be remembered in segments divided among the locations. Recall, then, simply consisted of mentally retracing the journey. The memory of the specific locations remained the same and was used for new material.

More recent uses of mnemonics has produced the Peg system which uses rhyming nouns and numbers as mental pegs. Another is the phonetic system. Developed in the seventeenth century, it is a more sophisticated system that uses numbers represented by a consonant sound. The phonetic system requires more time to learn, but it is a powerful tool when mastered.

There are numerous techniques available today for developing a more effective recall. Some of them are based on recent research. For example, it has been discovered that there is a rhythm suitable for learning that allows brain cells a moment to rest between moments of recording data. The rhythm that works best is a continuous, monotonous sound that is spaced about ten seconds between beats.[3]

It is also known that short periods of concentration are preferable to long ones. I have found it particularly effective to read two or three pages in a book and then reflect on the material before proceeding. This is an effective method, especially if you are not going to take notes. It is a thoroughly aggravating experience to read a book, have it come up in conversation and not be able to remember a word of it.

Recitation is a particularly effective method of memorization, because it involves concentration and repetition and attaches both to the continual practice of recall. It forces the actual rehearsal of retrieval which is, after all, what you are trying to accomplish.

There are many effective techniques for using memory in learning. One of the most useful books I have found on the subject is *Your Memory* by Kenneth L. Higbee. The author writes about the phenomenon of "overlearning," which must be understood thoroughly before setting out to become an autodidact. Higbee says:

> Overlearning accounts for the fact that you can still remember some things you learned as a child (such as the multiplication tables, the alphabet, and how to ride a bicycle), even though you may not have used them for a long time. Overlearning also shows one reason why cramming for an exam does not result in retention of the material for very long after the exam—you have barely learned the material, so it is forgotten quickly.

Overlearning, says Higbee, is why we still remember the names of the people we went to school with years ago, but we do not remember the material that we studied during those years.[4]

Regarding our attitudes about memory Higbee writes:

Suppose you wanted to be good at golf, chess, math, or playing the piano. You would not expect to learn just one secret that would give you the skill. Rather, you would expect to learn techniques and principles, practice them, apply them, and thereby improve your skill. However, when it comes to memory, some people do not reason the same way. They do not work at it. When such a person finds out that improving memory takes effort, he may decide that he can make do with his memory as it is.

Higbee suggests that the basic principles that help learning and memory are: "meaningfulness, organization, association, visualization, attention, interest and feedback."

Learning through Media

After you determine your individual learning style you will know best how to proceed with your method of exploration. The explosion in media methodology and content—the same phenomenon that has caused us to begin to refer to ourselves as a knowledge or information society—is exponentially increasing the access to information and knowledge. Today we have books, magazines, newsletters, newspapers, data bases, television, VCR's, video disks, audio tapes, movies, computers, computer networks, seminars, self-help groups, associations, colleges, universities, free universities, tele-universities and many more methods of learning avenues available to us.

Why Study Language?

Educator Neil Postman said, "Language is an organ of perception." Indeed, we think in terms that cannot be described without language. Language is both liberating and limiting. The Japanese have seventeen different ways of saying *no*. In most cases the Chinese language calls for descriptions too specific for the use of such absolutes as *yes* and *no*. Language is how we express our thoughts. If we have feelings but cannot find words, what do we substitute?

The ability to use language effectively as a means for communicating with others is a fundamental characteristic that most successful people share. Yet most people never seem to make this cause and effect connection. They will attribute their success and the success of others to a multitude of possibilities, but seldom will they realize the power and influence that language has in the process. The study of language is crucial because it is the tool with which we apprehend everything else.

Writing to Learn

My own experience is that writing can be a useful process for self-discovery. If you want to clarify your knowledge about a particular subject or situation, and you are unsure how to proceed, you should probably try writing about it. If it's not clear when you start, it will be by the time you finish, which is, after all, the whole point. Writing is sort of a forced conversation with oneself. It is a direct link with the subconscious just as speaking is, but speaking usually doesn't engage the brain to the extent that the act automatically becomes a learning experience. Learning requires reflection. Speaking raises the issue, but writing synthesizes it through your entire repertoire of learning, experience and range of emotions. The appearance of your thoughts on paper reinforces the effort and strengthens the learning of you, the writer.

Books

It is useful to think of books as perspectives. The more you read the more perspectives you will have. The best book I ever discovered about reading was *How to Read a Book* by Mortimer Adler. My approach to reading has not been the same since. The copy I found at the library was written in 1940. The book has since been updated, but any copy is as applicable today as when it was first published. About reading and comprehension Adler wrote, "It is my honest belief that almost all of the great books in every field are within the grasp of all normally intelligent men, on the condition, of course that they acquire the skill necessary for reading them and make the effort."

I have adopted a modified version of the recommendations in Adler's book in which I categorize the purposes of reading for: information, understanding, entertainment or combinations of the three. I strongly recommend that you read *How to Read a Book* and develop a method compatible with your own style of learning.

Because books are perspectives, they serve as anchors for our knowledge and wisdom. Many books are timeless. Indeed, the wisdom of the ancients often has a ring of intelligence that one might expect to find in the generation that succeeded us, not one that lived over two thousand years ago. Mark Twain said, "A classic is something that everybody wants to have read, and nobody wants to read." The "classics," or "Great Books" as they are sometimes referred to, are intellectual treasures, once you lose your fear or aversion for them.

They are a part of our common inheritance, the legacy of human reason. If we can be dissuaded from reading them, or distracted from their importance, we must also say that we have been cheated out of what was rightfully ours. It is ironic that the experience of the great books is like that of a child eating asparagus. After many attempts, which may even include gagging, the child will sometimes reach the moment when asparagus tastes good. The aversion becomes a positive obsession.

The subject of reading is not complete until you add the dimension of discourse. In 1986 Mortimer Adler wrote *A Guidebook to Learning*. On the subject of reading and learning he wrote:

> What, then, shall autodidacts do? How should persons proceed who wish to conduct for themselves the continuation of learning after all schooling has been finished?
>
> The answer is in one way very brief and simple. Looked at another way it is rich and substantial enough to occupy a lifetime of learning in the pursuit of wisdom.
>
> The simple answer is: *Read and discuss!* Never just read, for reading without discussion with others who have read the same book is not nearly as profitable as it should be for the mind in its effort to understand what has been read. As reading without discussion can fail to yield the full measure of understanding that should be sought, so discussion without the substance for discussion that good and great books afford is likely to degenerate into chit-chat or be little more than an exchange of opinions and personal prejudices.

I would argue that failure to fully discuss what we read on a regular basis is the primary reason that many of us do not know our own minds, or are simply without opinion. Schopenhauer warned us that it is dangerous to read about a subject without thinking about it first. He argued that when we read, the author thinks for us. If we spend too much time reading, we lose the capacity for thinking. Thomas Jefferson, on the other hand, was a voracious reader. In a letter to John Adams he wrote that he could not live without books. Jefferson clearly never lost his capacity for thinking—compare the rich ideological discourse which occupied his life with that of your own, and you can gain an idea of the significance of discourse. Jefferson never lost his capacity for thinking, and neither will we, if we examine other people's words with the mettle of our own experience and temper them through a continuing dialog with others.

My greatest pleasure in reading comes from discovering ideas which immediately strike a nerve. It's almost as if the author says something which fits perfectly with my own experience, or is something that I have suspected, but never consciously acknowledged. For example, E.F. Schumacher is the first person I can remember who wrote that what we don't know for sure about ourselves should maintain our attention. This simple assertion hit me with the resounding profundity of a left hook to the jaw. Here was an idea that suddenly explained why the way we are educated doesn't make sense. The quotations used throughout this book were selected because, in a similar sense, each struck a nerve.

Where to Find What You Want

The techniques that follow have saved me a great deal of time and effort. Try them, and in a short time you will be able to devise your own shortcuts for finding information.

The Library

If you feel as if you have no clue as to what you are genuinely interested in, the library can be a good place to find out. Spend all day there if you can, simply browsing through and seeing what type of books you are drawn to. Make a list as you go of the titles which you find interesting. This procedure may take a while, but a pattern will develop. In time, the list will offer enough insight for you to proceed, until such time that you no longer have any doubts about where your interests lie.

There are several excellent library guides available. Two that I highly recommend are: *Your Library*, by William Katz, and *How to Look Things Up*, by Bruce L. Felkner. The problem that most of us have when we enter the library is not finding a lack of material on our subject, but finding too much. Using these guides is not likely to solve that problem, but it will help you to narrow the scope of your search somewhat.

Libraries have changed vastly over the last few years, and the "old fashioned" card catalog has just about disappeared overnight. Instead, most modern libraries provide this service with on-line computer facilities. These are usually well designed and very easy to use, even for the person without computer expertise. They also are much faster and less cumbersome than the old methods, making it possible to "scan" whole categories of information in very little time. The standard systems provide information not only by author and title, but also by general subject. You can even look for certain "key" words in a title, to make sure that you have access to absolutely everything in your area of interest. Regardless of the classification system your library uses, when you find the call number of one particular work, you'll discover right next to it many more related works in the same area. This is a benefit that allows you to quickly examine all the works your library has on a particular subject, without running all over the place looking for them.

One of the most important resources you can have is the librarian. Don't be shy about approaching the librarian when you are having trouble finding something or need help operating the equipment. Almost always you'll find people well-trained in their field and dedicated to assisting you. Often they remove the frustration from your search in a matter of moments by suggesting other available resources. They also are invaluable in instituting library-to-library loans.

Most everything you'll be looking for can be found by using the reference section of the library. Each reference leads you to another reference, which in turn leads you to another. At first this seems frustrating and mind-boggling, but as you continue your research you'll begin to narrow the search. And, as most reference material is divided and sub-divided into more usable categories, you'll soon find yourself zeroing in on just exactly the right piece of information.

Bookstores

Bookstores today are changing rapidly. Many of the chain stores have on-line ordering systems and some have customer terminals to allow you to browse as if you were in the library. The biggest drawback for today's bookstore is in finding specialized or narrow-interest books. Bookstores maintain a profit margin by quickly turning their inventory, and in order to do that they must carry titles for which there is a lot of demand. However, many bookstores are adding a measure of competition by offering quick special order service. I believe that in the future bookstores will add many features of personalized service. One of these might include maintaining a customer interest profile to identify publications that customers might be interested in buying if told of them.

Books in Print

Books in Print is published by the R.R. Bowker Company, of New York. It is continually updated and is available for reference in most libraries and many bookstores. It has three major categories: subject, titles and authors. If you are trying to keep abreast of a particular subject, use the subject and author categories on a regular basis. Make a list of those authors who are prolific in your area of interest and check *Books in Print* regularly for new books they may have written. If you are determined to develop expertise in the field, write the authors themselves or the publishers, and ask to be notified of their new releases. One final note: just because a book is listed as "out of print" doesn't always mean that it is not available. Check your library first, and if it doesn't have it, perhaps a copy can be located through an inter-library loan service. If all else fails, ask your local bookstore to recommend an out-of-print book finding service for you.

Directories

It is useful to think of directories as your own department managers or assistants. Most directories are regularly updated, so, in effect, they continually look out for material which you might be interested in. Directories save time. There is no reason to spend hours piecing together information that someone else with years of experience does on a regular basis.

Technological Perspective

If your enrollment in the continuing body of reason is primarily for the pleasure derived from one of the new technological disciplines, and you ground your knowledge sufficiently to place it in philosophical context, then your attention will probably be directed to the cutting edge of discovery that drives today's specialized magazines, newsletters, data bases, networks, seminars, university research labs and high-tech business ventures. There are many such technological disciplines where knowledge is developing so fast that by the time a book is ready for print it is out of date. These areas of discovery should be of some interest to us all, simply because we know from our past experience that our artifacts shape our behavior. We build models which we then use to model ourselves.

We have reached such technological capability that we are on the cusp of inventing our own future. Technology offers a method of control that has never before been available—we are moving so fast that we can associate cause and effect while there is still time for course correction. Knowledge brings responsibility. Knowledge that is growing faster than we can categorize it demands that we develop intellectually to the extent that we can keep technology in human perspective. This is the single greatest charge of *Self-University*. A liberal education is no longer a luxury. It is a necessity for the preservation of freedom and democracy.

CHAPTER ELEVEN

Practicum in the Workplace

*But for the wisdom of business, wherein
man's life is most conversant, there be no
books of it, except some few scattered advertisements, that have no proportion to the
magnitude of this subject. For if books were
written of this as the other, I doubt not but
learned men with mean experience, would
far excel men of long experience without
learning, and outshoot them in their own
bow.*

                                        —Sir Francis Bacon

The hard reality is that the problem of economic necessity dictates
how most of us spend our time. It is necessary to get to the social level
of Maslow's hierarchy of needs before people can learn objectively. At
least that's what we perceive, though some argue rationally that it
isn't true. A hand-to-mouth existence hardly lends itself to the
pursuit of higher learning. So how do we become self-directed learners? How do we reverse a lifetime of conditioned behavior that has
left a distaste for learning?

The chapter discusses the importance of discovering what work
you want to do, exploring the option of returning to school, creating
your own credentials, using learning resources in the workplace, and
taking advantage of the open or free university.

The first step is to review the past, understand why we are the
way we are, just as we have done in earlier chapters. The only way to
become truly self-directed is to thoroughly understand how we
learned to be so self-limiting. We cannot recognize the symptoms if
we are continually pulled to regress and withdraw. We must clean
the slate, examine the origin of our beliefs, develop a sense of
philosophy and define a purpose or mission. To be self-directed in a
knowledge society means that we have to see ourselves as lifelong
learners. Self-education must become the journey and not the destination. Knowledge of the "law of reverse effort" quoted earlier by
Alan Watts will expand our horizons, once we realize just how little
we know of what is knowable.

Knowing What You Want to Do

A concentrated effort at developing self-knowledge will allow you to feel comfortable with the fact that you can make informed career choices, but do not expect this to happen overnight. After a lifetime of ignoring the need to study behavior, you will not suddenly free yourself into becoming an all-knowing individual. As time passes you will become better at making informed decisions about your work and your personal life, if you use the process of self-education as a life-centering experience. You will encounter people who view the study of behavior for the purpose of self-knowledge to be an act of self-indulgence, rather than of an act of intelligence. (This is a residue of sorts from the self-denial aspect of the Protestant work ethic.) But if you persist, soon you will be able to seek what you want based on your own definition of success. And you will have confidence that you can make intelligent course corrections along the way. If you are the only person who knows where you are going, then you are likely to be the only one to know when you have arrived.

Thousands of people walk into personnel agencies or prospective employers' offices each day for job interviews with only a vague idea of what they want to do or what they are really good at. This fact causes many people to stay in a line of work for which they are unsuited, but for which they are qualified. They rely on previous experience because it seems easier than the process of breaking into a new field.

After you have decided what you want to pursue, what you do next depends on how much discrepancy exists between where you are and where you want to go. If you are presently employed by an organization in which you intend to stay, you need to enlist the organization's assistance in reaching your maximum contribution. If you are seeking an entry-level position for the first time, you may be in for a difficult qualifying and credentialing experience. If you have an entrepreneurial urge, and many self-educated people do, then you have only to educate yourself so as to sufficiently minimize the risk of your enterprise. Ways to create your own credentials will be covered later in this chapter, but first it is necessary to take a look at economics and the credentialing process.

Returning to School and the Question of Economics

If money is an important factor, you can base your decision on an equation similar to this: Determine the total cost of the education necessary to qualify for the position you seek. Then, estimate the additional amount of money you will earn as a result of the credentials you are trying to obtain. Take your current age and determine the remaining years you expect to work. Now you have the basis for an economic decision.

For many adults, returning to a traditional school for a four-year curriculum simply cannot be justified on the basis of economics. The feeling of accomplishment that you receive from educational achievement may exceed by far any financial compensation you might expect, which is in itself an argument for the nontraditional method of obtaining a degree. Nontraditional programs differ from self-directed inquiry in that the students follow a curriculum established by the institutions. They differ from traditional programs in allowing students to choose their own approach to the task. A nontraditional program is considerably less expensive and more likely to meet the needs of those who work, although some of these programs still insist upon ridiculous requirements such as physical education courses designed for nineteen-year-olds. (For that matter, what is the value of such a course for a nineteen-year-old?) All other things being equal, a nontraditional degree from a respected institution is likely to achieve the purpose intended by the person who earns it. It will not generate the impact of a degree from an Ivy League school, but then neither will one from anywhere else. Do not confuse nontraditional educational programs with "diploma mills" where money is simply exchanged for a certificate.

If you have a significant number of college credits already, it may be smart to continue—especially if you are near completion of a degree. Likewise, if you have an undergraduate degree, a traditional Masters program might be well worth considering. Still, if a person is forty years old and perfectly capable of breezing through a Masters program without any detectable difficulty, why should he or she be required to go back and pick up an undergraduate degree as a prerequisite? In the distant future there will likely be some flexibility in the linking of degrees, but for the present the structure is set. For example, you must complete a Bachelor of Science or Bachelor of Arts degree before you are eligible to enter a Masters program, and a Masters is necessary for most Doctorate programs. There are some combined Masters/Doctorate programs.

An equally important consideration is whether you are seeking credentials you lack, even though you believe you are already qualified. If this is the case, your time might be much better spent in trying to document your learning rather than accepting the traditional premise that a curriculum is naturally superior to your experience.

A great many adults have returned to school in the pursuit of credentials which, once obtained, are not likely to land them a job. It is of critical importance to make a thorough investigation of a field that you want to enter. I once heard the famed motivational speaker, Earl Nightingale, say that almost anyone can become an expert in his career field by simply spending one hour a day studying. I believe it absolutely, but I would add that the time to start is before you enter the field. What you learn may change your mind. Millions of people spend years in jobs but know little more of the nature of their industry as a whole than the average person on the street. It's easy to stand out as someone who knows what's going on in a particular industry, simply because most of the others know only about the specific function that they perform and no more.

How Much Learning in a Degree?

It is useful to keep in mind just how much learning a four-year college degree entails in terms of actual hours. This becomes a useful comparison when you are documenting your prior learning experience. Colleges and universities vary in their requirements, but most consist of twelve quarters or eight semesters at forty-five hours per week, which computes to a total of 6,480 hours for an average four-year degree. This assumes that for each hour in class two are spent outside studying. The figure is subjective, but it gives you something with which to compare to your own experience. When you break this down further and examine how many actual hours are applicable to the job you are seeking, they will be much less. In fact it is often shocking to learn how little study in some fields is required in order to earn a degree.

Now consider the motivational orientation of the student and the quality of the institution. If motivation is external (just going through the motions), the student's experience is likely to be vastly different than the one whose motivation is internal (highly interested). The experience you already have may far exceed, in a practical sense, what you can expect to learn from a traditional school. If you can demonstrate this convincingly, you may open that door you have long considered closed. Examine a college curriculum in your area of interest and compare your experience. Cornelius Hirschberg, author of *The Priceless Gift*, concluded that he had given himself an equivalent of at least five liberal arts college degrees by reading on trains, buses, subways and during his lunch hour over a period of forty-five years.

Masters degrees range from thirty to sixty credit hours, depending on the institution, the program and the individual student's background. Using the same formula of one hour in class for every two hours outside of class, the total for a Masters is an additional 1620–3240 hours, or one to two years of full-time attendance.

Doctorates average around an additional 100 credit hours, or 5,400 hours. However, a dissertation is also required, and that often ranges in the thousands of hours, 3,000–4,000 is average. So we have a range of between 14,000 and 20,000 hours from the start of college to a Ph.D. It seems formidable until you conclude that there are 8,760 hours in a year, 87,600 in a decade, and 219,000 in a quarter century. Just one or two hours of study per day can make an incredible difference over a lifetime; it can quickly add up to expertise and is without a doubt a short-cut to a better quality of life. The great aspect of self-education is that *you control* your time. Therefore, you have the ability to eliminate all but quality effort, and to greatly reduce the time necessary to gain knowledge and expertise.

The Open or Free University

The open or free university is primarily a phenomenon that has developed as a backlash to traditional education. These are places where anyone can learn and anyone can teach. They can be excellent places to round out your education in areas where you already have some experience, but need to enter into a dialog with others in order to put your learning in clearer perspective. You can do this by comparing theory with your experience and the experience of others. The open university can also be a place where you can document your learning experience through the recognition of others who have also developed similar expertise.[1] Bill Draves, author of *The Free University*, wrote of some of the general stated purposes of the free university as follows:

1. To transform higher education.
2. To supplement the traditional university and provide a place for innovation and experimental concepts.
3. To provide a place for radical political thought to be expressed and promoted.
4. To change society.
5. To help individuals change and grow.
6. To sustain the counterculture.
7. To be an alternative self-supporting institution.
8. To provide lifelong learning opportunities for adults.
9. To link knowledge and action.
10. To preserve the First Amendment freedom of speech and allow citizens the right to teach or learn any subject they want.

Creating Your Own Credentials

If you are seeking credentials toward a position for which you already believe you are qualified, you may not really need the credential. You may only have to demonstrate convincingly that you are already eminently qualified. Being thoroughly acquainted with a field before you seek qualification is the only way you can determine this. There are some occupations where there is absolutely no way around a credential, such as an engineer, doctor or dentist. However, there are many occupations that appear to require certification but, in fact, prefer experience. Sometimes the experience is much easier to come by than the credentials or certificate, even though it may mean starting at a lower level and at a lower salary than you intended.

Experiential Learning

The Achilles heel of credentialism is evidenced by the growth of nontraditional degree programs that award credit for experiential learning. Over 500 colleges and universities currently offer some type of nontraditional program, and the practice is growing rapidly. These programs usually include a method for assessing and awarding credit for prior learning. They also allow for completing work off-campus, usually through correspondence.

Today many educational institutions have little choice but to try to attract adult enrollment in continuing education, because there are not enough young people entering college (the baby bust). Also, most educational institutions have been put on notice by the marketplace that there is not a sufficiently demonstrated relationship between the education students are getting and the work they are doing afterwards.

Nontraditional education is a method to get credit for the learning we gain from practical experience. Nontraditional educational alternatives will increase. Indeed, during the Nineties we may witness "credential wars" between educational institutions. A struggle is going to exist for some time, as some of the older institutions are likely to resist nontraditional education and will try to discredit it.[2] But for the long term, experiential education is here to stay, because communications technology is tearing away the walls of the traditional university. Colleges and universities will change with the times, or they will cease to exist in their present form. The fundamental reason is that access to information is continually getting easier.

Experience is often more desirable than education. For example, the federal government will allow a person to substitute education in lieu of experience for the vast majority of its jobs. Section 3308 of Title 5, United States Code, provides that no minimum educational requirement will be prescribed in any civil service examination except for such scientific, technical, or professional positions the duties of which the Office of Personnel Management decides cannot be performed by a person who does not have this education. Section 3308 also provides that OPM will make its reasons for these decisions a part of the public record. This restriction includes all formal schooling whether at grade school, high school or college level.

There are so many federal jobs that will accept experience in lieu of education that there is not enough room to list them all in this chapter. The list of jobs that do require minimum educational requirements is only three pages long and includes occupations such as aeronautical research pilot, archaeologist, computer scientist, ecologist, economist, mathematician, physicist, statistician and zoologist.

Private companies can be even more liberal than government in accepting experience in lieu of educational credentials. Consider the drastic difference between starting out in a position that doesn't pay very well in order to get your foot in the door and thus gain experience, and attending school with only the possibility that you might start at a higher level, if indeed you are able to obtain the position once you gain your credential. In such a case it would be practical to say that, if all you needed was to get some experience under your belt, you could add to your low beginning hourly wage the amount that you would have spent to become qualified. For example, if your college tuition and expenses are estimated at $10,000 a year, and you determined that you could enter your desired field at a lower than expected salary (say at $10,000 a year to start) you could then say that your salary is $20,000 per year because of the $10,000 you save. Then it doesn't seem so bad to have to start at the bottom. Just be sure that proof of competence – and not a rigid requirement for traditional credentials is the means for advancement. This kind of information is not particularly hard to come by, although most people fail to find out in advance. All you have to do is learn the educational levels of the people currently in the field or company in which you wish to work. If there are road blocks because of educational requirements, they will quickly become apparent.

There is often a significant discrepancy in the advice you get from school counselors about what you will need to qualify for a particular job or career field. Before you pursue a field of study with the specific intention of qualifying for a job, be sure to ask a significant number of potential employers about what you need to qualify for employment.

Proof of Competence

If you could kick a football accurately for a long distance, consistently pitch a baseball past the best hitters or score with a basketball at will, then finding a place on a team would in most cases be as simple as attracting the attention of the coach to your special skills. It should be that easy in the workplace, but that's not always the case. What is exciting today is that rapid change is exerting tremendous pressure on those who hold positions through unearned privilege. Today's organization is dominated by uncertainty and intense competition. During such times organizations need people who can do more than answer questions. They need people who can ask the right questions. When competition increases, competence becomes critical.

Credentialing, licensing and job performance standards are usually written by those who have already met the requirements—experience shows that they rarely set requirements that will hold themselves to any future difficulty in achievement. They are much more likely to devote their energy to restricting themselves from future competition by making entry for others difficult. This tends to create arbitrary requirements that have little to do with competence and results in mediocre performance standards. Mediocrity simply does not cut it in a global marketplace. It is probably true that in many fields, at least for the short term, credentialing is going to get worse. But technology and communications are providing a double-barreled shot at the privileged professional. First is the fact that access to knowledge through communication technology is continually getting easier. This enables people to act by adding value to information without restriction. In other words, if you can and do add value it is easily recognizable. What method you used is of little importance. For example, I don't care about the educational level of the person who wrote the software that I am using to write this chapter; I am satisfied that it works. The second blast comes from the premise that through the same communication channels it is easier to get the coach's attention long enough to watch you perform. Computer graphics—in a work environment where almost every activity searches for a means of reducing itself to numeric data for computer evaluation—offers many unique opportunities for calling attention to your work.

It is a generally accepted, common sense social edict that the person with the better educational credentials will outperform the person with less education, but as I've already pointed out, socially accepted "common sense" is often based on incorrect assumptions. Study after study confirms that, while formal education may offer an individual more options in the approach to work, it has little if any value as an indicator of performance. The exception is the case of self-education, where the results are empowerment and an increase in one's perceived locus of causality. The desire to perform well is a much better predictor of performance than any history of educational accomplishment.

Many of today's managers are in critical need of people who can provide solutions. All you may have to do in such a case is get their attention and then prove that you can indeed provide what is needed. But once you have their attention, you must be able to do more than articulate your enthusiasm. Remember that organizations have their share of articulate incompetents. Your evidence must be compelling.

Another aspect of today's opportunity for the self-educated comes from the old saying that the world gets out of the way for the person who knows where he or she is going. This is especially true today. Demonstrate that you know how to use the new computer equipment just delivered to your company, and watch people get out of your way. Or as Harvey Mackay, author of *How to Swim With the Sharks Without Being Eaten Alive,* stated, "There is always a place in the world for anyone in the world who says, 'I'll take care of it.'"

During rapid change, training in major companies is a game of "catch-up." New methods and techniques appear while the training department is still juggling with fundamentals. For the individual capable of self-training, change is an opportunity to demonstrate superior performance. Demonstrate that you are capable of meeting challenges head-on with minimal assistance, without outside direction and based solely on your own motivation, and hard-pressed managers will run interference for you as if you were a wide receiver in the NFL.

Portfolio Development

In my opinion, the best way to prove your competence to gain employment or a promotion is to follow a method like the one used in pursuing nontraditional degrees: simply identify and then document your experiential learning. Many colleges and universities offer such programs, usually called a portfolio development course or something similar. I highly recommend the process, even if you decide to not follow through with a request for credit for other than the course itself. I completed the portfolio development course at Alaska Pacific University and found it to be a completely worthwhile experience.

The portfolio development process is a good demonstration of the differences that subtly exist between most traditional classroom experiences and genuine self-directed learning activities. The instructor's role in portfolio development is facilitative, not directive. If you are unused to this type of approach it may be frustrating at first. However, once you begin to realize the extra intrinsic satisfaction that you get from self-directed versus instructor-directed learning activities, you will be able to genuinely appreciate the difference between pedagogy and andragogy (self-directed learning).

There are numerous approaches to identifying learning experiences in these types of classes, and they vary with each institution. The process that I followed at Alaska Pacific University consisted of formulating a goal statement, preparing a chronological resume, writing an autobiography, a worksheet, a reading list, a competency statement, and submitting a request for college credit in recognition of the experiential learning that I was able to successfully document.

Your goal statement would simply be an effort to clarify your intentions by describing specifically what it is you want to accomplish. If you have difficulty beginning, start by eliminating what you know that you don't want to do.

The next step is a chronological resume that is a complete history of your work life. This is for you, not an employer. List each job that you have ever held and what you did specifically. It doesn't matter how many pages it takes. The next step is to write an autobiography. I thought this was silly and almost talked myself out of doing it, but I am glad that I went ahead. Writing your own autobiography in ten to thirty pages is an exercise that takes a lot of discipline, at least it did for me. It is, however, an extremely valuable experience to help clarify your basic orientation to the future by putting the past in better perspective. After you write your autobiography you may have to go back and adjust your goal statement because of the insight you received from the experience.

Whether or not you intend to follow such a plan, I highly recommend three books. Two are by Richard Bolles: *What Color Is Your Parachute?* and *The Three Boxes of Life.* The third is *Self-Directed Learning* by Malcom Knowles. There is no need to try to repeat the advice that they have already given so clearly. Besides, it would take three more books. These guides will be invaluable to you in making career decisions.

If your goal is to become an independent scholar, educator Ronald Gross has written a wonderful book, *The Independent Scholar's Handbook: How to turn your interest in any subject into expertise.* This is by far the best work I have found on the subject of independent scholarship. Gross covers independent scholarship from messy beginnings to intellectual partnerships.

In writing this book I have relied on the works of many learned people who achieved academic expertise without a college degree: James Feibleman, Herbert Spencer, Buckminster Fuller, Erik Erikson, and Eric Hoffer, for example. Lacking a degree did not keep these men from getting an education or from gaining recognition for what they learned.

Assessing Prior Learning

In assessing what you have learned it is important to realize that it is common for us to grossly underestimate what we have learned from experience and to overestimate what others have learned through formal education. We have a sense of depth relative to learning only when it is specific; otherwise we have no internal sense of accumulative measurement to indicate that we are making progress. To get a true sense of the knowledge you have gained from experiential learning, you must be methodical and careful not to overlook skills and knowledge that you assume everyone else has, but in fact does not. Studies conducted by Canadian educator Allen Tough show that the average person engages in seven distinct learning projects each year for a total of 700 hours of learning. Yet when we are asked what we learned last year the mind goes blank—unless the question is specific.

It is fairly easy to remember a computer course on the Macintosh, which subsequently led to the learning of four new program applications, just as it is easy to recall attending a seminar on improving our supervisory skills. But it is much harder to realize that from a difficult experience with a subordinate during a performance review, we may have achieved a major learning breakthrough which will be forever useful in dealing with such problems in the future. Or that through the process of trial and error we achieved a significant method for developing new sales promotion strategies. This type of learning is the type we most often overlook; yet is not that difficult to document, and many employers acknowledge it to be of principal value.

The next exercise is to develop a worksheet based on your resume. On it you list what you did, what you already knew, and what you learned from the experience. This is also a highly illuminating exercise. If you have been in the workplace for many years, it is likely that you have learned a great deal more than you ever would have considered. You will be in for a pleasant surprise. Next prepare a reading list of anything you have read pertinent to your learning experiences. The next step is to match your learning experience with the courses offered by the institution. Then prepare a competency statement based on the worksheet. This is a declarative assertion of skills that you have gained through experience.

It now becomes a matter of ingenuity to put together the necessary documentation that will prove beyond any reasonable doubt that you do possess these skills. Your examples may be exhibits of the work itself, licenses, certificates, essays, letters of accomplishment from former employers or any number of methods that clearly establish evidence of your past performance and learning experience. The final step in this process is to offer this documentation to the respective course instructors for review, so that they can each make an assessment based on your learning experience and award you college credit accordingly. Examples of the material used in the portfolio process such as goal statements and worksheets may be found in Susan Simosko's excellent book *Earn College Credit for What You Know.*

Documentation For Employment

Here is an opportunity that is almost totally overlooked, but it may be the single most important point in my assertions about credentialism. It is simply this: the same principle used in the process of documentation for college credit can also work in obtaining the job in the first place. In other words, you can document your past learning experience and offer it to an employer as evidence of your qualifications, just as you would to a learning institution to obtain academic credit. If possible, do both.

I have checked this out with personnel directors, and many of them are extremely impressed by someone who applies for a job able to back up his work history with documented learning experience. Someday this may be a commonplace effort, but for now and the next few years it is a new approach and very impressive.

This method of documentation has substance and specifics, unlike many diplomas and fancy resumes that aren't backed up with performance. For the past few decades the focus has been on resumes; but once you get the interview, the focus will shift. Employers are aware that resume fraud is on the increase, especially for the better jobs. When you can document what you say, it expresses a great deal about your ability to think objectively and organize your efforts. Any employer or personnel director with a lot of experience has been "burned" numerous times by people whose great claims of experience later prove to be untrue. They are likely to view hiring a person with verified learning experience and well-documented background as being much less risk to themselves and their company.

Learning Resources in the Workplace

There are numerous sources for learning in organizations, e.g., managers/supervisors, peers, training departments, workshops, etc. If your organization has a performance appraisal review system, you can use it as a means for setting your learning objectives. Unfortunately, most performance appraisal systems do more harm than good, because very few managers possess the people skills to use them effectively. Having your own plan for learning objectives allows you a certain degree of control in steering your performance appraisal into a positive, productive experience. It will be impressive simply that you have already identified your own learning objectives. Discuss your performance objectives with your supervisor and plan your learning objectives accordingly. If you need to document your learning experience for credentialing purposes, have your supervisor formally acknowledge that you have achieved the specific objectives. This accomplishes two things: The first is the documented evidence of your competence; the second is acknowledgment from your boss.

Management

Managers and supervisors are themselves good sources for learning. In fact, one of the best learning relationships is to have a supervisor or manager as a mentor. This can be a valuable experience for both parties. The mentor adds to the sophistication of his own or her own knowledge by teaching, and the learner has the added benefit of objective job performance feedback.

Peers

Learning from peers in the workplace is a day-to-day occurrence in most organizations, but it is incredibly underutilized. Most outside consultants will readily admit that the solutions to many organizational problems lie in being able to tap the expertise that already exists in an organization but is not known.

Learning from peers is almost never used as objectively as it could be. If you examine the backgrounds of your co-workers, you may be amazed at the diversity. A great deal of it may not seem relevant, but it is diversity that allows people to amplify their experience using the techniques of pattern matching and judging similitudes. These are techniques for solving problems which appear to have no connection but which are solvable by similar methods. For example, the solution to a personnel problem may be similar to that of a technological innovation, but the connection is not obvious. Sometimes the person who offers the solution doesn't even understand the connection consciously, but will have used the process of pattern matching and judging similitudes unconsciously. The point is: where there is wide diversity of experience there are often many solutions to problems.

A technique I suggest for initiating peer learning is to first assess the depth of the available resources by taking an inventory of the group's experience. Compile a group resume as if the group were one person; then have one individual act as facilitator. Let the group decide what a person with this particular resume should be qualified to do for the organization. If you have a group of people with a rich, diverse background of experience, you will be amazed at the potential you are not using, potential that no one ever would have guessed existed. At this point let the facilitator assist the group in developing group learning objectives based on the premise that instruction will come from those with appropriate experience. From here you can easily set your own learning objectives and have the benefit of your own in-house training department. This can be an exceptionally productive effort for small companies.

There are numerous benefits to be derived from this process. The potential worth and value of each individual in the group will be elevated. Individuals' self-esteem will rise. They will see the group in a new perspective. And perhaps the most important result of all is that once the synergistic possibilities of the group's talents are known, the "expectations" of everyone will be raised.

The Training Department

The purpose of the training department, though seemingly simple, is often highly misunderstood within an organization. Each training department is likely to have its own mission statement, but the larger the organization, the bigger the misunderstanding. The difficulty arises because of the many different perceptions managers and employees have as to what the training department's purpose is. Sometimes this difference in understanding about how the training department is supposed to respond to problems is enormous. I have often heard managers say that it would be easier to bring in an outside consultant than to give a training objective to their own training department. I am not suggesting this as an indictment of training departments, it's just that formal training in organizations is not well understood because of conflicting opinions about training objectives.

For individuals interested in training for specific objectives, the training department can be an invaluable source of assistance. My experience has been that most training personnel genuinely like to be helpful. They can be a great source for books, films, commercially packaged training courses, trade publications, in-house training packages and a multitude of references for outside sources. They can also be extremely helpful in assisting you in the documentation that you might need to prove your competence in a particular area. Many training departments award certificates for the completion of their training classes. In special cases they may be persuaded to offer a certification document that is specific to your own unique requirements.

If a training department is unavailable to you, the best place to look for training assistance is your local library. Look for trade publications, books, films, associations and newsletters in your field of interest. An increasing number of libraries now offer computer database search services, through which you can conduct key word searches of thousands of printed sources.

Seminars

The self-help seminar industry is primarily divided into technical and nontechnical fields. Seminars in the technical field range from those offered by institutions of technical excellence on the cutting edge of discovery to fraudulent imitations of valid institutions designed to fleece those eligible for student loans. The nontechnical field is what I call "the common sense industry." Selling common sense has become a multi-billion dollar industry. Paradoxically, common sense should dictate that this is not possible. But the common sense premise upon which most businesses are founded is forgotten with the expansion that follows initial success. People are added to the organization with objective agendas that are light years away from the original product or service idea. At this point quality and service often begin to deteriorate, and departments emerge with objectives so diverse that they may as well be different companies (indeed, in the future they may be). The unanimous solution often suggested to combat the problem is "training." There are many professional training organizations that offer excellent opportunities for learning. Indeed there are some that offer in one course more insight and methods for developing self-knowledge than you may have received in years of traditional education. There is, however, a paradox that you need to be aware of or you may become quickly disillusioned by outside training. If you are self-employed you will not likely be affected, but if you work in an organization you may come away with a renewed sense of enthusiasm and empowerment, only to be met with a wall of resistance when you try to demonstrate your learning within the organization that sent you for the training in the first place.

The bottom line is that organizations spend millions on advice and then do not take it. This process itself is destabilizing because it creates elevated expectations that seem to fall from anticipated "excellence" to status quo. The newly-learned common sense solutions seem to dissolve when the recipients attempt to use what they have learned within the bureaucracy of the organization. The hung-over feeling that lingers among employees who have had such experience is one of frustration and guilt. They often accept the blame themselves for not being able to use their newly acquired knowledge. The result is that people become busy with busyness to make up for the fact that they are not reaping the anticipated progress. Or, as the saying goes, when you lose sight of your objective, you redouble your efforts. The only way to insulate yourself from this phenomenon is to study the dynamics of organizations themselves so that you will not be frustrated by the nature of organizational policy.

Another common mistake made by many of us who attend seminars is our failure to genuinely assimilate the new information. Many of us seem incapable of any more familiarization with new material than would be expected in a formal classroom, regardless of our level of interest in the subject matter. Even if the subject is really interesting we default out of habit to inadequate methods of study. In other words, we read it, look it over, discuss it briefly and promptly forget it. I believe the single most important point in this section of *Self-University* is to truly understand and to utilize the methodology of overlearning. Failure to overlearn new material is a contributing factor that causes organizations not to take the advice which they have paid for by sending their employees to seminars. Because the organization by nature is slow to change, the new information will be forgotten before the organization is ready to adapt it. It usually goes something like this: After a few months someone will say "I remember something about that, what did professor what's-his-name say about it at last summer's seminar?" And after a few blank looks from those who attended, somebody will come up with a point or two. To attend a seminar or class is to simply be made aware of new information, but to develop expertise—our stated purpose—requires far more of us. It means the new information must be assimilated by over-learning if it is to become a part of our repertoire of usable knowledge.

Maintaining Your Edge

To be dealt with effectively, the problem of credentials must be understood. Today many people pursue credentials that make little economic sense. The pursuit of the credential often costs more than can be recovered, and in some cases will not even produce a job. The fast times we live in are full of brick walls, though some have large windows of opportunity. Before you can recognize opportunity, you must understand yourself well enough to know what it is you want to do. Not knowing what we really want to do exacts a penalty. Unless we discover our right livelihood by accident, we are condemned to engage in work activities for which we continually run out of enthusiasm. People who approach employers with little idea of what they are looking for have little hope of being perceived as a valuable addition to the staff. Experienced employers know that credentials are not always a reliable indicator of future performance, and many will adjust their policy to offer an opportunity for the person who makes a good case for doing so.

Whenever you are able to gain a significant learning experience in your organization, use your associates and supervisors to document the experience. You can even follow the same process for courses you take outside the organization, provided of course, that you prepare evidence of your learning beyond any reasonable doubt. Again this accomplishes two objectives: It prepares you for the future by offering proof of what you know, and it focuses attention on your present accomplishment. When you think about it, this is the only type of strategy that makes sense in times of rapid change and uncertainty.

True knowledge takes place in the form of synthesis when theory and experience meet. None of us should be without either. The experienced individual who scoffs at the theorist and the theorist who belittles those who only have experience are each at a severe disadvantage. If you have only one, seek the other; combine the two and offer a thesis or a declarative argument as a means of documenting your knowledge. Do this and you will be far ahead of others.

Personal success and advancement in today's organization is most easily understood when you view the process as an exercise in self-marketing. Like any product, the more you know about it the better you are able to sell it. The process of self-education, which enables you to do this, is really only a method of simply living your life as if you were really interested in it.

Afterword

The first man who, having enclosed a piece of ground, bethought himself of saying This is mine, and found people simple enough to believe him, was the real founder of civil society. From how many crimes, wars and murders, from how many horrors and misfortunes might not any one have saved mankind, by pulling up the stakes, or filling up the ditch, and crying to his fellows, "Beware of listening to this impostor; you are undone if you once forget that the fruits of the earth belong to us all, and the earth itself to nobody."

—Jean Jacques Rousseau

In the preface of this book, I said that the process of my own self-education changed my views on a myriad of subjects. The greatest influence has been a dramatic change in my definition of value which seems to be forever in the process of reshaping. What we learn in a practical sense suggests that, for most of us, the term value has more of an economic meaning than any other.

Much of the economic philosophy that divides world opinion today can be traced to the work of Adam Smith and Karl Marx. In 1776 Smith defined value as follows:

> The word value, it is to be observed, has two different meanings, and sometimes expresses the utility of some particular object, and sometimes the power of purchasing other goods which the possession of that object conveys. The one may be called "value in use;" the other, "value in exchange." The things which have the greatest value in use have frequently little or no value in exchange; and, on the contrary, those which have the greatest value in exchange have frequently little or no value in use. Nothing is more useful than water: but it will purchase scarce anything; scarce anything can be had in exchange for it. A

diamond on the contrary, has scarce any value in use; but a great quantity of other goods may frequently be had in exchange for it.

In describing the virtue of self-interest Smith used the still famous metaphor of the invisible hand:

> The greatest value, he intends only his own gain, and he is in this, as in many other cases, led by an invisible hand to promote an end which was no part of his intention. Nor is it always the worse for the society that it was no part of it. By pursuing his own interests he frequently promotes that of the society more effectively than when he really intends to promote it.

Ninety-one years later Karl Marx also saw an invisible hand, but he deemed its power to be exploitive instead of unintentionally altruistic. Marx's assessment was based on the despicable working conditions of the poor which he witnessed firsthand.

Regardless of your political ideology, it is difficult to study the works of these two men without concluding that they were brilliant. While Marx's idea of a classless society is noble, I believe if it were possible, Smith's methods would be better for attaining it. Smith's invisible hand is a powerful, useful force, so long as it is attached to a head which is capable of objectivity. Neither man during his time could anticipate the incredible power to come from technological development. Smith said "nothing is more useful than water: but it will scarce purchase anything." How do we define value when it is clear that what we are doing "for exchange" is contaminating what we assume to be available "for use," as is the case with ground water throughout America and the world's oceans? How much would we be willing to pay for clean water if we could scarce find any? It seems clear to me that Marx underestimated the power of self-interest and that Smith overestimated its unchecked benefit to society. With knowledge comes responsibility, and it is painfully clear that the latter is not keeping pace with the former. We continue to focus on our self-interest to the exclusion of any felt responsibility for the process of government or the state of our environment, and we allow our educational system to remain a fundamental part of the problem. If you think that today's young people are prepared intellectually to champion the ideals of democracy, you have only to watch their reaction when they receive their first paycheck to change your mind. They are shocked by the deductions withheld from their check. So, whose government and what problems have they been studying?

The solution to a myriad of the world's problems today lies somewhere in a clear definition of what constitutes value. We confuse value with wealth and wealth with money, yet money is only a symbol of wealth which enables us to avoid the inconvenience of bartering for our goods. It has become a constant source of dissonance for me that we lean so heavily in favor of efficiency over equity. I ended Chapter Nine on a high note by saying that we should find replacements for our natural resources among the stars, but simply re-thinking how we use our resources would not only make this unnecessary, it would exponentially increase our quality of life. Our actions suggest we prize efficiency over any other virtue, yet we waste more resources in its pursuit than any other nation in the world. We confuse quantity with quality and pretend that because something is good, more is always better. We assume that all work adds value, but some work, as I've said, is not only without value but adds a negative value.

Indeed, there is a vast range of value attributable to work: some has great value (intelligent work), some is merely busyness (wasted or meaningless work), and some is demonstrably harmful (destructive work). Don't misunderstand my simplistic descriptions (attributing value to only three types of work) by thinking that intelligent work is solely the product of intellectual contemplation. Proper disposal of garbage is intelligent work.

The majority of us blindly accept the edict that all three types of work are more important than people. We think that as long as everyone is employed, all is well. Only a few of us look beyond our own personal interests to the extent that we call attention to the differences. And those of us who do, are shouted down as doomsayers and naysayers whose motives are subversively suspect because of our audacity to question authority or raise questions which illuminate the need to deal with problems we would rather not discuss. We label people as environmentalists and radicals so as to be forewarned not to listen to them, for if they catch us unaware, they may strike a nerve of truth which we are ill prepared to deal with.

We are poised to grow at any cost, often admiring those who are exceptionally busy (even if we suspect their efforts are destructive), while we hold the poor in contempt for their inability to participate. For example, we would be much better off to pay people to do nothing rather than to "work" at growing tobacco. We can say the same for scores of chemicals we produce whose value above ground is insignificant when compared to the damage they cause upon reaching their final destination in our water wells. Which in the long term costs more, remedying the damage of destructive work, or the costs associated with the welfare of the poor? The latter is inconsequential compared to the former, so why is this such an emotional issue? Why do we continue to blame the poor for most of our economic ills?

We have peculiar ways of attributing value to the efforts of others. For example, we abhor inactivity when we infer it to be an unwillingness on anyone's part to work for self-support, and we will begrudge them charity. On the other hand, if someone aspires to devote his life to spiritual contemplation, many of us will enthusiastically subsidize that person's support over a lifetime. This action would seem to suggest that we do have a sense of value independent of activity as long as we approve of the intentions of the individual. If we modified this bent of cultural bias just a little, we might see the wisdom of substituting education for spiritual quest, and thereby attributing a value to education so that people in the ghetto might be subsidized to learn their way out of poverty. Would this be terribly different from paying farmers not to grow crops?

Don't take my emphasis on helping people out of the ghetto as an assumption that everyone there is guilty of being unemployable. Ghettos are scabs across the face of America, and are in reality a middle class problem. There are many people in the slums, as I've said, who have no confidence in their ability to have an effect on their environment. But the ghettos also contain the working poor, imprisoned through the subtleties of undetectable prejudice. For every law that guarantees equality of opportunity, there are a thousand subtle ways of denying opportunity without appearing to break the law. If we set aside our emotions and consider this problem objectively, it cannot be denied that the growth of ghettos is a threat to national security. "United we stand. Divided we fall." "We are only as strong as the weakest link." We grew up repeating these sayings, but failed to learn their meaning. The simple truth is that whether you call it racial bias, gender bias or class bias, we exhibit little tolerance for people who are different from ourselves. We do not allow people into the mainstream who appear as if they have just arrived or as if they do not belong. Herein lies the largest obstacle and the greatest misunderstanding on the part of the middle class, as B.F. Skinner has demonstrated: experience shapes behavior, not the reverse. For example, we do not act like soldiers until we are sufficiently adjusted to being in the military; likewise we do not act like college students until we have been to college. Yet before we extend the vast array of opportunities afforded members of the middle class to people who live in the ghetto we demand that these people behave as if they have never lived there. We confound our understanding of this problem by focusing on the exceptions. For example, if you corral a herd of wild horses, or imprison a group of humans behind a fence, a few will escape, some will go over the fence and some under, but to point to the escapees as examples of the path to freedom is ludicrous. If freedom is seriously your goal, you demolish the fence.

The prejudice of the middle class constructs barriers at the borders of the ghetto as surely as if they were prison walls. These barriers however, are much more effective than walls because they exist only as abstractions; their existence is difficult to prove. We deny such barriers exist, but the barbs of prejudice are strong – we just don't want to see them.

We point to the Soviet system and their obvious lack of freedom and say that socialism doesn't work. The Soviets, in turn, point to our "street people" (homeless) and say that capitalism doesn't work. But it would be a more accurate assessment for an alien space traveler passing close by earth to make the observation that human society doesn't work. We are expeditiously committing suicide by destroying the conditions that make our planet livable; "for exchange" is clearly destroying "for use." Almost every society participates to some degree without due reflection on the consequences. The alien observer might conclude that the only rational humans on this planet are the simple tribesmen, who are totally without technology, and the world's poor people, whose lack of excessive consumption places them in greater harmony with their surroundings. He might also find it paradoxical that humans develop economic systems for creating and exchanging value and then promptly become prisoners of those same systems. Indeed, he would conclude that humans cannot comprehend solutions to problems which appear to lie outside their economic systems, such as protecting the global environment. This is a problem which is unequivocally more important than the human systems for measuring value for exchange.

Each time we try to address these issues, we conclude by throwing up our hands and saying, "But who is going to pay for it?" Alan Watts reminds us that money doesn't and never did come from anywhere. Money is simply a way of measuring real wealth (our food products and natural useable resources). For example, during a depression real wealth is not lost, we still have the land, the natural resources, the livestock and our crops. It is only our system for measurement which has failed. For this reason Watts predicted in the Sixties that by the year 2000, if we could and would understand this confusion of symbol with reality (money versus wealth) we would

reverse many of our economic practices. He believed we would eliminate taxes and create a national credit versus a national debt system
in which each of us by nature of citizenship would have equity in the
form of a credit, directly tied to the productivity of our machines
which, after all, are designed to put us out of work.[1] Watts was wrong.
We are not yet wise enough nor sufficiently startled or frightened by
an environment which is poised to bite back with increasing fero-
ciousness, if we continue on our present course without trying to
adjust our world economies into models with humanitarian and
environmental congruence. Huge budget deficits are evidence that
there are some things we value above our system for measuring what
we loosely call productivity, even if those things are irrational.

Cooperation and competition are two of the fundamental
mechanics with which we persevere, but if we survive as a species, I
believe it will be because we learn to keep the two in better perspective and more equitable relationships. We speak of competition as
being the "engine" of our economy, and it is clearly a powerful force. I
would argue that capitalism has created better conditions for more
people than any other system on earth, but the engine of our planet
runs on organic life forces which are being radically altered by our
system for exchange. Our capabilities for changing our environment
escalate daily, while our means of assessing the impact remains
primitive. The "greenhouse" effect is prima facie evidence that millions of invisible hands are at work which are in no way attached to a
head. Tropical forests burned in South America affect the global
atmosphere as do the industrial emissions of developed countries.
Nuclear reactor failure anywhere threatens people everywhere. The
unassailable notion of global interdependence is in no way better
demonstrated than by the fact that water from the same oceans wash
the beaches of many nations. Toxic waste dumped anywhere, in any
ocean, is a threat to mankind.

Nobel Laureate Konrad Lorenz has said that the only legitimate "intake" power source on earth is solar. Everything else puts the
world in debt "to a completely callous and uncompromising creditor."
Nuclear power plants seem to me to be similar to the Great Pyramids
of Egypt, but in reverse. For example, we estimate that thousands of
workers must have died building the Great Pyramids, and although
their original purpose was not economic, today they bring thousands
of people and millions of dollars to Egypt. Nuclear power plants, on
the other hand, justified by economics, cost billions to construct,
injure thousands, last twenty or thirty years and leave a storage
residue problem for 20,000 years.[2] Is this viable long-term planning?

Overpopulation is a crucial world problem, but addressing the issue by allowing millions of humans to starve to death demonstrates the same incredible mentality that says we have to manufacture thousands of nuclear weapons in order to achieve the negotiating posture necessary to destroy them. Such logic is madness, and the only thing I find more unbelievable is the fact that millions of us support these actions without a second thought, many with a great deal of enthusiasm.

The more I study the world economy and world politics, the more firmly I am convinced that we are precariously treading a path laden with extraordinary possibilities for the betterment of human-kind and simultaneously booby-trapped with a multitude of opportu-nities for devastation, including the total annihilation of humanity.

The crux of the issue is hidden by our confusion over value and activity or symbol and reality. I still hold the conservative belief that the family is the foundation of our moral strength. I believe its greatest enemy is an economy based on indefinitive value and indiscriminate busyness. We know that during the formative years the quality of child care sets an orientation for personal development that may last a lifetime. Yet, for millions of families, the daily struggle for economic survival is so great that children are left to fend for themselves. By the time the parents achieve an economic status which will allow for them to spend time with their kids, if indeed they do, the opportunity to influence behavior is past. We would never accept a manufacturing process where it is so easy to see design flaws without making the necessary adjustments. Why then do we try to produce taxpayers this way? I used to refer to people who argued that we should be concerned with such problems as "bleeding-heart liberals," but today I see these positions as being based on reason. On the other hand, my former conservative view of society's disenfranchised as the cause of our ills I now see as ludicrous, a purely emotional, bleeding-heart, non-thinking approach. A heart damaged for a purely emotional reason is a bleeding heart, regard-less of the convictions of its owner. I believe many of us have assumed attitudes like these from spending years in a workplace dominated by the assumptions of classical management. We no longer believe in the assumption that everyone in the workplace is lazy or cannot be trusted to be productive without an overseer. However, we have been judged by this measuring stick and confused about our definition of value for so long that we still apply these non-thinking assumptions to everyone who is outside the workforce, regardless of their reasons for being left out.

As long as we act as if indiscriminate activity equals value—while knowing full well that much of our activity is adding negative value and is, in fact, killing our planet—then we are complicit in sending the world the message that efficiency is what we view as the moral fiber that binds us together. Thus we continue to judge others not by their wisdom or their contribution to our collective knowledge, but rather by whether or not they are busy. Actions have consequences, and sometimes there is value in no action at all.

The raw resource energy we waste while feigning affection for efficiency is unbelievable. By simply doubling our efforts at recycling raw materials we could equal the energy savings of more than a dozen nuclear reactors.[3] This waste upon which our economy depends is at the crux of a moral issue that we refuse to acknowledge. The issue is simply this: even though there are enough food resources in the world to put an end to starvation, there are clearly not enough natural raw resources for everyone to waste them as we do. I hold out a hope that as we begin to perceive ourselves as a knowledge society, we may replace the value of busyness with one of thoughtfulness and objectivity. I believe a true knowledge society cannot escape the conclusion that humanity is worth its weight in equity because of the explicit interdependence which binds our interests as a species. Such equity assumes that people really matter and that each person, simply by nature of being human, is worth enough real wealth (food, shelter, and education) to be afforded the opportunity to cooperate and compete in making the world a better place to live. If we are able to maintain objectivity, at some point we must buy into a social contract which rises above the national symbols we use to protect our own versions of reality.

We must temper our cultural bias with a species bias. Either we reduce the role of competition from that of an engine to that of a carburetor, or we set the engine of competition at full throttle to create a desired state of environmental quality. I believe it would be entirely appropriate to create a world environmental quality bank in which nations could earn cash credit value for either ceasing destructive environmental activities or by finding alternatives for pursuing them in the first place. Such a mechanism would empower undeveloped countries to establish a reasonable equity and bypass the need to industrialize, thus avoiding the contribution to world pollution which would inevitably follow. A similar approach will be necessary on a local level. People cannot be expected to set aside their own economic interests, if there are no practical alternatives. For example, it is one thing to say we should stop making certain products, but it is quite another problem when it is your employer who is making those products. Until we deal with environmental problems by offering economic alternatives, it can truthfully be said that we have not dealt with them at all. The same is true for the arms race. Until there are economic alternatives to replace the hundreds of thousands of jobs in the defense industry, we will continue to produce weapons at full capacity regardless of the state of our adversarial relationships. John Naisbitt's prescription of "thinking globally and acting locally" is entirely appropriate and long past due.

We are near a time when television documentaries about the sorry state of the environment are overshadowed by panicked legislators shouting at each other on the evening news in an attempt to avoid blame for environmental blunders that affect the lives of millions of people. The damage will be so devastating that we will wonder at our ability to have blindly allowed these catastrophes to happen in the first place. My hope is that the thoughts I've presented about process, freedom, and responsibility will cause you to reach the simple conclusion that "we," you and I, are the "head" which has the power and obligation to see that busy hands are responsible and accountable. We must acknowledge that as the ratio of information to mass increases, so does our capacity for change, as well as our responsibility for that change. We need to engage in constant discourse on the definition and character of what we construe to be value and the true nature of freedom. People who have strong convictions about the future produce leaders with clear visions, not the reverse. The availability of scouts and wagon masters did not cause the settling of the West during the nineteenth century; rather, it was the popular desire to go West that produced scouts and wagon masters.

I believe strongly in individual initiative, individual responsibility, individual freedom, hard intelligent work, and the pursuit of individual happiness. But I also believe the evidence is clear that we have abdicated individual responsibility to such an extent that the quality of human life, if not life itself, is in jeopardy. Today's problems call for radical solutions. I am not advocating that we abandon technology, just that we lean it toward intelligent use. The greatest danger our present course poses is in reaching a stage of environmental damage that is irreversible. Our history suggests we are slow to act unless toxic waste comes seeping into our own backyards, and then we are too emotional to deal with the problem rationally. Protecting the environment calls for a sincere commitment from many nations. It is a delusion to think that the damage already done can be cleaned up out of business profits, because the damage is far too great. It is also a mistake to think we can fix the damage quickly; it will take long-term, well-thought-out approaches of the kind we have little experience in making. By attacking meaningless and destructive work I am not by any means suggesting that we replace destructive activity with idleness. On the contrary, I believe we should set about with all of the energy and enthusiasm that America can muster to replace the brawn of industrialism with the brains to survive the next century. And to do so requires that we become autodidacts and that we empower our children to do likewise. Voltaire said that "not to be occupied, and not to exist, amount to the same thing."

In the final analysis, we are back to the question of value. Social critics increasingly argue that America has lost its shared vision of the future. In other words, we lack something to stand for – a cogent argument for existence, a shared desire for posterity. We are said to lack commitment. It is an argument which can be stated for many nations. A positive future for America and the world demands cooperation which may be attainable only through a common desire, something people can stand for despite their many differences. A shared vision that transcends religions and political systems and enables the cooperation necessary for us to live in harmony among ourselves and the global environment. In other words, a positive future requires a third definition of value, a universal explanation which makes a strong case for commitment by all those who assent. We need to subordinate "for use" and "for exchange" to a higher definition of value such as "for life."

My own experience suggests that life continually offers us glimpses of genuine value only at the point of catastrophe. A near-death experience, or the death of someone close will, for a short period of time, cut through all the pretentiousness of our culturally built realities and leave little doubt about what does and does not constitute value. All the simple things we take for granted and scarcely acknowledge suddenly stand out. We feel somewhat in awe and a little stupid for never having fully realized how simple value is to define when time has run out. It is only then that many of us can put our economic system in perspective and see clearly and undoubtedly that genuine value has little to do with, and is infinitely more important than money. Don't misunderstand my point: I'm not saying money is not important to people; I'm saying people are more important than money. I believe the ability to override culture and recognize genuine value at life's ebb is common to all humans. Human survival may depend upon understanding this commonality.

Notes

Chapter One: Why We Are the Way We Are

1   I heard Dr. Elisabeth Kuebler-Ross say something similar to my opening statement, "All humans are born into the world with the capacity for unconditional love and compassion," in the spring of 1988 at a seminar for Humana Hospital in Anchorage, Alaska. The assertions that follow are mine.

2   Alvin Toffler. *The Third Wave*, page 348.

3   Paul Chance. "Master of Mastery," *Psychology Today*, April 1987, page 46.

4   W. Baird Whitloch. *Educational Myths*, page 75.

5   Stephen S. Young. "The Next Revolution in Education," *The Futurist*, March-April, 1986, page 60.

6   Malcolm Knowles. *Self-Directed Learning*, page 14.

7   U.S. Department of Education. *What Works*, 1986, page 33.

8   Marilyn Ferguson. *The Aquarian Conspiracy*, page 283. Ferguson uses the term "pedogenic illness."

9   William W. Lowrance. *Modern Science and Human Values*, page 11.

10   Leon Martel. *Mastering Change*, page 65.

11   James Gleick. *Chaos*, pages 11-56.

12   Allan Bloom. *The Closing of the American Mind*, page 43.

13   The assertion that there is no shortage of food in the world is based on a report titled, "The Right To Food," by Jose Antonio Viera-Gallo, and on *World Hunger: Ten Myths* by Frances Moore Lappe and Joseph Collins. The assertion that there are 3000 calories available for every human on earth appears on page 8. This figure is for grains alone and does not include meat products.

14   I wrote to numerous organizations for help in estimating how many people have from starvation died in this century, but to no avail. No one, including the World Health Organization, seems to want any part in such an estimate.

15   Hendrickson, Robert. *More Cunning Than Man: A Social History of Rats and Men*, page 32.

16   The estimates of U.S. military war dead from all wars were taken from *1987 Information Please Almanac*, 40th edition, Houghton Mifflin Co., Boston, MA.

17   The traffic fatalities number is based on estimates by the U.S. Department of Transportation.

18   Deaths from cigarette smoking are based on estimates from the U.S. Department of Health and Human Services. According to FY88 report IB87032, the 1988 federal government tobacco subsidy was approximately $434 million.

19   Cancer deaths in 1985 numbered 461,563; in 1986 the figure was 472,000; in 1987 it was 483,000; and for 1988 the estimate is 494,000. These figures are from the American Cancer Society. Estimates of cancer research funding by the federal government were based on Report FY88 by Michael E. Davey, coordinator Science Policy Research Division. This information was not easy to find. After several letters to government agencies I finally received help from the office of Alaska's U.S. Senator Ted Stevens in locating the figures which are still somewhat vague.

20   The estimated U.S. Defense budget for 1988 according to FY88 report IB87129, is $291.5 billion. The estimate for cancer research for 1988 is slightly less than $1.5 billion, according to FY88 report IB87129.

21   Audrey Haber, and Richard P. Runyon. *Psychology of Adjustment*, page 11.

Chapter Two: Media and Manipulation

1   Michael Hutchison. *Megabrain*, page 310.

2   Denise Winn. *The Manipulated Mind*, page 194.

3   Ibid., page 135.

4   Ibid., page 196.

5   Thomas W. Keiser, and Jacqueline L. Keiser. *The Anatomy of Illusion*, page 52.

6   Ibid., page 76.

7   The fact that barely 75 percent of U.S students graduate from high school and only one in five has a college education appears in the *1988 World Almanac and Book of Facts*.

Chapter Three: Self-Knowledge-the Foundation of Self-Education

1   Michael Hutchison. *Megabrain*, page 151.

2   Marilyn Ferguson. *The Aquarian Conspiracy*, pages 163, 166.

3   Robert E. Kelley. *The Gold Collar Worker*, page 159.

4   F.H.C. Crick. *The Brain*, page 13.

5   Michael Hutchison. *Megabrain*, pages 28, 90.

6   David Lewis, and James Greene. *Thinking Better*, page 6.

7   Lawrence J. Greene. *Kids Who Underachieve*, pages 57, 58.

8   John Naisbitt, and Patricia Aburdene. *Re-Inventing the Corporation*, page 135.

9   Robert J. Trotter. "Three Heads are Better than One," *Psychology Today*, August 1986, Vol. 20, no. 8, page 60.

10   William H. Van Hoose. *Midlife Myths and Realities*, page 36.

11   Alan B. Knox. *Adult Development and Learning*, pages 419, 420, 421.

12   Jerold W. Apps. *The Adult Learner on Campus*, pages 89, 90.

13   Michael Hutchison. *Megabrain*, page 44.

14   Edward De Bono. *De Bono's Thinking Course*, page 3.

15   Michael Hutchison. *Megabrain*, pages 28, 33, 38.

16   Alan Knox. *Adult Development and Learning*, page 434.

17   Jerold W. Apps. *The Adult Learner on Campus*, page 91.

18   Sharon Begley, et al. "Memory," *Newsweek*, September 29, 1986, pages 49, 54.

19   Joseph Alpher. "Our Dual Memory," *Science 86*, July/August 1986, page 46.

20   Kenneth L. Higbee. *Your Memory*, pages 17, 24.

21   Joseph Alpher. "Our Dual Memory," *Science 86*, July/August 1986, page 46.

22   William C. Miller. *The Creative Edge*, page 109.

23   Robert J. Trotter. "The Mystery of Mastery," *Psychology Today*, July 1986, page 36.

Chapter Four: The Personal Sciences

1   Edward L. Deci. *Intrinsic Motivation*, page 8.

2   Ibid., pages 9, 17.

3   Denise Winn. *The Manipulated Mind*, page 61.

4   Frank G. Goble. *The Third Force*, page 44.

5   James K. Feibleman. *The Stages of Human Life*, page 156.

6   Anne Roe, and Patricia W. Lunneborg. "Personality Development and Career Choice," an essay from *Career Choice and Development*, page 32.

7   Edward L. Deci. *Intrinsic Motivation*, page 83.

8   James K. Feibleman. *Understanding Human Nature*, page 43.

9   Edward L. Deci. *Intrinsic Motivation*, pages 84, 85.

10   Daniel Yankelovich. *New Rules*, pages 235, 236, 244, 245.

11   Frank G. Goble. *The Third Force*, page 54.

12   Edward G. Olsen, and Phillip A. Clark. *Life Centering Education*, page 112.

13   I made the statement that Socrates was a man who knew that he did not know, but in *The Trial of Socrates*, author I.F. Stone suggests otherwise. This is an intriguing book. Stone worked over ancient texts for ten years and taught himself Greek in the process. Stone offers a powerful argument which suggests that Socrates was quite a different person than the one we have been led to believe. I recommend this book highly.

Chapter Five: Motivation

1   Edward P. Morgan. *Inequality in Classroom Learning*, page 125.

2   Edward L. Deci. *The Psychology of Self-Determination*, page 213.

3   Edward L. Deci. *Intrinsic Motivation*, page 91.

4   Edward L. Deci. *The Psychology of Self-Determination*, page 38.

5   Benjamin D. Singer. *Learning for Tomorrow*, page 25.

6   Alan B. Knox. *Adult Development and Learning*, page 371.

7   James K. Feibleman. *The Stages of Human Life*, pages 151, 152, 153.

8   Lewis M. Andrews. *To Thine Own Self Be True*, page 12.

9   Audrey Haber, and Richard P. Runyon. *The Psychology of Adjustment*, page 35.

10   Anne Rosenfeld, and Elizabeth Stark. "The Prime of Our Lives," *Psychology Today*, May 1987, page 66.

11   Audrey Haber, and Richard P. Runion. *The Psychology of Adjustment*, 224, 227.

Chapter Six: The People Sciences

1   Peter F. Drucker. *Toward the Next Economics and Other Essays*, pages 96-106. Drucker explains why classical management is a misinterpretation of the work of Frederick W. Taylor.

2   Mortimer J. Adler. *We Hold These Truths*, page 146.

3   E.F. Schumacher. *Good Work*, page 50. This is a great book which puts technology in clear human perspective.

4   Marilyn French. *Beyond Power*. The author offers a powerful argument for the switch from a patriarchal society to one of matriarchal leadership.

Chapter Seven: The Methodology of Inquiry

1   Edward De Bono. *De Bono's Thinking Course*, page 89.

2   Huey B. Long. *Adult and Continuing Education*, pages 10, 12, 32, 60.

3   James K. Feibleman. *Understanding Philosophy*, pages 48, 98, 219.

Chapter Eight: Understanding Credentialism

1   Mortimer B. Zuckerman. "Physician, Heal Thyself, " *U.S. News and World Report*, July 21, 1986, page 68.

2   Oxford Analytica, *America in Perspective*, page 68.

3   Robert Klitgaard. *Choosing Elites*, page 118.

4   William Abbott. "Work in the Year 2001," *1999 The World of Tomorrow*, page 104.

5   Bill Draves. *The Free University*, page 124.

6   John Harris, and William Troutt. *Credentialing Educational Accomplishment*, page 39.

7   Ernest L. Boyer. *College*, page 143.

8   Ronald Dore. *The Diploma Disease*, pages 5, 24.

9   James Burke. *The Day the Universe Changed*, pages 256-273.

10   Alfie Kohn. "How to Succeed without Even Vying," *Psychology Today*, September 1986, pages 24, 26 28.

11   Alfie Kohn. "Cooperating in the Classroom," *Psychology Today*, September 1986, page 27.

12   Jonathan Kozol. *Illiterate*, page 204.

13   Malcolm Knowles. *Self-Directed Learning*, page 85.

14   Michael Hutchison. *Megabrain*, page 83.

15   Brooklyn C. Derr. *Managing the New Careerists*, page 2.

Chapter Nine: The Possibilities of Tomorrow

1   This chapter is an assessment of the possibilities of the future based on my own self-education. In addition to the books mentioned in the text I was particularly influenced by the following works: *1999 The World of*

Tomorrow by William Abbott; *America in Perspective* by Oxford Ana-
lytica; *The Communications Revolution* by Frederick Williams;
"Libraries in the Year 2010" by S.D. Neill; *Computer Phobia* by Sanford
B. Weinberg and Mark Fuerst; *The Creative Edge* by William C. Miller;
"Population and Education" by Joseph F. Coates; "Illiterates with
Doctorates" by Peter H. Wagschal; *The Free University* by Bill Draves;
"Schools of the Future" by Marvin J. Cetron, Barbara Soriano and
Margaret Gayle; *The Great Conversation* by Robert M. Hutchins; "Atti-
tudes to Information Technology" by Nigel Kemp; "Information Tech-
nology and People: A Fresh view of the Relationship" by Frank Blacker
and David J. Oborne; "Educational and Social Implications" by Christo-
pher Dede; *The Networking Book* by Jessica Lipnack and Jeffrey
Stamps; *The New Achievers* by Perry Pascarella; "The Next Computer
Revolution" by Abraham Peled; *Videotext* edited by Efrem Sigel; *Working in the Twenty-First Century* edited by C. Stewart Sheppard and
Donald C. Carroll; *The Work Revolution* by Gail Garfield Schwartz.

Chapter Ten: Practicum

1   David Keirsey, and Marilyn Bates. *Please Understand Me: Character &
     Temperament Types*.

     The four temperament types of Hippocrates were the Sanguine, Chol-
     eric, Phlegmatic, and the Melancholic.

2   Kenneth L. Higbee. *Your Memory*, pages 120, 133, 135.

3   Shelila Ostrander, and Lynn Schroeder. *Superlearning*, page 68.

4   Kenneth L. Higbee. *Your Memory*, page 62.

Chapter Eleven: Practicum in the Workplace

1   If you would like information on how to start a free university in your
     community, write The Learning Resources Network, P.O Box 1448,
     Manhattan, KS 66502; phone: 913-539-5376.

2   John Harris, and William Troutt. *Credentialing Educational Accom-
     plishment*, page 57.

Afterword:

1   Alan Watts. *Does It Matter?* Alan Watts makes a good case for an
     economy based on equity rather than efficiency, and he describes in
     greater detail the fact that when our systems for exchange fail we still
     have the resources necessary to survive.

2   Konrad Lorenz. *The Waning of Humaneness*, page 177.

3   This is a conservative estimate based on the work of David Morris and
     Neil Seldman of The Institute for Local Self-reliance, 2425 18th Street
     N.W., Washington, D.C. 20009. According to their research, we could
     actually save the equivalant of 14 nuclear reactors if we would only
     return to recycling efforts similar to those of World War Two.

Annotated Bibliography

I found all of the works that follow to be useful, but I marked with an asterisk (*) those works which I thought the reader would find of particular importance.

Abbott, William. "Work in the Year 2001," in *1999 The World of Tomorrow: Selections from the Futurist*. ed. Edward Cornish. Washington, DC: The World Future Society, 1978.

*Adler, Mortimer J. *Aristotle for Everybody: Difficult Thought Made Easy*. New York: Macmillan, 1978.

*_____ . *A Guidebook to Learning: For the Lifelong Pursuit of Wisdom*. New York: Macmillan, 1986.

_____ . *How to Speak, How to Listen*. New York: Macmillan, 1983.

_____ . *The Paideia Proposal: An Educational Manifesto*. New York: Macmillan, 1982.

_____ . *Philosopher at Large: An Intellectual Autobiography*. New York: Macmillan, 1977.

_____ . *Reforming Education: The Schooling of a People and Their Education*. Boulder, CO: Westview Press, 1977.

_____ . *Ten Philosophical Mistakes*. New York: Macmillan, 1985.

*_____ . *We Hold These Truths: Understanding the Ideas and Ideals of the Constitution*. New York: Macmillan, 1987.

*Adler, Mortimer J. and Charles Van Doren. *How to Read a Book: The Classic Guide to Intelligent Reading*. New York: Touchstone/Simon & Schuster, 1972.
  – A must for anyone serious about learning.

Alpher, Joseph. "Our Dual Memory," *Science 86*, July/August 1986, p. 46.

Andrews, Lewis M. *To Thine Own Self Be True: The Rebirth of Values in the New Ethical Therapy*. Garden City, NY: Anchor Press, 1987.

*Apps, Jerold W. *The Adult Learner on Campus*. Chicago: Follett, 1981.
  – Highly recommended for anyone returning to school.

_____ . *Study Skills, For Those Adults Returning to School*. New York: McGraw-Hill, 1978.

Bardwick, J.M. *The Plateauing Trap: How to Avoid It in Your Career—and in Your Life*. New York: AMACOM, 1986.

Barnet, R.J., and R.E. Muller. *Global Reach: The Power of the Multinational Corporations*. New York: Simon & Schuster, 1974.

Baron, Joan B. and Robert J. Sternberg. *Teaching Thinking Skills: Theory and Practice*. New York: Freeman, 1987.

Batri, Ravi. *The Great Depression of 1990: Why It's Got to Happen—How to Protect Yourself*. New York: Simon & Schuster, 1987.

*Beane, J.A., and R.A. Lipka. *Self-Concept, Self-Esteem, and the Curriculum*. New York: Teachers College Press, 1984.
  – An outstanding book for understanding how the classroom affects self-esteem.

Begley, Sharon, Karen Springen, Susan Katz, Mary Hager, and Elizabeth Jones. "Memory," *Newsweek*, 29 September, 1986, pp. 49, 54.

Begold, C., R.J. Carlson, and J.C. Peck. *The Future of Work and Health: The Institute for Alternative Futures.* Dover, MA: Auburn House, 1986.

*Berger, Peter L. *The Capitalist Revolution: Fifty Propositions about Prosperity, Equality, and Liberty.* New York: Basic Books, 1986.

Bird, Caroline. *The Case Against College.* New York: D. McKay Co., 1975.

Blackler, Frank and David Osborne, ed. *Information Technology and People: Designing for the Future.* Cambridge, MA: MIT Press, 1987.

Bloom, Alan. *The Closing of the American Mind.* New York: Simon & Schuster, 1987.

*Bolles, Richard N. *The Three Boxes of Life: And How To Get Out of Them.* Berkeley, CA: Ten Speed Press, 1981.
 —One of the best self-help books available. Filled with practical information which we should have learned in school, but didn't.

*_____ . *What Color is Your Parachute?* Berkeley, CA: Ten Speed Press, 1986.
 —Don't look for a job without it.

*Boyer, E.L. *College: The Undergraduate Experience in America.* New York: Harper & Row, 1987.

*Brand, Stewart. *The Media Lab: Inventing the Future at MIT.* New York: Viking, 1987.
 —A must for anyone trying to make sense of technology.

*Bridges, William. *Transitions: Making Sense of Life's Changes.* Reading, MA: Addison-Wesley, 1980.

Brown, Duane, Linda Brooks and associates. *Career Choice and Development.* San Francisco: Jossey-Bass, 1984.

*Burke, James. *The Day The Universe Changed.* Boston, MA: Little, Brown, 1985.
 —The companion to the PBS television series with the same name. A great synthesis of history, technology and social science. If you have the opportunity to see it, don't miss it.

*Campbell, Joseph, Bill Moyers and Betty Sue Flowers, eds. *The Power of Myth.* New York: Doubleday, 1988.
 —Companion to the PBS television series with the same name. A wonderful synthesis of man and mythology. Available on video cassette.

*Capra, Fritjof. *The Tao of Physics.* New York: Bantam Books, 1975.
 —A lucid approach to the study of Eastern culture and Western science.

*_____ . *The Turning Point: Science, Society, and the Rising Culture.* New York: Simon & Schuster, 1982.

*_____ . *Uncommon Wisdom: Conversations with Remarkable People.* New York: Simon & Schuster, 1988.

Cetron, Marvin J. *Encounters with the Future: A Forecast.* New York: McGraw-Hill, 1982.

_____ . *Jobs of the Future: The 500 Best Jobs—Where They'll Be and How to Get Them.* New York: McGraw-Hill, 1984.

Cetron, Marvin, Alicia Pagano and Otis Port. *The Future of American Business: The U.S. in World Competition.* New York: McGraw-Hill, 1985.

Cetron, Marvin C., Barbara Soriano and Margaret Gayle. "Schools of the Future," *The Futurist,* August 1985, pp. 18-23.

Chance, Paul. "Master of Mastery," *Psychology Today,* May 1987, p. 46.

*Clutterbuck, David, ed. *New Patterns of Work.* New York: St. Martin's Press, 1985.
 —An insightful look into work patterns for the serious planner. More advanced than most management books on the subject.

Coates, Joseph F. "Population and Education," in *Education and the Future: Selected Articles on Education from The Futurist.* ed. Lane Jennings and Sally Cornish. Washington, DC: The World Future Society, 1980.

Combs, Arthur W. *Individual Behavior: A Perceptual Approach To Behavior.* New York: Harper, 1959.

Conger, D. Stewart. "Social Inventions," in *1999 The World of Tomorrow: Selections from the Futurist.* ed. Edward Cornish. Washington, DC: The World Future Society, 1978.

Coons, John E. *Education By Choice: The Case for Family Control.* Berkeley, CA: University of California Press, 1978.

Cornish, Edward, ed. *Communications Tomorrow: The Coming of the Information Society.* Bethesda, MD: World Future Society, 1982.

_____. *1999 The World of Tomorrow: Selections from the Futurist; A Journal of Forecasts, Trends, and Ideas about the Future.* Washington, DC: World Future Society, 1978.

Couger, Daniel J. and Robert A. Zawacki. *Motivating and Managing Computer Personnel.* New York: John Wiley & Sons, 1980.

Cousins, Norman. *Human Options.* New York: W.W. Norton, 1981.

Crick, F.H.C. "Thinking about the Brain," *Scientific American* Offprint, 1984.

Crosby, Philip B. *Quality Is Free: The Art of Making Quality Certain.* New York: New American Library, 1980.

Daloz, Laurent A. *Effective Teaching and Mentoring.* San Francisco: Jossey-Bass, 1986.

*DeBono, Edward. *De Bono's Thinking Course.* New York: Facts on File Publications, 1982.
 —This is a must for your own personal library. It is the best book I have found on thinking skills—easy to understand and practical for immediate use.

_____. *Six Thinking Hats.* Boston: Little, Brown, 1985.

Deci, Edward L. *Intrinsic Motivation.* New York: Plenum Press, 1975.

_____. *The Psychology of Self-Determination.* Lexington, MA: Lexington Books, 1980.

Dede, Christopher. "Education and Social Implications," *The Information Technology Revolution.* Cambridge, MA: MIT Press, 1985.

*Deming, W. Edwards. *Out of the Crisis.* Cambridge, MA: MIT Press, 1986.
 —One of the best modern management books in print.

*Derr, C. Brooklyn. *Managing the New Careerists.* San Francisco: Jossey-Bass, 1986.

Donaldson, Sam. *Hold On, Mr. President.* New York: Fawcett Crest, 1987.

Donnelly, William J. *The Confetti Generation.* New York: Henry Holt, 1986.

Dore, Ronald. *The Diploma Disease.* Berkeley, CA: University of California Press, 1976.

*Draves, Bill. *The Free University: A Model for Lifelong Learning.* Chicago: Association Press, 1980.

Drucker, Peter F. *The Frontiers of Management: Where Tomorrow's Decisions are Being Shaped Today.* New York: Truman Talley Books/E.P. Dutton, 1986.

_____. *Innovation and Entrepreneurship: Practice and Principles.* New York: Harper & Row, 1985.

*_____. *Toward the Next Economics and Other Essays.* New York: Harper & Row, 1981.

*Durant, Will. *The Story of Philosophy: The Lives and Opinions of the Greatest Philosophers from Plato to John Dewey.* New York: Pocket Books/Simon & Schuster, 1953.
 —This is an outstanding introduction to the subject of philosophy. Durant gives the reader insight by offering information about the personal lives of the great philosophers. I find it easier to understand abstract thought when I have some knowledge of the conditions which prompted it.

Ehrenfeld, David. *The Arrogance of Humanism.* New York: Oxford University Press, 1978.

Erikson, Erik H. *Adulthood: Essays*. New York: W.W. Norton, 1976.

Fallows, James. "The Case Against Credentialing," *The Atlantic Monthly*, December 1985, pp. 49-67.

*Feibleman, James K. *The Stages of Human Life: A Biography of Entire Man*. The Hague, Netherlands: Martinus Nijhoff, 1975.

_____ . *Understanding Philosophy*. New York: Horizon Press, 1973.

_____ . *Understanding Human Nature: A Popular Guide to the Effects of Technology on Man and His Behavior*. New York: Horizon Press, 1977.

_____ . *Technology and Reality*. The Hague, Netherlands: Martinus Nijhoff, 1982.

Felkner, Bruce L. *How to Look Things Up*. New York: William Morrow, 1988.

*Ferguson, Marilyn. *The Aquarian Conspiracy*. Los Angeles: J.P. Tarcher, 1980.
  –Ferguson has the gift of synthesis and the communicative ability to make complex issues easy to understand. A must if you want to understand the times in which we live.

Fowler, E.M. *The New York Times Career Planner*. New York: Times Books, 1987.

*French, Marilyn. *Beyond Power: On Women, Men and Morals*. New York: Ballantine Books, 1985.
  –This is a powerful book. It is a must if you want to put gender into sociological perspective.

Friedrichs, Guenter and Adam Schaff, ed. *Micro-Electronics and Society: A Report to the Club of Rome*. New York: New American Library, 1982

*Fuller, R. Buckminster. *Critical Path*. New York: St. Martin's Press, 1981.
  –Fuller offers a lifetime of thought on a myriad of political, economic, environmental, and ethical issues.

_____ . *R. Buckminster Fuller on Education*. Amherst, MA: University of Massachusetts, 1979.

Garfield, Charles. *Peak Performers: The New Heroes of American Business*. New York: William Morrow, 1986.

Gawain, Shakti. *Creative Visualization*. New York: Thorsons Publishers, 1978.

Glasser, William. *Positive Addiction*. New York: Harper & Row, 1976.

*Gleick, James. *Chaos: Making a New Science*. New York: Viking, 1987.

Goble, Frank G. *The Third Force: The Psychology of Abraham Maslow*. New York: Simon & Schuster, 1971.

Goldberg, S.R. and F. Deutsch. *Life-Span: Individual & Family Development*. Monterey, CA: Brooks/Cole Publishing Co., 1977.

Goodman, Paul. *Growing Up Absurd: Problems of Youth in the Organized System*. New York: Random House, 1960.

Greenberger, Martin, ed. *Electronic Publishing Plus: Media for a Technological Future*. White Plains, NY: Knowledge Industry Publications, 1985.

Greene, Lawrence J. *Kids Who Underachieve*. New York: Simon & Schuster, 1986.

Greenfield, P.M. *Mind and Media: The Effects of Television, Video Games, and Computers*. Cambridge, MA: Harvard University Press, 1984.

*Gross, Ronald. *The Independent Scholar's Handbook*. Reading, MA: Addison-Wesley Publishing Co., 1982.
  –A wonderful book about how to achieve expertise and recognition as an independent scholar.

*Gross, Ronald, ed. *Invitation to Lifelong Learning*. Chicago: Follett Publishing Co., 1982.

Haber, Audrey and Richard P. Runyon. *Psychology of Adjustment*. Homewood, IL: The Dorsey Press, 1984.

Halal, W.E. *The New Capitalism*. New York: John Wiley & Sons, 1986.

Half, Robert. *Robert Half on Hiring*. New York: New American Library, 1985.

Hammer, Signe. "Stalking Intelligence," *Science Digest*, June 1985, pp. 31-37.

Harman, Willis. *Global Mind Change: The Promise of the Last Years of the Twentieth Century.* Indianapolis, IN: Knowledge Systems, 1988.

Harris, John and William Trout. *Credentialing Educational Accomplishment: Report and Recommendations of the Task Force on Educational Credit and Credentials (With Analyses).* Washington, DC: American Council on Education, 1978.

*Harris, Thomas A. *I'm Okay–You're Okay.* New York: Avon Books, 1969.
  –A useful guide for self-discovery.

*Hawken, Paul. *Growing A Business.* New York: Simon & Schuster, 1987.

*_____ . *The Next Economy.* New York: Holt, Rinehart & Winston, 1983.

Harman, David. *Illiteracy: A National Dilemma.* New York: Cambridge Book Co., 1987.

Heller, R.K. *Deprogramming for Do-It-Yourselfers.* Medina, OH: The Gentle Press, 1982.

Hendrickson, Robert. *More Cunning Than Man: A Social History of Rats and Men.* New York: Dorset Press, 1983.

*Higbee, Kenneth L. *Your Memory: How It Works and How to Improve It.* Englewood Cliffs, NJ: Prentice-Hall, 1977.

*Hirsch, Jr., E.D. *Cultural Literacy: What Every American Needs to Know.* Boston: Houghton Mifflin, 1987.

Hirschberg, Cornelius. *The Priceless Gift.* New York: Simon & Schuster, 1960.

Hoffer, Eric. *The True Believer: Thoughts on the Nature of Mass Movements.* London: Secker & Warburg, 1952.

Holland, John H., Keith J. Holyoak, Richard E. Nisbett, and Paul R. Thagard. *Induction: Processes of Inference, Learning, and Discovery.* Cambridge, MA: MIT Press, 1986.

Hook, Sidney. *Out of Step.* New York: Harper & Row, 1987.

Houle, Cyril O. *The External Degree.* San Francisco: Jossey-Bass, 1973.

Hutchins, Robert M. *The Great Conversation: The Substance of a Liberal Education.* Chicago: Encyclopaedia Britannica, 1982.

*Hutchins, Robert M. and Mortimer J. Adler, eds. *Great Books of the Western World.* 54 volumes. Chicago: Encyclopaedia Britannica, 1952.
  –This set of books has been invaluable to me during the course of my own self-education. Many of the quotations in Self-University were taken from them to demonstrate that these works are just as applicable to us now as when they were written.

*Hutchison, Michael. *Megabrain: New Tools and Techniques for Brain Growth and Mind Expansion.* New York: William Morrow, 1986.

*Illich, Ivan. *Deschooling Society.* New York: Harper Colophon Books, 1971.

Jacobson, S. *Mind Control in the United States.* Santa Rosa, CA: Critique Publishing, 1985.

Janos, A.C. *Politics and Paradigms.* Stanford, CA: Stanford University Press, 1986.

Jennings, Lane and Sally Cornish, eds. *Education and the Future: Selected Articles on Education from the Futurist.* Washington, DC: The World Future Society, 1980.

Jones, Judy and William Wilson. *An Incomplete Education.* New York: Ballantine Books, 1987.

Judson, Horace F. *The Search for Solutions.* New York: Holt, Rinehart & Winston, 1980.

*Kanter, R.M. *Men and Women of the Corporation.* New York: Basic Books, 1977.

Katz, William. *Your Library.* New York: Holt Rinehart Winston, 1984.

*Keirsey, David and Marilyn Bates. *Please Understand Me: Character and Temperament Types.* Del Mar, CA: Prometheus Nemesis Book Company, 1984.

—This book offers a simple test which gives the reader a lot of information and insight into one's own character and temperament type.

Keiser, T.W. and J.L. Keiser. *The Anatomy of Illusion*. Springfield, IL: Charles C. Thomas, 1987.

Kelley, Robert E. *The Gold-Collar Worker: Harnessing the Brain Power of the New Work Force*. Reading, MA: Addison-Wesley, 1985.

Kemp, Nigel. *Information Technology and People: Designing for the Future*. Cambridge, MA: MIT Press, 1987.

Klitgaard, Robert. *Choosing Elites*. New York: Basic Books, 1985.

*Knowles, Malcolm S. *The Modern Practice of Adult Education: From Pedagogy to Andragogy*. Chicago: Follett, 1980.
    —A must for people entering the field of adult education as an instructor.

* _____ . *Self-Directed Learning: A Guide for Learners and Teachers*. New York: The Adult Education Co., 1975.

Knox, Alan B. *Adult Development and Learning*. San Francisco, CA: Jossey-Bass, 1977.

Kohlberg, Lawrence. *The Psychology of Moral Development*. San Francisco: Harper & Row, 1984.

Kohn, Alfie. "How to Succeed without Even Vying," *Psychology Today*, September 1986, pp. 22-28.

Kozol, Jonathan. *Illiterate America*. Garden City, NY: Anchor Press/Doubleday, 1985.

Kraut, Richard. *Socrates and the State*. Princeton, NJ: Princeton University Press, 1984.

Krout, J.A. *The Aged in Rural America*. Westport, CT: Greenwood Press, 1986.

LaBier, Douglas. *Modern Madness: The Emotional Fallout of Success*. Reading, MA: Addison-Wesley Publishing Co., 1986.

Lappe, Frances M. and Joseph Collins. *World Hunger: Ten Myths*. 4th ed. San Francisco: Institute for Food and Development Policy, 1982.

Lasch, Christopher. *The Culture of Narcissism: American Life in an Age of Diminishing Expectations*. New York: Warner Books, 1979.

*Lewis, D. *Thinking Better*. New York: Rawson, Wade Publishers, 1982.

Levine, Art. "Child Prodigies," *U.S. News and World Report*, 29 December, 1986, p. 93.

Lipnack, Jessica and Jeffrey Stamps. *The Networking Book: People Connecting with People*. New York: Routledge & Kegan Paul, 1986.

*Long, Huey B. *Adult and Continuing Education: Responding to Change*. New York: Teachers College Press, 1983.
    —This is a good overview of adult education from an educator's point of view. Long discusses the history of adult education, the implications of social, psychological and technological developments and new challenges for the future.

*Lorenz, Konrad. *The Waning of Humaneness*. Boston: Little, Brown. 1987.
    —This is a fascinating book by one of the world's most eminent and influential students of animal behavior. Lorenz offers a sociological interpretation of human behavior based on biological fact.

Lowrance, William W. *Modern Science and Human Values*. New York: Oxford University Press, 1985.

Lowy, L. and D. O'Connor. *Why Education in the Later Years*. Lexington, MA: D.C. Heath & Co., 1986.

*Lovelock, James. *The Ages of Gaia: A Biography of Our Living Earth*. New York: W.W. Norton, 1988.

Lundberg, Margaret J. *The Incomplete Adult: Social Class Constraints on Personality Development*. Westport, CT: Greenwood Press, 1974.

Mackay, Harvey. *How to Swim With the Sharks Without Being Eaten Alive*. New York: William Morrow, 1988.

Madsen, K.B. *Modern Theories of Motivation*. New York: Halsted Press, 1974.

Maeroff, Gene L. "An Exclusive Interview with Alvin Toffler," *Consumers Digest*, March-April 1985, pp. 87-90.

Martel, Leon. *Mastering Change: The Key to Business Success*. New York: Simon & Schuster, 1986.

Maslow, Abraham H. *The Farther Reaches of Human Nature*. New York: Viking Press, 1971.

Maslow, Abraham H. *Religions, Values and Peak Experiences*. New York: Penguin Books, 1987.

*Massey, Morris. *The People Puzzle: Understanding Yourself and Others*. Reston, VA: Prentice-Hall, 1979.
    —Massey draws a clear picture of how the environment shapes our attitudes into a cultural construction of perceived correct behavior. He has made several films which are available through the corporate training industry. Watch for them, as they are well worth seeing.

May, Rollo, Carl Rogers, Abraham Maslow, et al. *Politics and Innocence: A Humanistic Debate*. Dallas: Saybrook Publishers, 1986.

McClelland, D.C. *The Achieving Society*. Princeton, NJ: D. Van Nostrand, 1961.

McGuire, Willian and R.F.C. Hull, eds. *C.G. Jung Speaking: Interviews and Encounters*. Princeton, NJ: Princeton University Press, 1977.

McLeish, John Alexander Buchanan. *The Ulyssean Adult: Creativity in the Middle and Later Years*. Toronto, New York: McGraw-Hill Ryerson, 1976.

McLuhan, Marshall. *The Gutenberg Galaxy*. Toronto: University of Toronto Press, 1962.

*_____. *Understanding Media*. New York: McGraw-Hill, 1964.

*Meiland, Jack W. *College Thinking*. New York: New American Library, 1981.

*Miller, William C. *The Creative Edge: Fostering Innovation Where You Work*. Reading, MA: Addison-Wesley Publishing, 1987.

Milton, Ohmer, Howard R. Pollio, and James A. Eison. *Making Sense of College Grades: Why the Grading System Does Not Work and What Can Be Done About It*. San Francisco: Jossey-Bass, 1986.

Morgan, Edward P. *Inequality in Classroom Learning: Schooling and Democratic Citizenship*. New York: Praeger Publishers, 1977.

*Naisbitt, John. *Megatrends: Ten New Directions Transforming Our Lives*. New York: Warner Books, 1984.
    —Naisbitt provides simple methods of looking at the present which offer insight into possible futures. A must read if you are concerned about social transformation.

Naisbitt, John and Patricia Aburdene. *Re-Inventing the Corporation: Transforming Your Job and Your Company for the New Information Society*. New York: Warner Books, 1985.

Neill, S.D. "The Libraries in the Year 2010," in *Communications Tomorrow: The Coming of the Information Society*. Bethesda, MD: The World Future Society, 1983.

Neuman, Russell. "The Media Habit," in *Electronic Publishing Plus: Media for a Technological Future*. White Plains, NY: Knowledge Industry Publications, 1985.

Olsen, Edward Gustave. *Life Centering Education*. Midland, MI: Pendell Publishing Co., 1977.

Ostrander, Sheila. *Superlearning*. New York: Dell, 1979.

Oxford Analytica. *America in Perspective: Major Trends in the United States Through the 1990s*. Boston: Houghton Mifflin, 1986.

Pascale, Richard T. and Anthony G. Athos. *The Art of Japanese Management: Applications for American Executives*. New York: Warner Books, 1982.

Pascarella, Perry. *The New Achievers: Creating a Modern Work Ethic*. New York: The Free Press, 1984.

Pear, T.H. *The Moulding of Modern Man*. London: George Allen & Unwin LTD, 1961.

Peck, M. Scott. *The Road Less Traveled: A New Psychology of Love, Traditional Values, and Spiritual Growth*. New York: Simon & Schuster, 1978.

Peled, Abraham. "The Next Computer Revolution," *Scientific American*, October 1987, pp. 56-64.

*Peters, Tom. *Thriving on Chaos: Handbook for a Management Revolution*. New York: Alfred A. Knopf, 1987.
    –This is an excellent book dealing with management and the problems associated with rapid change.

Peters, Tom and Nancy Austin. *A Passion for Excellence: The Leadership Difference*. New York: Random House, 1985.

*Peterson, Merrill D. *Thomas Jefferson: A Reference Biography*. New York: Charles Scribner & Sons, 1986.

Pifer, Alan and Lydia Bronte, ed. *Our Aging Society: Paradox and Promise*. New York: W.W. Norton, 1986.

*Pirsig, Robert M. *Zen and the Art of Motorcycle Maintenance: An Inquiry into Values*. New York: Bantam Books, 1985.
    –One of those books that, once read, will dramatically change the way you think about things. If I could take only a handful of books to a deserted island, this would be one.

Pitts, Jr., Robert E. and Arch G. Woodside, eds. *Personal Values and Consumer Psychology*. Lexington, MA: Lexington Books, 1984.

Postman, Neil. *Teaching as a Conserving Activity*. New York: Delacorte Press, 1979.

*Postman, Neil and Charles Weingarten. *Teaching as a Subversive Activity*. New York: Dell, 1969.
    –A must for anyone who teaches, or who wants to achieve a better understanding about the role of the school in the learning process.

Pugh, George Edgin. *The Biological Origin of Human Values*. New York: Basic Books, 1977.

*Rachels, James. *The Elements of Moral Philosophy*. Philadelphia: Temple University Press, 1986.
    –Complex moral questions so clearly explained they become simple and easy to understand.

*Restak, Richard M. *The Brain: The Last Frontier*. New York: Warner Books, 1980.

*Riso, Don R. *Personality Types: Using the Enneagram for Self-Discovery*. Boston: Houghton Mifflin, 1987.
    –This is a great book for developing insight into the nature of your own personality.

Robbins, Anthony. *Unlimited Power*. New York: Ballantine Books, 1986.

Robeach, Milton. *The Nature of Human Values*. New York: The Free Press, 1973.

Roe, Anne and Patricia W. Lunneborg. "Personality Development and Career Choice," in *Career Choice and Development*. San Francisco: Jossey-Bass, 1984.

Rogers, C.R. *Freedom To Learn for the 80's*. Columbus, OH: Charles E. Merrill Publishing Co., 1983.

Rosenfeld, Anne and Elizabeth Stark. "The Prime of Our Lives," *Psychology Today*, May 1987, p. 66.

Russell, Bertrand. *The ABC of Relativity* (4th rev. ed.). New York: New American Library, 1985.

Russell, Cheryl. *100 Predictions for the Baby Boom: The Next 50 Years.* New York: Plenum Press, 1987.

Schumacher, E.F. *Good Work.* New York: Harper & Row, 1979.

*_____ . *Small Is Beautiful.* New York: Harper & Row, 1973.
    – A must for putting technology in perspective.

Schwartz, Gail Garfield. *The Work Revolution.* New York: Rawson Associates, 1984.

Sheppard, C. Stewart and Donald C. Carroll, ed. *Working in the Twenty-First Century.* New York: Wiley, 1980.

Sheehy, Gail. *Passages: Predictable Crises of Adult Life.* Toronto, New York: Bantam Books, 1981.

Sigel, Efrem with Joseph Roisen, Colin McIntyre, Max Wilkinson. *Videotext: Worldwide Prospects for Home/Office Electronic Information Services.* New York: Knowledge Industry Publications, 1980.

*Simosko, Susan. *Earn College Credit for What You Know.* Washington, DC: Acropolis Books LTD, 1985.
    – This is an excellent guide to nontraditional degree programs. Simosko breaks the portfolio development program into an easy-to-understand process. This book is also good for developing insight into how you might use similar methods for employment documentation purposes.

*Sinetar, Marsha. *Do What You Love, The Money Will Follow: Discovering Your Right Livelihood.* New York: Paulist Press, 1987.
    – Highly recommended as a tool for self-discovery.

_____ . *Ordinary People as Monks and Mystics.* New York: Paulist Press, 1986.

Singer, Benjamin D. "The Future-Focused Role-Image," *Learning for Tomorrow.* New York: Random House, 1974.

Skinner, B.F. *Upon Further Reflection.* Englewood Cliffs, NJ: Prentice-Hall, 1987.

Smith, Robert M. *Learning How to Learn: Applied Theory for Adults.* Chicago: Follett, 1982.

Solorzano, Lucia. "Education: Different Ways of Learning," *U.S. News and World Report,* 31 August, 1987, p. 62.

State of the World 1987: A Worldwatch Institute Report on Progress Toward a Sustainable Society, Annual Report. New York: W.W. Norton, 1987.

Stearn, Gerald E., ed. *McLuhan: Hot and Cool.* New York: The Dial Press, 1967.

*Stevenson, Leslie. *Seven Theories of Human Nature.* New York: Oxford University Press, 1987.
    – An excellent approach to the differences in Christianity and the theories of Freud, Lorenz, Marx, Sartre, Skinner, and Plato.

*Toffler, Alvin. *The Third Wave.* New York: Bantam Books/William Morrow, 1981.
    – The best overall book in print for putting today's society in perspective.

Toffler, Alvin, ed. *Learning for Tomorrow: The Role of the Future in Education.* New York: Random House, 1974.

Tough, Allen M. *Learning Without a Teacher.* Toronto: The Ontario Institute for Studies in Education, 1977.

Trotter, Robert J. "The Mystery of Mastery," *Psychology Today,* July 1986, p. 36.

_____ . "Three Heads are Better Than One," *Psychology Today,* August 1986, p. 60.

Underwood, Geoffrey, and Jean D.M. Underwood. *Information Technology and People.* Cambridge, MA: MIT Press, 1987.

Van Hoose, W.H. *Midlife Myths and Realities.* Atlanta, GA: Humanics Ltd, 1985.

Voss, Hans-Georg and Heidi Keller. *Curiosity and Exploration: Theories and Results*. New York: Academic Press, 1983.

Wagschal, Peter H. "Illiterates with Doctorates," *Education and the Future: Selected Articles from The Futurist*. Washington, DC: The World Future Society, 1980.

Warner, S.J. *Self-Realization and Self-Defeat*. New York: Grove Press, 1966.

Warren, Jonathan R. "Current Practices in Awarding Credits and Degrees," *Credentialing Educational Accomplishment*, Washington, DC: American Council on Education 1974.

Warren, Malcolm W. *Training for Results: A Systems Approach to the Development of Human Resources in Industry*. Reading, MA: Addison-Wesley, 1979.

Waterhouse, Philip. *Managing the Learning Process*. New York: McGraw-Hill, 1983.

Watson, Charles E. *Management Development Through Training*. Reading, MA: Addison-Wesley, 1979.

*Watts, Alan. *Does It Matter: Essays on Man's Relation to Materiality*. New York: Vintage Books, 1968.

–A fascinating look at man's confusion of symbol and reality.

* _____ . *The Wisdom of Insecurity*. New York: Vintage Books, 1968.

Weinberg, S.B., and Mark Lawrence Fuerst. *Computer Phobia: How to Slay the Dragon of Computer Fear*. Wayne, PA: Banbury Books, 1984.

What Works: Research About Teaching and Learning. Washington, DC: U.S. Department of Education, 1986.

White, Mary Alice, ed. *The Future of Electronic Learning*. Hillsdale, NJ: Lawrence Erlbaum Associates, 1983.

Whitlock, Baird W. *Educational Myths I Have Known and Loved*. New York: Schocken Books, 1986.

*Williams, Frederick. *The Communications Revolution*. New York: New American Library, 1983.

*Winn, Denise. *The Manipulated Mind*. London: The Octagon Press, 1983.

Witmer, J.M. *Pathways to Personal Growth: Developing a Sense of Worth and Competence, A Holistic Education Approach*. Muncie, IN: Accelerated Development, 1985.

*Yankelovich, D. *New Rules*. New York: Random House, 1981.

Young, Stephen S. "The Next Revolution in Education," *The Futurist*, March-April 1986.

Zuckerman, Mortimer B. "Physician, Heal Thyself," *U.S. News and World Report*, 21 July, 1986.

Index